Responsive Web Design with jQuery

Learn to optimize your responsive web designing techniques using jQuery

Gilberto Crespo

[PACKT] open source*
PUBLISHING   community experience distilled

BIRMINGHAM - MUMBAI

Responsive Web Design with jQuery

Copyright © 2013 Packt Publishing

All rights reserved. No part of this book may be reproduced, stored in a retrieval system, or transmitted in any form or by any means, without the prior written permission of the publisher, except in the case of brief quotations embedded in critical articles or reviews.

Every effort has been made in the preparation of this book to ensure the accuracy of the information presented. However, the information contained in this book is sold without warranty, either express or implied. Neither the author, nor Packt Publishing, and its dealers and distributors will be held liable for any damages caused or alleged to be caused directly or indirectly by this book.

Packt Publishing has endeavored to provide trademark information about all of the companies and products mentioned in this book by the appropriate use of capitals. However, Packt Publishing cannot guarantee the accuracy of this information.

First published: November 2013

Production Reference: 1181113

Published by Packt Publishing Ltd.
Livery Place
35 Livery Street
Birmingham B3 2PB, UK.

ISBN 978-1-78216-360-2

www.packtpub.com

Cover Image by Daniel Bertolino (alphaimagem@alphaimagem.com)

Credits

Author
Gilberto Crespo

Reviewers
Maria Gabriela Didoni
Joydip Kanjilal
Alex Libby
R.J. Lindelof
Carla Molina
Anirudh Prabhu
Paul Sprangers
Taroon Tyagi

Acquisition Editor
Rubal Kaur

Lead Technical Editor
Balaji Naidu

Copy Editors
Janbal Dharmaraj
Tanvi Gaitonde
Sayanee Mukherjee
Aditya Nair
Deepa Nambiar
Lavina Pereira
Laxmi Subramanian

Technical Editors
Veena Pagare
Manal Pednekar

Project Coordinator
Wendell Palmer

Proofreader
Bernadette Watkins

Indexer
Rekha Nair

Graphics
Ronak Dhruv

Production Coordinator
Aparna Bhagat

Cover Work
Aparna Bhagat

About the Author

Gilberto Crespo is a skilled frontend developer who started frontend developing using CSS2, HTML4, and tableless HTML in 2005. He has always focused on increasing his knowledge by following strong trends, such as HTML5, CSS3, and jQuery. In the past five years, he has helped improve the web development process by creating and spreading best development practices for CI&T where he currently works. For the past two years, he has been working exclusively on responsive websites on the job and supporting other web developers by answering questions on responsive websites. He has been connected with new technologies and design trends.

He is passionate about creating themes for Drupal CMS and websites' look and feel in general since 2011. Currently, he is writing technical articles and giving presentations in Brazil, sharing his knowledge with students and with the Drupal community and friends.

Outside of work, he enjoys a normal life, trying to learn something new every day.

Feel free to contact him at www.gilcrespo.com.

> I would like to thank my lovely wife Gabriela for her strong support and her patience with me. Also, I thank my parents and my friends who have supported me greatly in accomplishing this work.

About the Reviewers

Maria Gabriela Didoni has over 12 years of experience in the field of English Language Teaching. She has degrees in Portuguese and English, Spanish, and Translation. She attended these courses at Sagrado Coração University, Bauru, São Paulo. Maria also has a Post Graduation Certificate in Education from the same university, and has attended other English courses at the Vancouver English Center in Canada.

Joydip Kanjilal is a Microsoft Most Valuable Professional in ASP.NET, a speaker, and the author of several books and articles. He has over 16 years of industry experience in IT, with more than 10 years in Microsoft .NET and its related technologies. He was selected as **MSDN Featured Developer of the Fortnight (MSDN)** a number of times and also as Community Credit Winner on www.community-credit.com several times.

He has authored the books *Visual Studio Six in One*, Wrox Publishers; *ASP.NET 4.0 Programming*, Mc-Graw Hill Publishing; *Entity Framework Tutorial*, Packt Publishing; *Pro Sync Framework*, Apress; *Sams Teach Yourself ASP.NET Ajax in 24 Hours*, Sams Publishing; and *ASP.NET Data Presentation Controls Essentials*, Packt Publishing.

Joydip has authored more than 250 articles for some of the most reputable sites, such as www.msdn.microsoft.com, www.code-magazine.com, www.asptoday.com, www.devx.com, www.ddj.com, www.aspalliance.com, www.aspnetpro.com, www.sql-server-performance.com, and www.sswug.com. Many of these articles have been selected at www.asp.net—Microsoft's official site for ASP.NET.

He has years of experience in designing and architecting solutions for various domains. His technical strengths include C, C++, VC++, Java, C#, Microsoft .NET, Ajax, WCF, REST, SOA, Design Patterns, SQL Server, Operating Systems, and Computer Architecture.

He writes blog at `http://aspadvice.com/blogs/joydip`. His website is `www.joydipkanjilal.com` and he is avaliable on Twitter at `https://twitter.com/joydipkanjilal`. You can find him on Facebook at `https://www.facebook.com/joydipkanjilal` and on LinkedIn at `http://in.linkedin.com/in/joydipkanjilal`.

Alex Libby has his background in IT support—he has been involved in supporting end users for the last 15 years in a variety of different environments and currently works as a Technical Analyst, supporting a medium-sized SharePoint estate for an international distributor based in the UK. Although Alex gets to play with different technologies in his day job, his first true love has always been with the open source movement and, in particular, experimenting with jQuery, CSS3, and HTML5.

To date, Alex has written several books for Packt, including one on HTML5 technologies and another on jQuery Tools. In his free time, Alex enjoys helping out at the local amateur theatre, cycling, and photography.

R.J. Lindelof has been innovating in the frontend web development field since 1998 and has been in the software development industry since 1993. He owns and maintains hundreds of web properties for his company and clients. Since the first Smartphone was released, he has been an enthusiast and leader in this field. His specialty is web applications and bringing the power and scalability of applications to the Cloud.

Today, R. J. continues to develop responsive web applications and solutions for clients and is constantly learning new techniques. He trains and mentors fellow developers and is part of an ever-growing community of software craftsmen.

Carla Molina has extensive experience in the field of teaching, proofreading, and translating in the English language. She has translated and proofread scientific articles, websites, and other publications. Having lived in the United States for six years, she was able to attend a variety of English courses, and teach **ESL (English as a Second Language**) to immigrants, at a language school in New Jersey. She also received a degree in Liberal Arts after attending Essex County College, and is currently pursuing a second degree in Portuguese and English, at a university in Brazil. In 2012, she was given the opportunity to work as an English coach, at an IT company in the city of Campinas, São Paulo. Currently, Carla owns a language institution that offers customized English classes and translation services. In her free time, she enjoys photography, yoga, listening to music, and drawing.

Anirudh Prabhu is a Software Engineer at Xoriant Solutions with four years' experience in web designing and development. He is responsible for JavaScript development and maintenance in his project. His areas of expertise are HTML, CSS, JavaScript, jQuery, and SASS. He has received an M.Sc. Degree in Information Technology from Mumbai University.

He has also been a technical reviewer for the book *Pro Javascript Performance* by *Tom Barker*, *Apress*.

When he is not working, Anirudh loves reading, listening to music, and photography.

Paul Sprangers has been building the Web for over a decade now. After building Flash websites and taking baby steps through HTML with the help of the **save as HTML** feature in Microsoft Word, he finally saw the proverbial light; he now specializes in HTML, CSS, and jQuery.

In 2003, he teamed up with a few classmates and started Interactive Studios, a web firm in the south of the Netherlands. They are currently building websites and (custom) web software for regional, national, and international clients. They have recently launched the Dutch invitation web app at `EasyInvite.nl`.

You can find some of Paul's personal writing at `paulsprangers.com`, but be prepared for CSS/jQuery nerdiness and Apple discussions.

Taroon Tyagi is a blunt biped, known for using sharp phrases. He is a rationalist with optimistic fantasies who has a lust for food, technology, and knowledge.

Taroon is an interface and interaction designer who likes to be an advocate of zen simplicity and minimalism.

He loves designing good stuff, especially when no one is watching. When he is not creating, he can be found reading and writing across the Web, listening to music, and finding inspiration.

www.PacktPub.com

Support files, eBooks, discount offers and more

You might want to visit www.PacktPub.com for support files and downloads related to your book.

Did you know that Packt offers eBook versions of every book published, with PDF and ePub files available? You can upgrade to the eBook version at www.PacktPub.com and as a print book customer, you are entitled to a discount on the eBook copy. Get in touch with us at service@packtpub.com for more details.

At www.PacktPub.com, you can also read a collection of free technical articles, sign up for a range of free newsletters and receive exclusive discounts and offers on Packt books and eBooks.

PACKTLIB

http://PacktLib.PacktPub.com

Do you need instant solutions to your IT questions? PacktLib is Packt's online digital book library. Here, you can access, read and search across Packt's entire library of books.

Why Subscribe?

- Fully searchable across every book published by Packt
- Copy and paste, print and bookmark content
- On demand and accessible via web browser

Free Access for Packt account holders

If you have an account with Packt at www.PacktPub.com, you can use this to access PacktLib today and view nine entirely free books. Simply use your login credentials for immediate access.

Table of Contents

Preface — 1
Chapter 1: Exploring Responsive Web Design — 7
  Understanding the concept of responsive web design — 8
  Comparing responsive, fluid, and adaptive web — 9
  Adapting the screen with media queries — 10
  Mobile-first — 12
  Using wireframe tools — 13
  Exercise 1 – practicing mobile-first development in wireframes — 14
  Summary — 15
Chapter 2: Designing Responsive Layouts/Grids — 17
  Adapting the site using JavaScript — 18
    Adapt.js — 18
      How to do it — 19
    Respond.js — 19
      How to do it — 20
  How percentage gives flexibility to the structure — 20
    Converting pixel to percentage — 21
  What is a responsive grid system? — 24
    Responsive grid systems — 25
      Fluid Baseline Grid system — 25
      1140 Grid — 28
      Foundation4 — 30
  Photoshop grid templates — 33
  Setting up the meta tag of viewport before starting — 34
  Exercise 2a – creating the layout design for wireframes — 34
  Exercise 2b – using Foundation4 Grid to structure our website — 36
  Summary — 42

Chapter 3: Building Responsive Navigation Menu — 43
Designing a menu by improving its usability — 43
Most-used responsive navigation patterns — 44
Top nav — 45
How to do it — 46
Footer anchor — 47
How to do it — 48
The toggle menu — 50
The Responsive Nav plugin — 50
How to do it — 51
The select menu — 52
The TinyNav.js jQuery plugin — 52
How to do it — 53
Footer-only — 54
How to do it — 55
Multi toggle — 55
How to do it — 55
Toggle and slide — 58
How to do it — 58
The off-canvas menu — 60
The jPanelMenu jQuery plugin — 60
How to do it — 61
Exercise 3 – customizing menu using the toggle menu solution — 62
Summary — 63

Chapter 4: Designing Responsive Text — 65
Understanding and converting the text to relative units — 65
Relative unit – percentage — 66
Relative unit – em — 66
Relative unit – rem — 67
Improving your element dimensioning using the box-sizing property — 68
Customizing the font family for beautiful responsive titles — 70
Using Font Squirrel tool generating — 71
How to do it — 71
The FitText plugin — 74
How to do it — 74
The SlabText plugin — 75
How to do it — 76
Lettering — 77
How to do it — 78
The Kern.js tool — 80
How to use it — 80
Responsive Measure — 81
How to do it — 81

Exercise 4 – customizing the homepage title	82
Summary	**83**
Chapter 5: Preparing Images and Videos	**85**
Basic image resizing only using CSS	86
Using image breakpoints	86
How the picture tag works	88
Control of art direction for responsive images	88
Focal Point CSS framework	89
How to do it	90
Alternative solutions for the <picture> tag	92
Foresight – selecting the right image to display depending on the screen size	92
How to do it	93
Picturefill – the solution that most closely resembles the picture tag	94
How to do it	95
Responsive background images by using jQuery plugins	95
Anystretch – stretching your background easily	96
How to do it	97
Backstretch – creating a responsive background slideshow	98
How to do it	99
Dealing with high-density displays	100
How to do it	101
How to do it using Foresight	101
Making responsive video elements	102
FitVids – a quick win solution for responsive videos	103
How to do it	104
Exercise – creating different image versions for featured homepage images	105
Summary	**106**
Chapter 6: Building Responsive Image Sliders	**107**
Responsive image sliders	107
Elastislide plugin	108
How to do it	108
FlexSlider2 – a fully responsive slider	114
How to do it	114
ResponsiveSlides – the best of basic slides	119
How do to it	119
Swiper – performatic touch image slider	124
How to do it	125
Using the 3D flow style on Swiper	128
Slicebox – a slice animation when using slide images	129
How to do it	129

Introducing touch gestures to user experience	**132**
Implementing touch events with JavaScript plugins	**133**
QuoJS – simple touch interaction library	133
How to do it	134
Hammer – a nice multitouch library	134
How to do it	135
Exercise 6 – creating an image slider using the Swiper plugin	**135**
Summary	**136**
Chapter 7: Designing Responsive Tables	**137**
Responsive tables	**137**
Expandable responsive tables	**138**
How to do it	138
Extending the plugin	141
Stackedtables	**143**
How to do it using the table from the previous example	143
Horizontal overflow	**145**
How to do it	146
Header orientation flip	147
Link to full-table	**150**
How to do it	150
Exercise 6 – creating a responsive table of prices using the FooTable jQuery plugin	**152**
Summary	**153**
Chapter 8: Implementing Responsive Forms	**155**
Types and attributes of form inputs	**155**
The autocomplete feature with Magicsuggest	**156**
How to implement it	157
The date and time pickers feature	**158**
Pickadate – responsive date/time picker	159
How to do it	159
The tooltip feature	**161**
Tooltipster – modern tooltip feature	161
How to do it	161
Responsive form using IdealForms	**163**
How to implement it	163
Exercise 8 – creating a contact form using the IdealForms framework	**166**
Summary	**168**

Chapter 9: Testing the Responsiveness — 169
- Simulating a device using browser tools — 169
  - Using the Viewport Resizer website tool — 170
  - Using the Surveyor website tool — 171
  - Using the ScreenFly website tool — 172
- Opera mobile emulator — 173
- Tips for design testing of responsive websites — 174
- Exercise 9 – let's test our website in different screen sizes — 174
- Summary — 175

Chapter 10: Ensuring Browser Support — 177
- Checking the features the browser supports — 177
  - CanIUse.com — 178
  - MobileHTML5.org — 178
  - QuirksMode.org — 179
- Defining fallback — 180
- Feature detection tools — 181
  - CSS Browser Selector + — 181
    - How to do it — 182
  - Modernizr — 182
    - YepNope.js — 184
    - html5shiv — 184
- Polyfill implementations — 185
  - MediaElements.js — 185
    - How to do it — 186
  - SVG — 187
    - How to do it — 187
  - Respond.js — 189
    - How to do it — 189
- Summary — 189

Chapter 11: Useful Responsive Plugins — 191
- Plugins for website structure — 191
  - Creating simple responsive structures using Columns — 192
  - Using Equalize for element dimension adjustment — 195
  - Implementing a card website layout with Packery — 197
- Plugins for menu navigation — 199
  - Creating a side menu with Sidr — 199
  - Knowing about EasyResponsiveTabstoAccordion — 201
  - Adding flexibility to your menu with FlexNav — 203
- Miscellaneous — 206
  - SVGeezy — 206
  - Prefix free — 207

Magnific Popup	208
Riloadr	210
Calendario	212
Summary	**216**
Chapter 12: Improving Website Performance	**217**
Using a content delivery network	**217**
Making fewer HTTP requests	**218**
Using conditional loaders	218
Consolidating and minifying resources (JavaScript and CSS)	218
CSS Sprites	219
Reducing the size of payloads	**220**
Progressive JPEG	221
Image optimization	222
Simplifying pages with HTML5 and CSS3	222
Testing website performance	**223**
PageSpeed Insights	223
YSlow	224
WebPagetest	226
Mobitest	226
Summary	**228**
Index	**229**

Preface

The Web no longer concerns only desktop or notebook devices. Web technology has now spread to various devices ranging from large desktop monitors to tablets, Smartphones, smart TVs, and outdoor displays. It has also increased the functionality and interfaces of sites and the way we interact with them.

Making a website *responsive* is not an option anymore. Hence, this is the time to hone our developing skills using grid system frameworks and providing a differentiated and enriched user experience.

In this book, we achieve all this using CSS3 and jQuery, which offer great integration options between devices, OSs, and different browser versions. Another advantage of using jQuery is the speed of development achieved by using plugins maintained by the collaborative community. We do not need to reinvent something that is already done! Furthermore, improvements are always welcome and your collaboration to the community will help everybody.

What this book covers

Chapter 1, *Exploring Responsive Web Design*, begins by explaining the concept of responsiveness created by generating wireframes for websites and adapting it to different screens. The chapter goes on to explain the mobile-first concept.

Chapter 2, *Designing Responsive Layouts/Grids*, helps you make flexible website structures and then focuses on explaining the usage of responsive grid systems and how it improves agility during development.

Chapter 3, *Building Responsive Navigation Menu*, has several analyzes and step-by-step implementations for each navigation menu pattern; this helps in the choice of the right option for each situation.

Preface

Chapter 4, *Designing Responsive Text*, explains the conversion of text to relative units and then their customization for beautiful and responsive heading titles.

Chapter 5, *Preparing Images and Videos*, explains handling high-resolution images in different formats. It then goes on to explain the art of direction importance when viewing images on Smartphones.

Chapter 6, *Building Responsive Image Sliders*, explains four different image-slider plugins and their implementation and shows useful touch libraries complementing the interaction.

Chapter 7, *Designing Responsive Tables*, delves into managing the different approaches for creating responsive tables, solving the difficulties faced while adjusting width for different screen sizes.

Chapter 8, *Implementing Responsive Forms*, discusses the highlights of form element features that improve the user experience by filling the form in on mobile devices and a good, responsive form framework.

Chapter 9, *Testing the Responsiveness*, discusses ways to perform responsive testing across various browsers and device platforms so as to prevent unexpected behaviors.

Chapter 10, *Ensuring Browser Support*, explains fallback and why it is deemed important. It then goes on to explain how to detect each browser feature that does / might not work for that browser and provides the correct support for these errors.

Chapter 11, *Useful Responsive Plugins*, shows different plugins for website structure, menu navigation, and so on, complementing the solutions already seen in other chapters.

Chapter 12, *Improving Website Performance*, explains major ways to analyze website performance using online tools and recommends tips to get better results.

What you need for this book

All the knowledge acquired by you after reading this book will be better assimilated if you already have an idea of the website you want to convert into a responsive one, because it can be made during the chapter exercises.

The list of software you will need is Apache HTTP Server, Adobe Photoshop CS5 or earlier, some code editor such as Sublime Text 2, and Internet browsers, such as Firefox and Chrome. Also, for testing the examples and exercises, it will be good for you to have mobile devices such as Smartphones or tablets.

Who this book is for

Responsive Web Design with jQuery and CSS3 is aimed at web designers who are interested in building device-agnostic websites. Some exposure to jQuery, CSS3, and HTML5 will be beneficial.

Conventions

In this book, you will find a number of styles of text that distinguish between different kinds of information. Here are some examples of these styles, and an explanation of their meaning.

Code words in text, database table names, folder names, filenames, file extensions, pathnames, dummy URLs, user input, and Twitter handles are shown as follows: "The HTML5 specification includes new structural elements, such as `header`, `nav`, `article`, and `footer`."

A block of code is set as follows:

```
.orientation_landscape .div-example {
  border: 2px solid red;
}
```

When we wish to draw your attention to a particular part of a code block, the relevant lines or items are set in bold:

```
<svg width="96" height="96">
  <image xlink:href="svg.svg" src="svg.png" width="96" height="96" />
</svg>
```

New terms and **important words** are shown in bold. Words that you see on the screen, in menus or dialog boxes for example, appear in the text like this: "clicking the **Next** button moves you to the next screen".

> Warnings or important notes appear in a box like this.

> Tips and tricks appear like this.

Reader feedback

Feedback from our readers is always welcome. Let us know what you think about this book—what you liked or may have disliked. Reader feedback is important for us to develop titles that you really get the most out of.

To send us general feedback, simply send an e-mail to feedback@packtpub.com, and mention the book title via the subject of your message.

If there is a topic that you have expertise in and you are interested in either writing or contributing to a book, see our author guide on www.packtpub.com/authors.

Customer support

Now that you are the proud owner of a Packt book, we have a number of things to help you to get the most from your purchase.

Downloading the example code

You can download the example code files for all Packt books you have purchased from your account at http://www.packtpub.com. If you purchased this book elsewhere, you can visit http://www.packtpub.com/support and register to have the files e-mailed directly to you.

Errata

Although we have taken every care to ensure the accuracy of our content, mistakes do happen. If you find a mistake in one of our books—maybe a mistake in the text or the code—we would be grateful if you would report this to us. By doing so, you can save other readers from frustration and help us improve subsequent versions of this book. If you find any errata, please report them by visiting http://www.packtpub.com/submit-errata, selecting your book, clicking on the **errata submission form** link, and entering the details of your errata. Once your errata are verified, your submission will be accepted and the errata will be uploaded on our website, or added to any list of existing errata, under the Errata section of that title. Any existing errata can be viewed by selecting your title from http://www.packtpub.com/support.

Piracy

Piracy of copyright material on the Internet is an ongoing problem across all media. At Packt, we take the protection of our copyright and licenses very seriously. If you come across any illegal copies of our works, in any form, on the Internet, please provide us with the location address or website name immediately so that we can pursue a remedy.

Please contact us at `copyright@packtpub.com` with a link to the suspected pirated material.

We appreciate your help in protecting our authors, and our ability to bring you valuable content.

Questions

You can contact us at `questions@packtpub.com` if you are having a problem with any aspect of the book, and we will do our best to address it.

1
Exploring Responsive Web Design

These days, the word responsive is one that we are hearing a lot in the website development environment, isn't it? No worries, together we will see the real meaning of it and its impact on our website development.

One factor that influences decision making (but is sometimes ignored) when starting the development process is the number of devices and different screen sizes that we need for previewing the responsiveness of website layout. Some time ago, we used to work with some definitions of website dimensions, for example, 1024 pixels. This happened because we thought the only way to access the content was on a desktop. But, as you know, technology is bringing us more and more devices (that can show websites), improving the way we interact with sites, such as large desktop monitors, tablets, smartphones, smart TVs, outdoor displays, and other good things.

These advances in mobile technology and the quick evolution of website navigation and viewing techniques have pushed everyone to review the concept of limited dimensions of sites, to start thinking of a structure that can adapt itself, and to offer the right content for each situation.

In this chapter we will learn:

- Understanding the concept of responsive web design
- Comparing responsive, fluid, and adaptive web
- Adapting the screen with media queries
- Mobile-first concept and tips
- Using wireframe tools
- Practicing mobile-first development in wireframes

Understanding the concept of responsive web design

I cannot start this theme without citing *Ethan Marcotte*, who released the book *Responsive Web Design* in 2011, which has become a reference for many other books and articles from across the frontend community.

In my understanding of Marcotte's book, the meaning of responsive web design is to provide different experiences for the user to see the same site depending on the available screen area. Technically speaking, it involves the use of the following three main techniques:

- Flexible grid-based layout
- Flexible images and video
- Smart use of CSS splitting the website behavior (media queries)

More details about each technique will be shown later, but just to clarify this concept visually, have a look at the following example, which represents a website as displayed on a small device (smartphone) on the left, medium device (tablet) in center, and on a large screen (desktop) on the right:

> There are many more challenges than just creating fluidic dimensions and applying some media queries.

We will talk about many minor and major challenges throughout the book. Some of them are:

- Replacing mouser-over events with touch events
- Facilitating the filling of data in the form fields
- Prioritizing the content
- Site loading optimization

Comparing responsive, fluid, and adaptive web

Responsive web design is a little different from fluid design. Fluid design is about adjusting the website's structure and dimensions automatically (by using relative units for widths, such as em or percentage) but does not offer a varied approach to the user to see the content layout.

Also, it would be fair to say that responsive web design is not a unique solution for all mobile device challenges. As we saw before, responsive web design is an idea, and can give the user a better experience when implemented correctly, but it may not work for everyone or every device. This is the reason we should improve our knowledge of new technologies.

There is a quote that I like very much, written by *Aaron Gustafson*, the author of the *Adaptive Web Design* book:

> *"Adaptive Web Design is about creating interfaces that adapt to the user's capabilities (in terms of both form and function)."*

> Adaptive web design implements new HTML5 functionalities only for newer devices, say to provide an enhanced experience. It misses out these functionalities on older devices, thus ensuring that the basic setup still works on them.

There are many ways to implement adaptive features. The following are the most common practices to achieve them:

- Using jQuery plugins to enable the touch event interactions in mobile devices (more in *Chapter 6, Building Responsive Image Sliders*)
- Transforming common table structures into responsive tables (more in *Chapter 7, Designing Responsive Tables*)
- Visual customization of form elements only for desktop (more in *Chapter 8, Implementing Responsive Forms*)
- Using geolocation functionality to bring more relevant content to the user
- Changing information hierarchy where the correct priority of content is set

Diego Eis, a Brazilian known to disseminate some best practices and the creator of the `Tableless.com.br` website, drew up an excellent comparison between responsive web design and non-responsive web design in one of his articles. Imagine if we were planning to travel to two or more destinations, you would certainly organize many clothing combinations such as jackets, pants, shorts, and shirts which would result in one big heavy bag. This is because you never know what the climate will be like in each place. In the same way, to be prepared for all events, sometimes it can slightly reduce the performance of the website..

Adapting the screen with media queries

Luke Wroblewski, author of popular web design books and a good reference for many articles, posted a recent device-sizes classification announced by technology companies as follows:

- 4"-5" smartphones
- 5"-6" phone / tablet hybrids
- 7"-8" tablets
- 9"-10" tablets
- 11"-17" laptops and convertibles (tablet/laptop)
- 20"-30" desktops

Labels such as smartphone are just friendly labels as long as we know that the responsive web design makes the structure respond to the device's screen resolution, not to the type of device. But, we must analyze if it is better to offer a different approach for a specific width. This is the improved feature of this module, where CSS2.1 was focused on media types such as print, screen, and handheld; in CSS3, the focus is on media features.

Media queries are mostly used and most browsers adopt it natively (Firefox 3.6 and above, Safari 4 and above, Chrome 4 and above, Opera 9.5 and above, iOS Safari 3.2 and above, Opera Mobile 10 and above, Android 2.1 and above, and Internet Explorer 9 and above). And now, here comes the question: what about IE6-IE8? For these browsers there is a known lightweight solution called **Respond**, which helps a lot when support for old browsers is needed (more in *Chapter 10, Ensuring Browser Support*).

Trying to keep concise on this topic, the following are the features mostly used when we are specifying media queries:

- Width: `min-width` / `max-width`
- Height: `min-height` / `max-height`
- Orientation: It checks whether a device is portrait or landscape in orientation
- Resolution: For example, `min-resolution: 300dpi`

Check the following CSS code for a better understanding of the use of media queries and their syntax:

```
/* Standard desktop screens */
@media only screen and (min-width:1025px) {
  CSS GOES HERE
}
/* Tablets */
@media only screen and (min-width:481px) and (max-width:1024px) {
  CSS GOES HERE
}
/* Smartphones */
@media only screen and (max-width:480px) {
  CSS GOES HERE
}
```

Just to clarify this code, the following figure is a visual interpretation of this code, where it shows that the layout could be displayed in different ways depending on the device's screen:

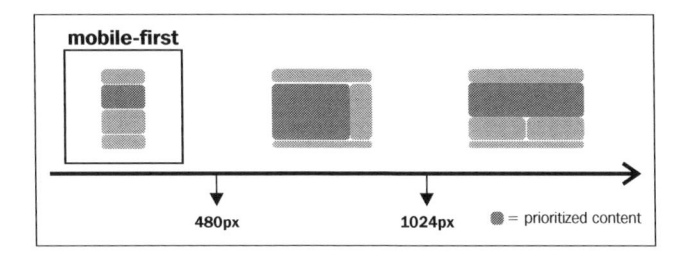

> **Downloading the example code**
>
> You can download the example code files for all Packt books you have purchased from your account at http://www.packtpub.com. If you purchased this book elsewhere, you can visit http://www.packtpub.com/support and register to have the files e-mailed directly to you.

Mobile-first

Let's start this section by analyzing the use case of this project:

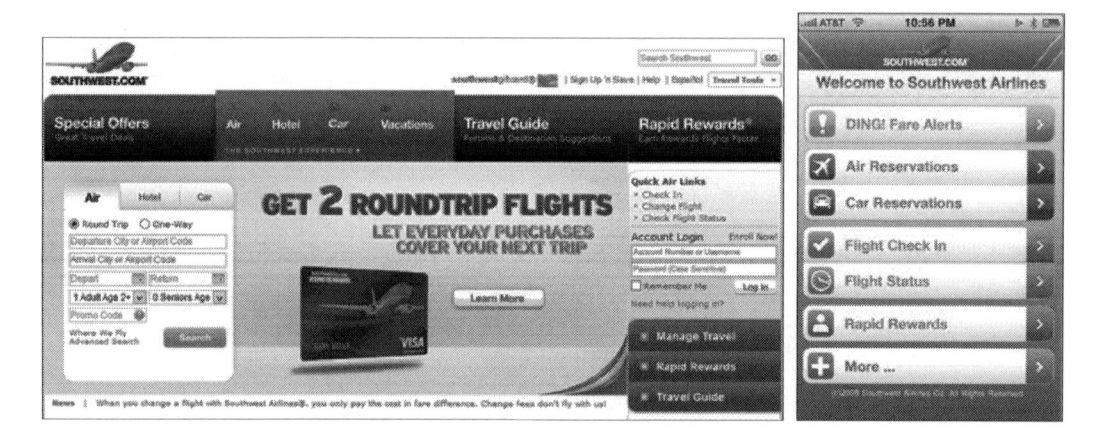

This result is commonly seen when the project starts with desktop-first, and the web design creation just fills the blank space with banners or pictures, less relevant links, animations, and so on. We are probably forgetting the obvious and basic flow that the user follows. We know that sometimes these other items look important to the project, but it is evident that this project design requires an information architecture review.

In the previous example, we can notice (on the right side) how simple the communication with the user can be, and it may be more efficient with less visual clutter. And that is the trend: make it simple. The next quote by *Bill DeRouchey* summarizes it:

> *"Designing the mobile app first forced us to strip down to essentials."*

> In other words, mobile-first is good for business because objectivity brings money. The content you are adding to your website is valuable and important to the end user. The implementation of these new features will allow visitors to have a far better user experience with quicker and more intuitive access to content on the go.

In this case, when the mobile-first concept was applied, a specific link could be found only on the interior pages. However, the objective of the homepage is to direct the user to the correct page, following the website flux information. For non-relevant links this scenario is acceptable.

Take a look at the following screenshot, and notice the many differences about the organization of information and focus on important links in a desktop version:

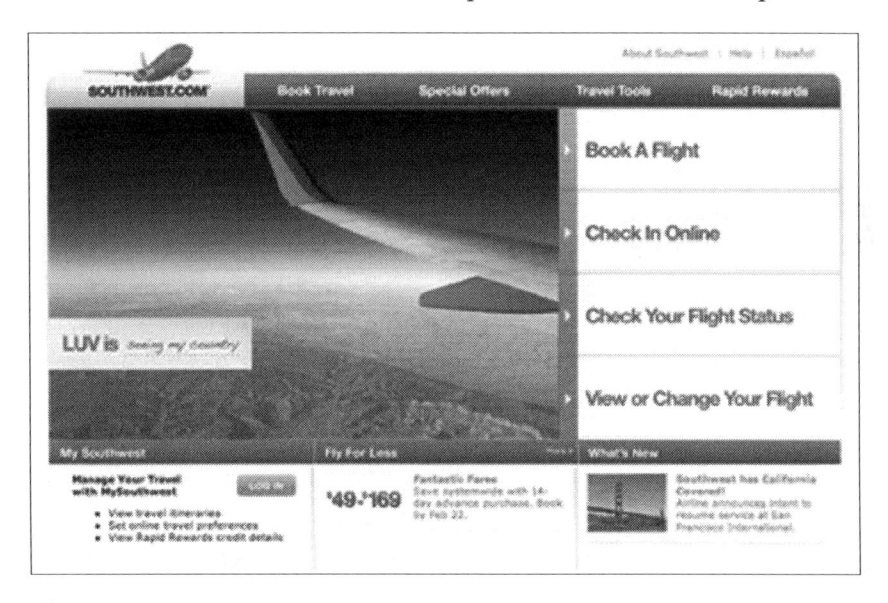

Using wireframe tools

Wireframe is a visual guide that helps to craft your website structure, and its main focus lies in functionality, behavior, and priority of content. It should be the first step of any project because it makes it easier to analyse the information architecture and arrangement of the visual elements.

Exploring Responsive Web Design

Wireframe.cc (http://wireframe.cc/) is an easy way to start our project. This tool is great to do something quick but with low fidelity. For detailed works, there are better tools such as Balsamiq Mockups or Pencil.

The usage of Wireframe.cc is very simple. After entering in the tool's site, perform the following:

1. On the top-left corner choose the device.
2. Then click on setting to redefine our container width if necessary.
3. Now click-and-drag to draw.
4. After this, select the appropriate stencil.
5. If you chose a wrong stencil, just double-click on it to edit it.

> When you finish using the wireframe, do not forget to click on the **Save** button that will generate a URL for further access.

Exercise 1 – practicing mobile-first development in wireframes

Visit http://mediaqueri.es/ and take your time to get inspired. Let's start our website project creating three website wireframes for these dimensions: smartphone, tablet, and desktop, by applying the mobile-first concept.

The following three wireframes will be used as reference for *Exercise 1*:

Summary

In this chapter, we reviewed the concept of responsive web design. We have also learned what mobile-first is. We learned about the media queries and how they can be different on our site implementation. We also created a wireframe drafting our site. This will connect us to the next chapter which will code this wireframe.

Now, let's move on in our project by learning how to use the three distinct responsive grid systems: Fluid Baseline Grid, 1140 Grid, and my favorite Foundation4 Grid. Also, we will look at adapting the website's behavior by using JavaScript. All of these topics will be explained in the next chapter.

2
Designing Responsive Layouts/Grids

"To think about the web responsively is to think in proportions, not pixels."

The previous quote by *Trent Walton* summarizes the ideas in this chapter because, when we are working with responsive design, we must think about fluidity, adaptation, and not about being pixel perfect. This is the reason that the habit of checking pixel-by-pixel is in a fast decline.

But, there are two ways to solve this problem and keep our site responsive:

- Performing the site conversions using a little math to ensure a good result
- Using responsive grid systems where you pick a bunch of columns and keep your code within this column using relative dimensions

These advances in mobile technology and the quick evolution of websites' techniques have pushed everyone to review the concept of the limited dimensions of sites and start to think in terms of a structure that will adapt itself and offer the content required for each situation.

In this chapter, we will learn the following:

- Adapting the site using JavaScript
- How viewing objects in the percentage format gives flexibility to the structure
- How to assimilate features of responsive grid systems
- How to code three different responsive grids
- How to Photoshop grid templates
- How to set up the `meta` tag of `viewport` before starting
- How to implement wireframes using Foundation4 Grid

Adapting the site using JavaScript

As we saw in the previous chapter, we may use media queries to identify the current available area and render specific design customizations. This property is very useful, but does not work in older browsers, such as Internet Explorer 8 and older. There are two main solutions we will take a look at that handle media queries very well: **Adapt.js** and **Respond.js**.

Let's undertake further analysis of the characteristics of each solution and see what it offers in addition to capturing the device dimensions dynamically (much like the `@media` query does) as an alternative to projects that need support for older browsers.

Adapt.js

The following are the characteristics of Adapt.js:

- After capturing the browser's dimensions, Adapt.js serves only the CSS that is needed, when it is needed
- It has a very lightweight file

Some points that should be considered before adopting it are as follows:

- This analysis of the size of the browser window is done on demand and short delays may occur in order to render the correct CSS
- The script must be inserted at the beginning of the code (in the `head` tag) and the initial loading of the page may take a bit longer.

There are some default CSS files and media queries that come with Adapt.js as a suggestion, which can be used on our site. The following are the files provided by `http://adapt.960.gs/` by default:

DEFAULT CSS FILES & WIDTHS	
File Name	**Screen Width**
mobile.css	below 760px
720.css	760px to 980px
960.css	980px to 1280px
1200.css	1280px to 1600px
1560.css	1600 to 1940px
1920.css	1940px to 2540px
2520.css	above 2540px

How to do it

After you download and place the files in your project, add the following piece of code in the `<head>` tag. In the following code, we are able to change the default path of the CSS file, the frequency of dynamic adaptation (once or whenever each window changes), and the CSS files based on ranges:

```
<noscript>
  <link rel="stylesheet" href="assets/css/mobile.min.css" />
</noscript>
<script>
  var ADAPT_CONFIG = {
    path: 'assets/css/',
    dynamic: true,
      range: [
    '0px    to 760px   = mobile.min.css',
    '760px  to 980px   = 720.min.css',
    '980px  to 1280px  = 960.min.css',
    '1280px to 1600px  = 1200.min.css',
    '1600px to 1940px  = 1560.min.css',
    '1940px to 2540px  = 1920.min.css',
    '2540px = 2520.min.css'
    ]
  };
</script>
<script src="assets/js/adapt.min.js" />
```

Respond.js

The Respond.js files can be downloaded from `https://github.com/scottjehl/Respond`. The following are the characteristics of Respond.js:

- This solution seems to be easier than Adaptive.js
- It has a lightweight file
- You will need to first check if the browser really requires this script, executing it only if needed
- There are two useful APIs helping us to debug

The cons are as follows:

- It also has a certain delay in executing the correct CSS choice at the right time

How to do it

After you download and place the files in our project, just add the following code in the `head` tag and it will execute the solution:

```
<script src="js/respond.min.js">
```

> Respond.js uses the `@media` query that we already should be using in our code and applies the styles dynamically. There is no extra work!

How percentage gives flexibility to the structure

Some old websites, and even recent ones, that do not care about the flexible structure, still use pixel as the unit of measurement. Pixel provides us greater control of its structure and accuracy. But, nowadays, we no more have control over where the website will be displayed (as we saw in *Chapter 1, Exploring Responsive Web Design*), which generates the need to build flexible structures where elements may stretch and fit the dimension.

Percentage always works as it is related to the value declared in its parent element. So, if a `div` tag is of size 50 percent and its parent element has 600 px, the `div` tag will be of the size 300 px, as the following figure shows:

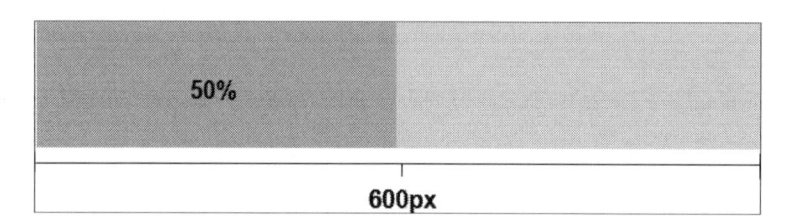

The same applies to a percentage where its parent element is of 50 percent of the actual size of an object, the `div` tag that is of 50 percent of the size will look like it is 25 percent, maintaining proportions. Let's see the following figure:

But, the question is: what if we do not set the width of our parent element? *Maurício Samy Silva* explains this very well in his blog at http://www.maujor.com/blog/2013/03/08/por-que-height-100-nao-funciona/. In this case, the parent element takes the default width of our current viewport. In other words, with each resizing of the browser window, this width changes automatically and this event is exactly what gives us the power of flexible structure.

Going back to the previous example, where `div` is set to 50 percent, it visually appears to be half the size of the usable area as shown in the following figure:

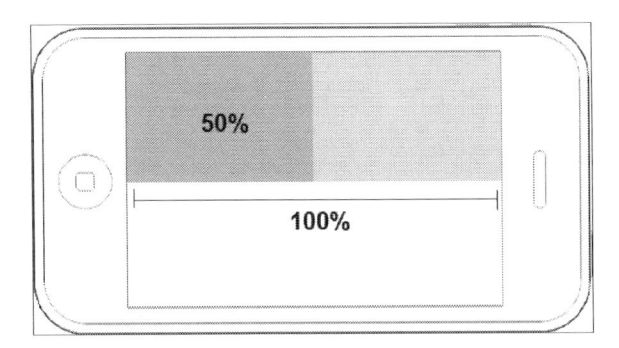

Now that you've seen the importance of the fluidity of the structure, another important task is to transform the padding and margins as well as the percentage. It has an impact, for example, when we need a big horizontal padding showing on large screens because, if the same website is seen on a smartphone and the padding has been defined in pixels, it will take a lot of space on the screen.

We could make an exception to the rule for mobile phones, decreasing this blank space. But, try to imagine the hard work that we would have to do for all the elements! The best option is to convert this spacing from pixel to percentage.

Converting pixel to percentage

The topic of converting pixel to percentage is important because this is where the magic starts to unfold; in other words, we will see with an example how to abandon the absolute size in pixels and convert it to percentage. The process of converting pixel to percentage should be used especially if the purpose of our project is to have greater flexibility in controlling the elements.

Let's practice converting the following sample pixel-based structure into percentage:

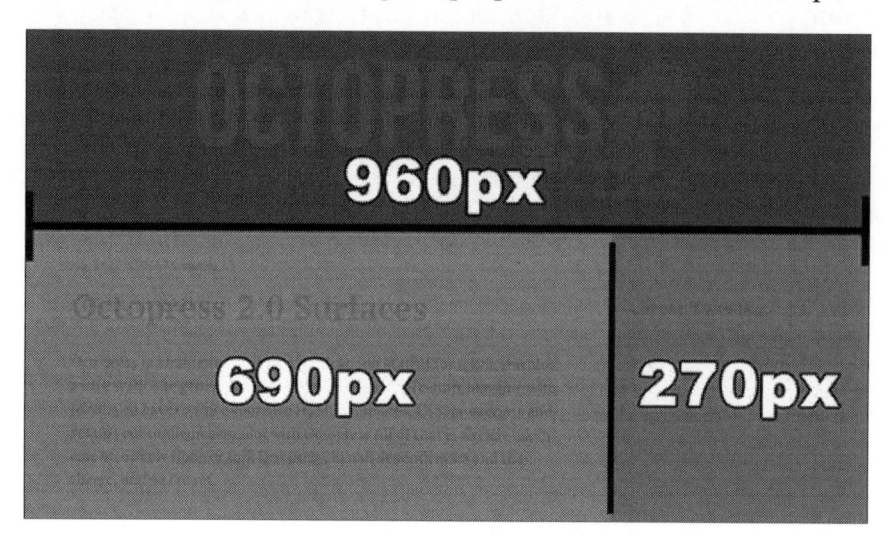

The following code is a sample of the CSS code representing the details in the previous screenshot:

```css
#wrap {
  width:960px;
}
#content {
  width:690px;
  float:left;
}
#right-sidebar {
  width:270px;
  float:left;
}
```

Let's see the magical formula: *Target / Context = Result*.

In the previous formula, *Target* is the original element width in pixels, which is 690 in the following code, *Context* is the width of its container, which is 960, and *Result* is the flexible value:

```css
#wrap {
  width:100%; /* container 960 */
}
```

```
#content {
  width:71.875%; /* 690 ÷ 960 */
  float:left;
}
#right-sidebar {
  width:28.125%; /* 270 ÷ 960 */
  float:left;
}
```

> Sharing a bit of my experience, I would suggest putting the original values ahead of the result. This makes a difference when we want to convert the size again and we forget the original pixel value.

Also, I would like to emphasize the importance of not rounding up the math result. This is important for accuracy about the flexibility of the elements, preventing undesired breaks.

The following figure is the result of conversion to a flexible structure:

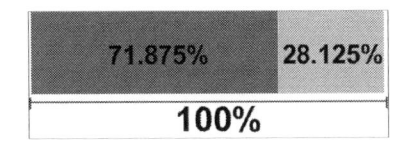

71.875%	28.125%
100%	

To help make this conversion easier, there is a tool named **Flexible Math** that may be found at `http://responsv.com/flexible-math/`. This site does exactly the math necessary for pixel conversion as long as it is based on the parent element size (as we've seen in the previous section).

There is also another kind of conversion that is from em to px of font sizes and line heights, but we'll learn about it in more detail in *Chapter 4, Designing Responsive Text*. Although we are talking about EM, the magical formula used will be the same, requiring some attention on other determined points.

We'll see in *Chapter 5, Preparing Images and Videos*, that not specifying the size of the `<img>` tag is only the first step to scaling the image. Later, we'll see in detail how to make images fluid and also some ways to display images and videos in the best-suited way for each situation.

If we have a lot of work with math conversions and it is consuming a lot of time, we should think of another way of doing it. There is a more convenient and faster solution to get this flexible structure, the name of which is the responsive grid system, as we will see in the following section.

What is a responsive grid system?

A grid system itself may be labeled as a development kit or a small collection of CSS files that will help us develop websites quickly. Some of them have a fixed width of columns (that may vary depending on the tool used). Columns are a grid system's smallest unit of measurement. Most grid systems contain 12-16 columns. Gutters are margins used to create space between columns.

In addition, grid systems save development time if the design is made grid-based. Sometimes, the layout creation may be limited by the use of columns, but this is not too common. The advantages of grid systems are that they help us achieve better readability and balance the visual weight, flexibility, and overall page cohesiveness.

To better understand how the grid system works, look at the following screenshot and notice that the header region's width could be measured as 12 columns (full width) and the **Sidebar** region as only 3 columns:

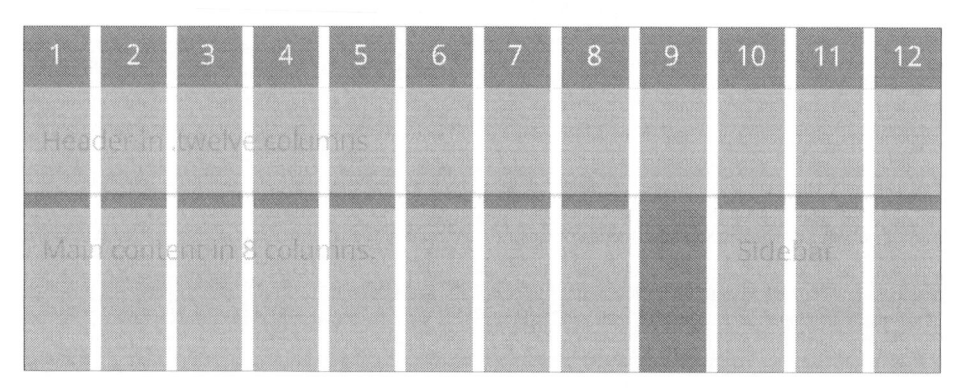

When shouldn't we use a grid? Implementing a grid will probably be impossible if your site's layout uses irregular column sizes and irregular gutters.

Here comes the question: what are the main differences between the responsive grid system and the non-responsive grid system?

The following are the distinguishing characteristics of the responsive grid system:

- It must have different traits at different sizes
- It must be fluid between breakpoints
- It must have enough control to decide which columns will transform and at which point
- Classes should ideally still make sense at all breakpoints

Responsive grid systems

Now, we are going to see three different systems to apply, but for our progressive understanding, I would like to start with describing the less complex systems and then those with more options and resources.

> Read all these grid systems before you choose the one that matches your project best. Also, there are other types of responsive grids that I have not tried to implement in a real project yet.

Fluid Baseline Grid system

The objective of this development kit is to provide ease and agility in developing for responsive websites. The Fluid Baseline Grid code (http://fluidbaselinegrid.com/) is simple, lightweight, non-intrusive, and is able to be customized depending on the needs of the project.

This grid system is based on a three-column folding layout: one column for mobile devices, two for tablets, and three for desktops and beyond. Let's see its usage.

To set the code this way, we just need to use the class g1 when we want the content to fill just one column of the structure; then, g2 for two columns and g3 for three columns. Look at the following sample of code:

```
<div id="content">
    <div class="g2">
        ...
    </div>
    <div class="g3">
        ...
    </div>
    <div class="g1">
        ...
    </div>
</div>
```

The following figure is a preview of this code:

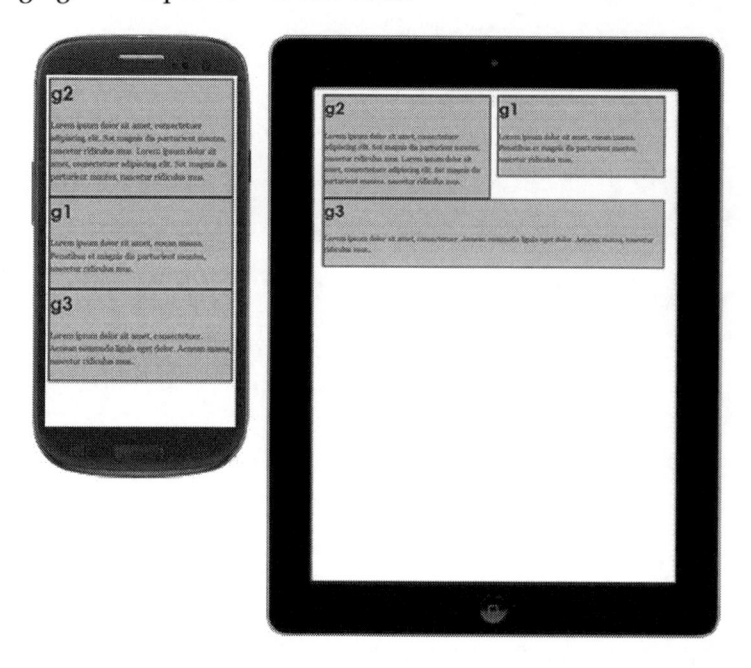

Now, let's see a website sample first and then try to code a structure using the classes:

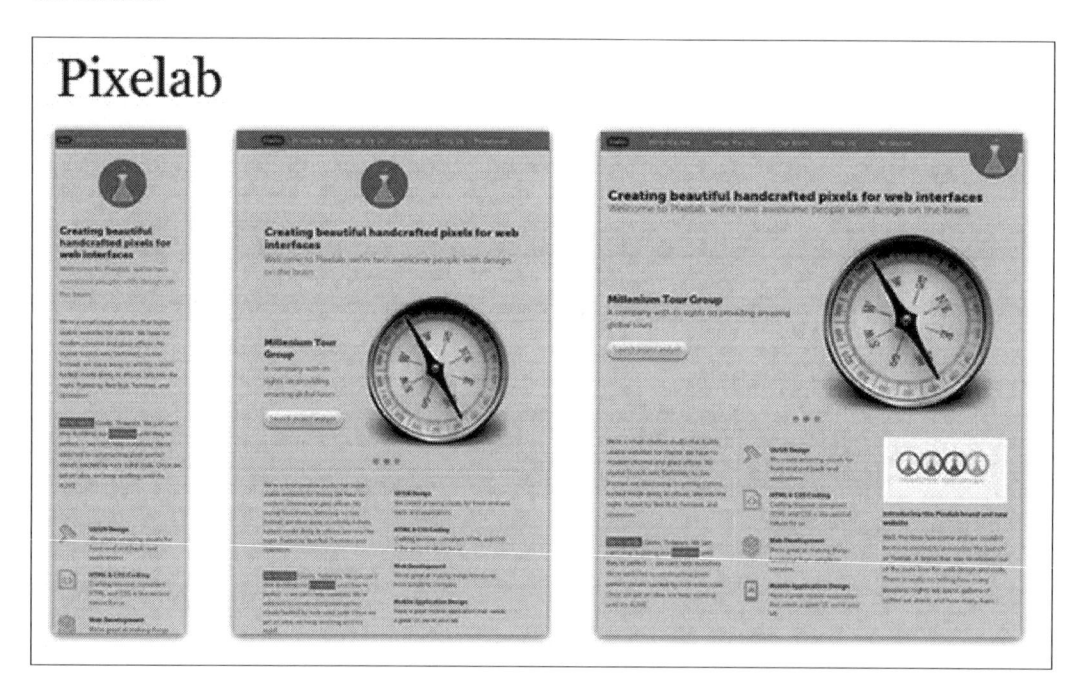

The HTML result should be the following:

```
<div id="content">
    <div class="g3">
        ...
    </div>
    <div class="g1">
        ...
    </div>
    <div class="g1">
        ...
    </div>
    <div class="g1">
        ...
    </div>
</div>
```

Did you notice that the compass image was hidden on the mobile phone screen? In this case, the solution was to hide the carousel on the mobile CSS and show it on the tablet CSS (and desktop as well).

The major advantages to using Fluid Baseline Grid are as follows:

- Fluid columns
- Baseline grid with beautiful typographic standards
- Responsive design behaviors
- Uses Normalize.css to fix common browser inconsistencies
- Simple file structure containing only the minimum number of files to get started
- Polyfills support for IE6/7/8: Respond.js (media queries) and html5shim (HTML5 elements)

Fluid Columns are defaulted to a minimum three-column folding grid with columns around 31 percent wide and gutters 2 percent wide between columns. If the website design requires more columns, it's not a problem, because it may be changed in the CSS code.

The Baseline Grid brings the cross-browser solution to typography, improving the readability and creating better harmony within the text. The main fonts used are Georgia and Futura and they can easily be changed to match the project's needs.

Fluid Baseline Grid is designed for mobile-first and provides common breakpoints to our implementation of responsive design. The CSS code is prepared to start customization from the small screen and suggest differences on content displays, depending upon the usable area in the device. As long as it is based on columns, the Fluid Baseline Grid is divided into: one column for mobile devices, two for tablets, and three for desktops and other devices.

1140 Grid

The 1140 Grid (http://cssgrid.net/) has a simple structure. Its objective is to offer more agility in code development when we define the width of each main element. It was divided into 12 columns that will or will not be merged for your ease, depending on your preference. But, when this project was designed, the width dimension was limited to a maximum of 1280 px. If the project does not require display on a big device, 1140 Grid works very well for all other smaller dimensions.

To clarify, the following code shows how, in fact, you can do it:

```
<div class="container">
    <div class="row">
        <div class="onecol">
            ...
        </div>
        <div class="twocol">
            ...
        </div>
        <div class="threecol">
            ...
        </div>
        <div class="threecol last">
            ...
        </div>
    </div>
</div>
```

The following figure shows the result:

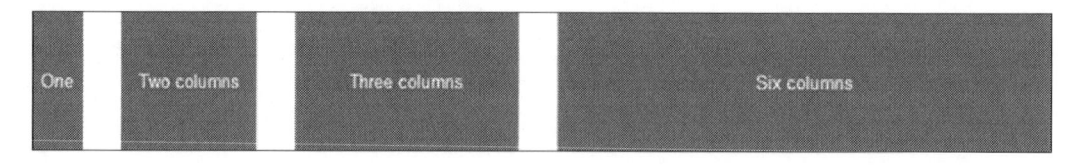

As part of our knowledge assimilation process, let's go back to the Pixelab sample and code using the 1140 Grid:

```
<div id="container">
   <div class="row">
        ...
   </div>
   <div class="row">
        <div class="fourcol">
          ...
        </div>
        <div class="fourcol">
          ...
        </div>
        <div class="fourcol last">
          ...
        </div>
   </div>
</div>
```

The row class centers the inner columns and defines `1140px` as `max-width`.

The classes, `.onecol`, `.twocol`, `.threecol`, `.fourcol`, `.fivecol`, `.sixcol`, `.sevencol`, `.eightcol`, `.ninecol`, `.tencol`, `.elevencol`, and `.twelvecol` can be used for each column. Also, they will be used in any combination within a row that adds up to twelve columns or less. In the last element, remember to add a class `last` too; that will remove the extra margins.

In comparison with Fluid Baseline Grid, one of the few differences is that the 1140 Grid would have already implemented more columns (providing more options to a developer), but Fluid Baseline Grid developers are free to implement it there if they need it.

In addition to the simple structure, Grid 1140 is also highlighted by the following characteristics:

- CSS code prepared to scale images
- Gutters based in percentages
- Browser support (except for IE6)
- Minimal file structure
- Downloadable PS template

Foundation4

Foundation4, `http://foundation.zurb.com`, is a complete framework with many components inside. They are predefined and stylized so professionally that they will serve as the basis for our projects. Focusing only on the grid component of Foundation4 surprises us again as it provides many options.

This framework is different due to its download area, where it shows the screen shown in the following screenshot, because it gives developers the freedom to start their project in the way that best suits them (if they already have some knowledge about grid in general):

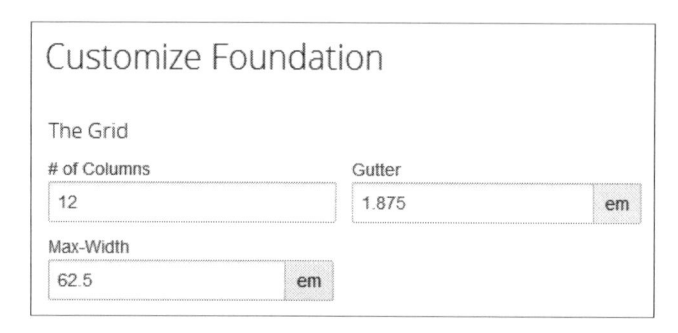

```
Customize Foundation

The Grid
# of Columns            Gutter
12                      1.875                em
Max-Width
62.5         em
```

But, no worries; if you are still learning about it, by default, it comes with most-used values such as 12 columns and 62.5 em (1000 px) of maximum screen size.

There are other good features in Foundation4 which are as follows:

- Predefined HTML classes.
- Small and large grids.
- Nesting our grid.
- Offsets.
- Centered columns.
- Source ordering.
- Mobile-first.
- Normalize and Modernizr scripts supporting browsers.
- There is no support for browsers such as Internet Explorer 7 and older. Also, Internet Explorer 8 has limited support for the Grid and some UI components such as the Input Switcher.
- To work with Internet Explorer 8, Foundation4 drives developers to use a complementary solution from its previous version which may be found at `http://foundation.zurb.com/docs/support.html`.

This framework deserves more attention because it has more options and advantages. That is the reason we see their characteristics in detail. In the next examples, we will use 12 columns as suggested by the tool as reference.

Foundation4 has a bunch of predefined HTML classes that help our development a lot because all the code is already created and we just need to call it using the class name. In the following example, we see a small class and the number of columns that the element will occupy:

```
<div class="row">
 <div class="small-3 columns">...</div>
 <div class="small-6 columns">...</div>
 <div class="small-3 columns">...</div>
</div>
```

The following figure shows the result:

| 3 | 6 | 3 |

Notice that the sum of 3, 6, and 3 is equal to 12. Also, there is an option to change the class from small to large. If we swap these classes, when we are decreasing the browser width reaching upto 768 px, each <div> tag takes up the maximum width. There is the possibility of having these two classes together—the content being shown for the small screens with dimensions smaller than 768 px—and for large dimensions, the width is as given the previous example.

In this case, the code would look as follows:

```
<div class="row">
 <div class="small-6 large-5 columns">...</div>
 <div class="small-6 large-7 columns">...</div>
</div>
```

Foundation4 Grid allows for nesting down as far as we would like. This technique is normally used to perform a quite complex design implementation or to better position the form elements. The following code is a sample of its usage:

```
<div class="row">
 <div class="small-8 columns">8
   <div class="row">
     <div class="small-3 columns">3 Nested</div>
     <div class="small-9 columns">9 Nested</div>
   </div>
 </div>
 <div class="small-4 columns">4</div>
</div>
```

Designing Responsive Layouts/Grids

The following figure shows the result:

8		4
3 Nested	9 Nested	

We can create additional space between columns in a row using `offset`. Manipulating this parameter, we may align the column as we want. Remember that all the offset comes to the left of element. Again, the sum of numbers should be equal to 12. Let's see this in the following example, where the first `div` tag fills two columns, then there are two columns offset, and then another `div` tag fills eight columns:

```
<div class="row">
  <div class="large-2 columns">2</div>
  <div class="large-8 large-offset-2 columns">8, offset 2</div>
</div>
```

The result is as follows:

2	8, offset 2

The `centered column` class was created to position a specific column (not the content inside) to the center of the row. Foundation4 offers two classes: `large-centered` and `small-centered`. As we've seen before, a small version will be shown as it is not overridden by a large version. For example, if we want to display a `div` tag filling six columns and that is centered (for small and large versions), we should use the following code before:

```
<div class="row">
  <div class="small-6 small-centered columns">6 centered</div>
</div>
```

The following is the result:

6 centered

Maybe the following feature is a little confusing, but it is very useful when we want to order the source code to be placed on top of our relevant content. To do this, we just need to use the classes `push` and `pull`. The following feature will also affect each version separately (using `small` or `large` before the function, that is, `large-push-8`) or the two versions together:

```
<div class="row">
  <div class="small-4 push-8 columns">4</div>
```

[32]

```
    <div class="small-8 pull-4 columns">8, last</div>
</div>
```

The following is the result:

8, last	4

Photoshop grid templates

To facilitate the visualization of columns while creating our design, there is a Photoshop plugin named Guideguide.

The Guideguide plugin (http://guideguide.me/) is supported for some versions of Photoshop, which are: CS5, CS6, and CC. However, if you have Photoshop CS4, Version 2.03 of this plugin will work, but it will no longer be updated with new features. This is a tool that guides us in creating custom guidelines for our Photoshop documents.

After installing the Guideguide plugin and creating a blank file, when we are accessing it in Photoshop, it will open the window shown in the following screenshot; I suggest filling it with the initial values shown, if you are not too familiar with grids:

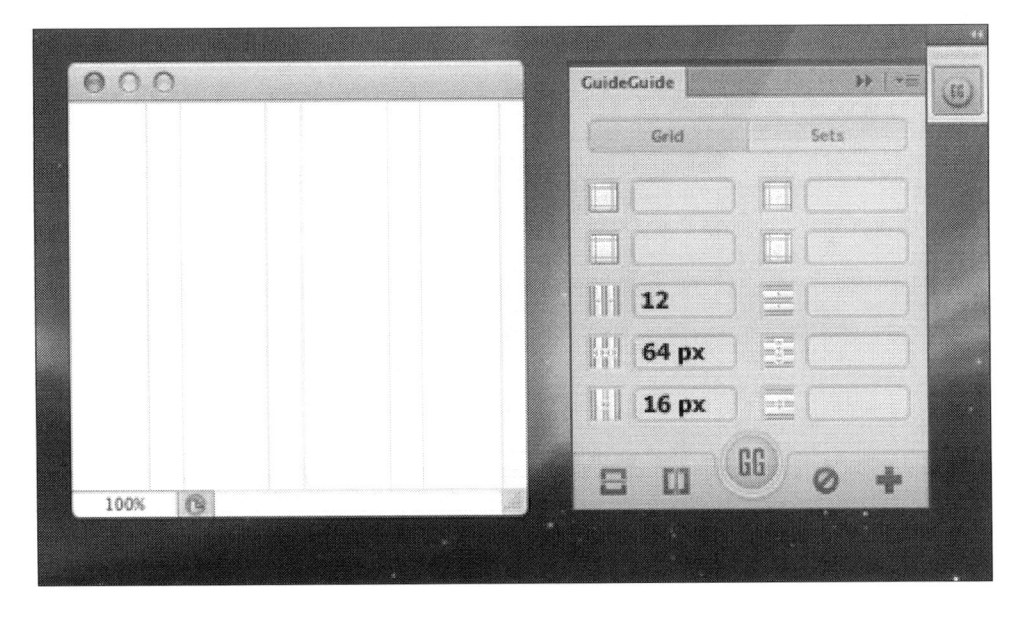

Then, clicking on the **GG** button, it will create guidelines in our document which will be very useful in layout creation.

Setting up the meta tag of viewport before starting

The `meta` tag of `viewport` works by displaying just a portion of the full viewable area. This configuration is very important when we are crafting a responsive website because, without it, the mobile device browser will return a zoomed-out version of the website to the user. There is no standard syntax for its usage, but all common mobile browsers support the following tag:

```
<meta name="viewport" content="width=device-width">
```

Other features such as `initial-scale` can be used to define the `meta` tag of `viewport`, which may prevent the user from opening the website in the zoomed-in mode and `maximum-scale` will restrict the user from zooming in on the content. The following code is an example of `viewport` restricting the user experience, giving no permission to use the zoom feature:

```
<meta content="width=device-width, initial-scale=1, maximum-scale=1"
name="viewport">
```

Exercise 2a – creating the layout design for wireframes

Now that we already have the wireframe and knowledge of how to operate the columns of the grid, we need to adapt the wireframe to fit the main elements in the columns, as shown in the following screenshot:

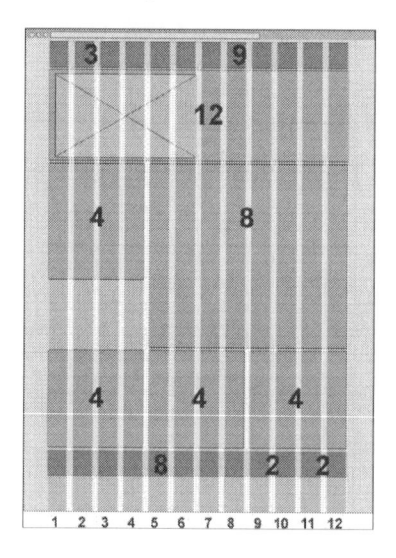

After that, it's about time we colorize it and imagine offering the user the best experience for all devices.

Based on the wireframe from *Exercise 1* in *Chapter 1, Exploring Responsive Web Design*, the following screenshot shows a suggestion for the layout design:

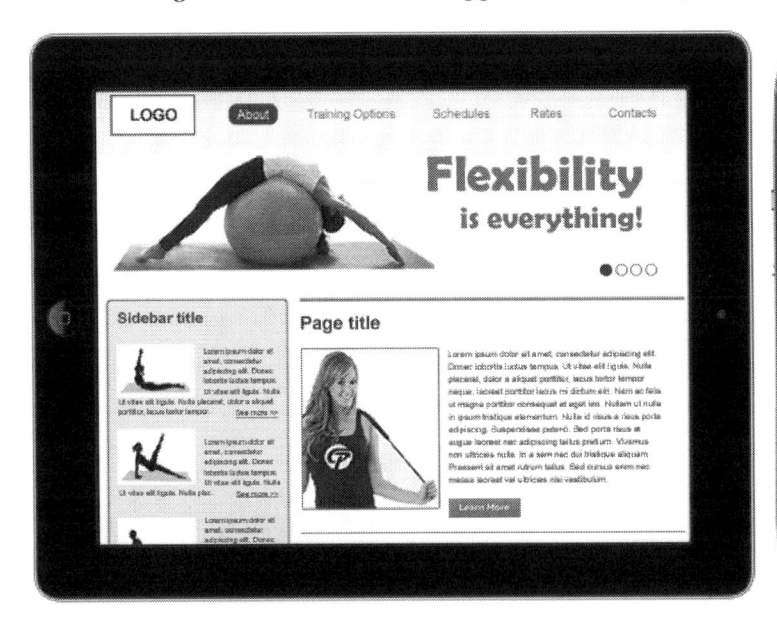

When we are customizing the main elements, remember to keep it inside the guidelines, which will make the next step easier. Otherwise, we'll consume more time to code it than expected.

Designing Responsive Layouts/Grids

The following screenshot shows how the main elements fit in columns:

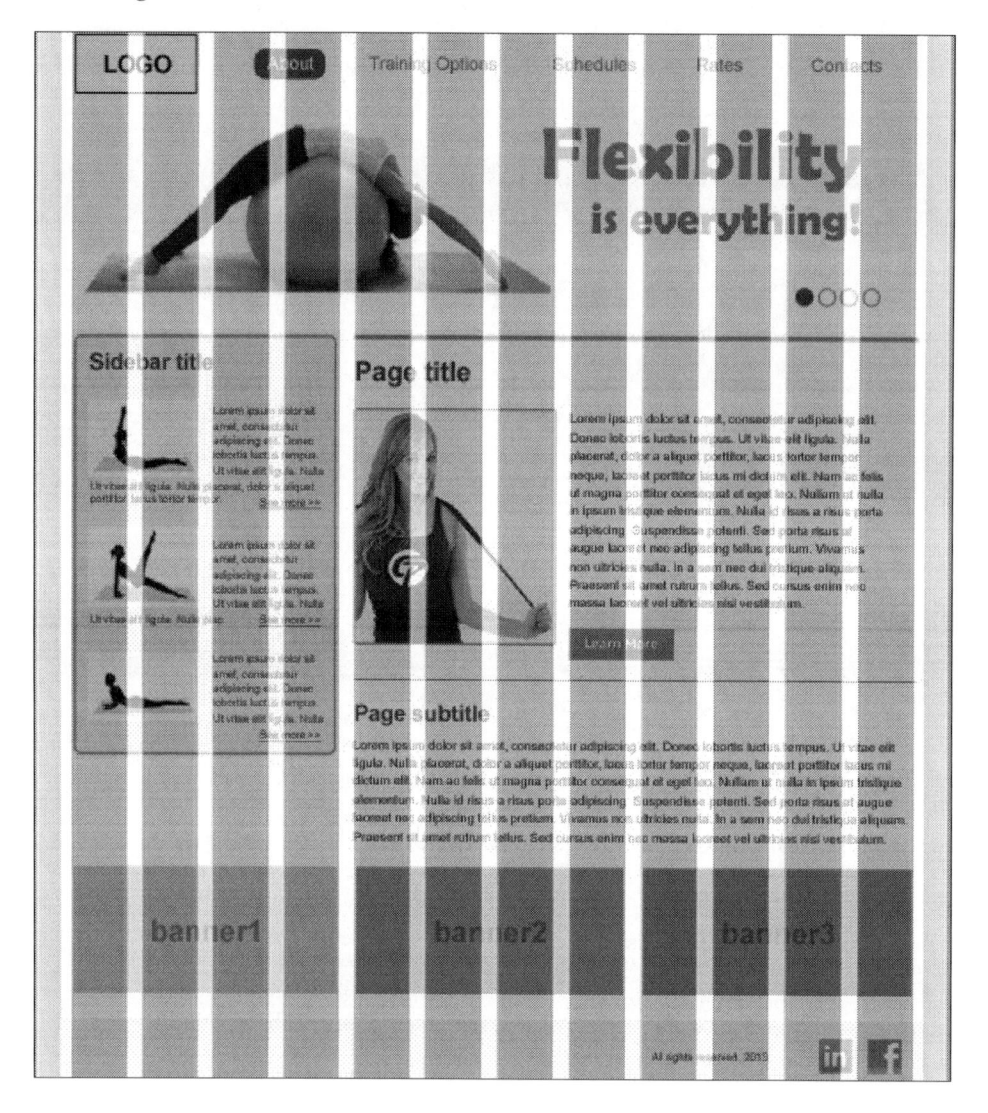

Exercise 2b – using Foundation4 Grid to structure our website

After seeing the use of some Responsive Grid Systems (starting from a simpler solution and going for a more complete solution), let's structure our code using the Foundation4 Grid, creating the response quickly, and without writing one line of CSS code to do that. Also, remember to configure the viewport in the `<head>` tag.

Using the Foundation4 Grid, perform the following recommended steps:

1. Start coding the HTML script.
2. Identify the rows in the structure and add a `row` class to the existent element or to a new `div` tag.
3. Measure how many columns each main element will fill and set this value in the classes.

Let's see how it is done in the following HTML:

```html
<!DOCTYPE html>
<html lang="en">
<head>
 <meta charset="utf-8" />
 <meta name="viewport" content="width=device-width" />
 <title>Responsive Web Design using jQuery & CSS3</title>
 <link rel="stylesheet" href="css/foundation.css" />
</head>
<body>
 <header class="row">
    <a class="large-3 columns" href="#">LOGO</a>
    <nav class="large-9 columns">
      <ul>
        <li><a href="#">About</a></li>
        <li><a href="#">Training Options</a></li>
        <li><a href="#">Schedules</a></li>
        <li><a href="#">Rates</a></li>
        <li><a href="#">Contacts</a></li>
      </ul>
    </nav>
 </header>
 <div class="row">
    <section class="small-12 columns">
      <img src="http://placehold.it/960x230" alt="FPO for slideshow" />
    </section>
 </div>

 <div class="row">
    <section id="content" class="large-8 push-4 small-12 columns">
      <article>
         <h2>Page title</h2>
         <p>FPO text: Lorem ipsum dolor sit amet...</p>
         <p><a href="#" class="button learn-more">Learn more</a></p>
      </article>
```

```html
      <article class="subcontent">
         <h2>Page subtitle</h2>
         <p>FPO text: Lorem ipsum dolor...</p>
      </article>
   </section>
   <aside class="large-4 pull-8 columns">
      <h2>Sidebar title</h2>

      <div class="row">
         <div class="small-4 large-12 columns">
<img src="imgs/aside-1.jpg" class="img-aside" />
      <span>FPO text: Lorem ipsum dolor...</span> <a href="#">See more</a></div>
         <div class="small-4 large-12 columns">
<img src="imgs/aside-2.jpg" class="img-aside" />
<span>FPO text: Lorem ipsum dolor...</span> <a href="#">See more</a></div>
         <div class="small-4 large-12 columns">
<img src="imgs/aside-3.jpg" class="img-aside" />
      <span>FPO text: Lorem ipsum dolor...</span> <a href="#">See more</a></div>
      </div>
   </aside>
 </div>

 <section id="banners" class="row">
    <div class="small-4 columns">Banner1</div>
    <div class="small-4 columns">Banner2</div>
    <div class="small-4 columns">Banner3</div>
 </section>

 <footer class="row">
    <p class="large-2 small-9 large-offset-8 columns">All rights reserved. 2013</p>
    <p class="large-2 small-3 columns">icons</p>
 </footer>
</body>
</html>
```

In this code, I broke one extra line, making it easy to see each row, and also highlighted the classes used by the grid. Let's observe the sum of the columns from each row:

1. `small` = 12 columns
2. `small` = 12 columns (4 + 4 + 4) and `large` = 12 columns (one column per line)
3. `small` = 12 columns (4 + 4 + 4)
4. `small` = 12 columns and `large` = 12 columns (2 + 8 + 2)

The following screenshot shows the result without writing any CSS code, in a device with a width greater than 768 px:

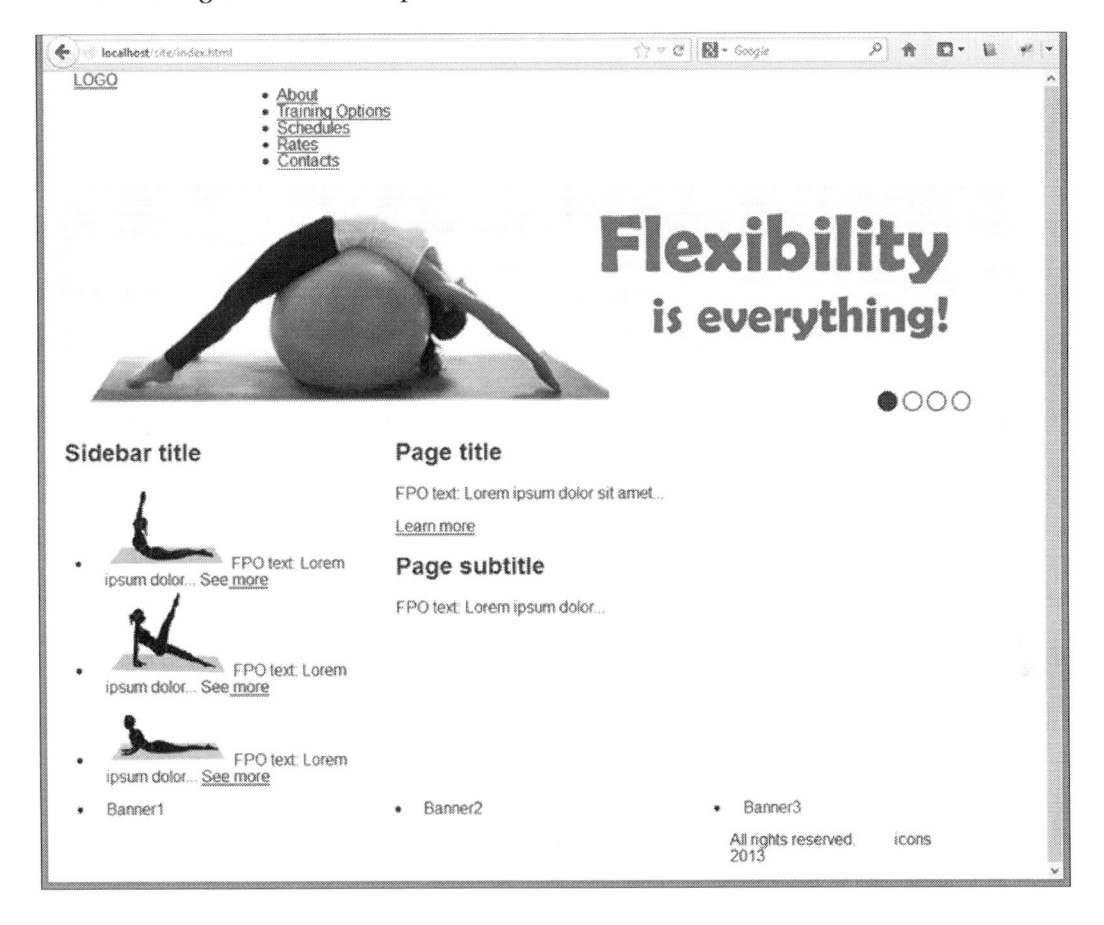

Designing Responsive Layouts/Grids

The following screenshot shows the same site in a device with a width less than 768 px:

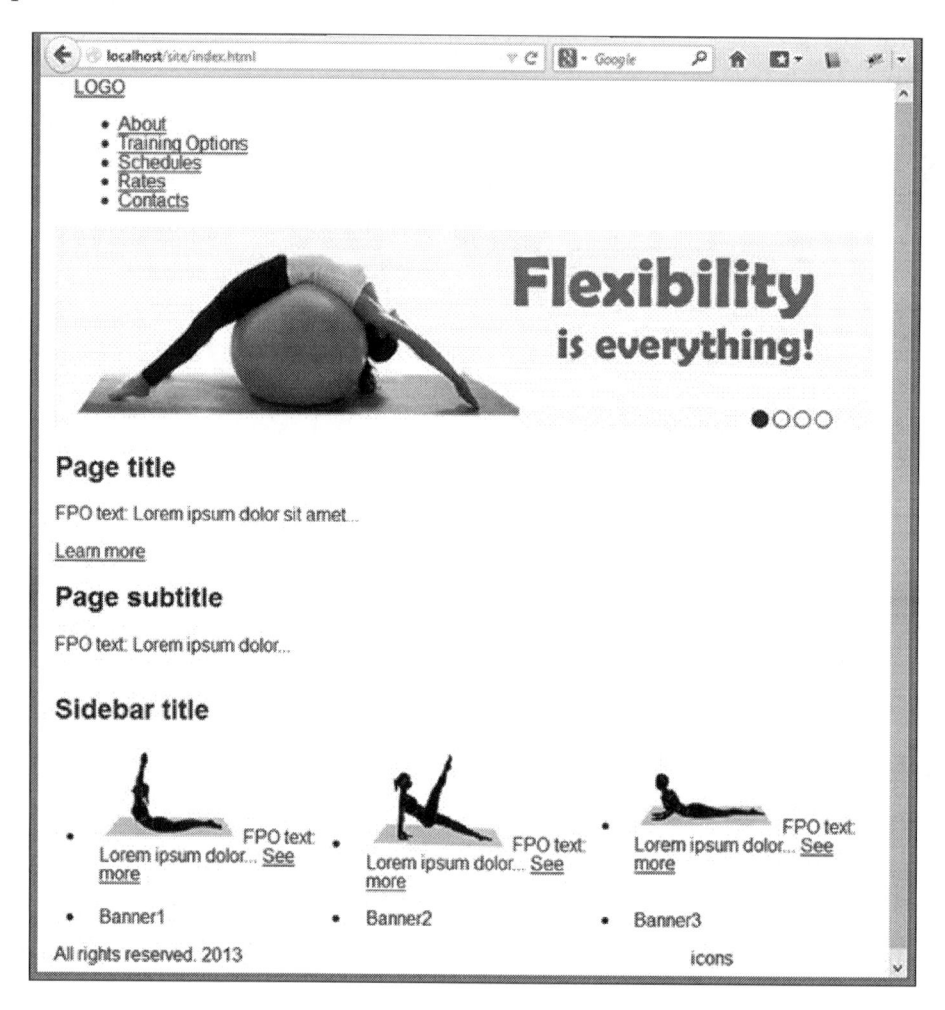

Be calm; the website still looks horrible because this is only the first step of the project. We need to do some visual adjustments to complete our mission.

> I would suggest that you search for some beautiful images to use in your website, improving its look and feel. Otherwise, you can go to http://placehold.it/ to create a placeholder reserving the space for images.

[40]

It is a good approach that avoids altering the CSS that comes with the solution. In this case, we'll create a new CSS file and include it on our website. In the `header` section, after the Zurb Foundation CSS file, include your own CSS code:

```
<link rel="stylesheet" href="css/mystyle.css" />
```

Inside this CSS, we are splitting the customization into three parts, applying the cascade style, and avoiding duplicating parts of the code:

- Both versions
- Small version (lower than 768 px)
- Large version (greater than 768 px)

The following code is used at the beginning of customizing from our site. Feel free to use it as long as it is only a suggestion to match the layout.

```
#banners div {
  text-align: center;
  height: 100px;
  line-height: 100px;
  background: #f65050;
}
#banners div:first-child {
  background: #7ddda3;
}
#banners div:last-child {
  background: #506ff6;
}
@media only screen and (max-width: 48em) {
  .subcontent,
  aside span {
    display: none;
  }
  aside .img-aside {
    display: block;
    margin: 0 auto;
  }
  aside div {
    text-align: center;
  }
}
@media only screen and (min-width: 48em) {
  aside .img-aside {
    float: left;
  }
}
```

Summary

In this chapter, we have learned three different ways to render the specific CSS code using JavaScript solutions: Adapt.js, Respond.js, and Breakpoints.js. We now also understand how to convert pixels to percentages by doing the math and discovering the result. We have also learned what the responsive grid system is and how to use each type of the responsive grid system.

Finally, we have started to code our site using grid (based on the wireframe from *Chapter 1, Exploring Responsive Web Design*), which connects to the next chapter, in which we will cover the different ways to implement responsive menu navigations such as the Toggle menu, the off-canvas menu (such as Facebook), and others.

3
Building Responsive Navigation Menu

The `header` section is an important section when a website is being built. There are some common elements in this area such as a logo, a login, navigation options, a sign-up option, and a search field. But planning this area is not too easy because if we put all the elements together, we will give our users a messy navigation. Another option is to reserve a lot of space for our header, but it will probably hide more content above the fold on smartphones. The expected result is to occupy a small amount of space for your header and to handle that space efficiently in order to display those elements.

In this chapter, we will analyze some types of navigation menu, when it is the correct situation to use each one in a clear and intuitive way, and to avoid frustrating users. That's why crafting our navigation menu in a way that will allow users to easily and clearly see the main and sub-items in it is important to us.

In this chapter we will:

- Design a menu improving its usability
- See most-used responsive navigation patterns and how to code each type
- Apply our recently gained knowledge by doing the exercise

Designing a menu by improving its usability

On responsive websites, especially for those which are using the mobile-first concept, the content is the main reason the user is visiting our site, so we must provide a reasonable space to show the content before the fold.

In order to provide this space, we need to handle the way we display the menu better so that we will be able to offer another view of it, depending on the device.

Anyway, the goal is the same: to make it easier for users to find what they are looking for without drastically affecting the useful area. When the menu is organized, we give the users the freedom to choose where they want to navigate to through our site.

The truth is that there is no answer for the duel between these two interfaces: the top and left navigation menus. Sometimes the navigation works well in one context; however, it may not work as well in another. To figure out which navigation is best for our site, it is important to understand the different contexts where the top and left navigation menus work best. Let's analyze this battle in five rounds:

- **Scanning**: In this, the left navigation menu wins because it occupies less space to show all items and facilitates a vertical scanning (more natural for users).
- **Page space**: In this, the top navigation wins because it uses a minimal vertical space, reserving the content area just for content.
- **Item priority**: For this round, there is a draw between the top and left navigation menus. The top navigation does not have the same weight among the items as the leftmost item will be read before others following the reading sequence. But, it depends on the type of content.
- **Visibility**: For this round, there is a draw between the top and left navigation menus. The top navigation menu is easier to see because it is usually near the logo. In the left navigation, some items may be hidden below the fold.
- **Topics and interests**: For this round, there is a draw between the top and left navigation menus. If our site has a variety of content for a widespread audience (for example, e-commerce sites), the left navigation menu would be better for these users because they have a range of interests and are the ones who will choose which items they want to see. However, for specific topics, the top navigation menu fits better because finding the high-priority items quickly is more important.

Most-used responsive navigation patterns

Planning mobile navigation is not an easy task because we need to provide unobtrusive and quick access to specific content in a responsive way and depending on the objective of the website. After a long study, *Brad Frost*, in his research of popular menu techniques, summarized some trends and established patterns for menu type concepts.

According to his article (http://bradfrostweb.com/blog/web/responsive-nav-patterns/), the navigation patterns are:

- Top nav
- Footer anchor
- Toggle menu
- Select menu
- Footer-only
- Multi toggle
- Toggle and slide
- Off-canvas

Let's inspect each one, see how they look, and understand which approach fits better with your project.

Top nav

The Top nav pattern is the most-viewed pattern on the Internet because it requires a little extra work for its adaptation. To implement this solution, we only need to keep the menu at the top, as we can see in the following screenshot:

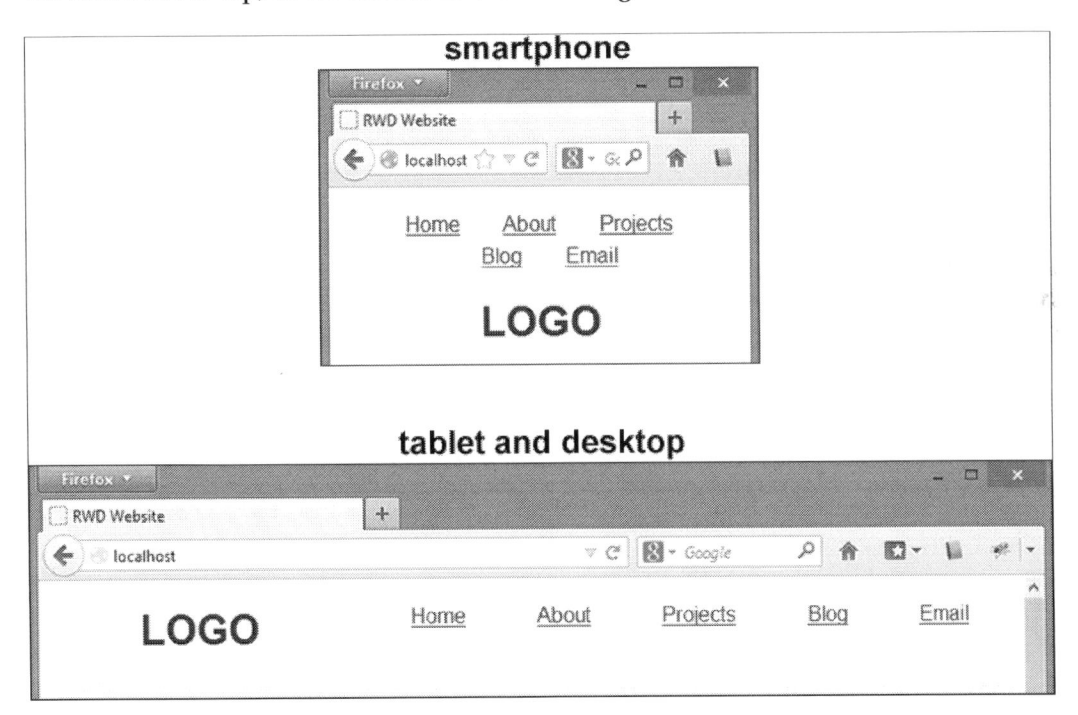

Building Responsive Navigation Menu

How to do it...

In this situation, as shown in the previous screenshot, it is showing the menu above the logo on the smartphone. So, let's code this HTML script to understand the changes:

```
<nav id="site-nav">
  <ul>
    <li><a href="#">Home</a></li>
    <li><a href="#">About</a></li>
    <li><a href="#">Projects</a></li>
    <li><a href="#">Blog</a></li>
    <li><a href="#">Email</a></li>
  </ul>
</nav>
<h1 id="logo">LOGO</h1>
```

If you prefer to rearrange these elements (display logo on top and then the menu), you need to invert the order of elements, moving the `<h1>` tag before the `<nav>` tag in the code.

Unfortunately, the `<nav>` tag is not supported for Internet Explorer 8 and lower. However, this tag has a good semantic meaning and I recommend its usage. We will see in *Chapter 10, Ensuring Browser Support*, how to handle it using `Html5shiv` with `Modernizr`. By adopting the mobile-first concept and using this first block of code in CSS, we may customize the menu to be displayed by filling the horizontal area with tiny horizontal margins and aligning the menu in the center:

```
/* mobile-first */
#site-nav ul {
  list-style: none;
  text-align: center;
  padding: 0;
}
#site-nav li {
  display: inline-block;
  margin: 0 5%;
  line-height: 1.5;
}
#logo {
  text-align: center;
  clear: both;
}
```

For screens more than 768 px, the menu width is reduced to 70 percent and floated to the right. Also, the logo is now floated to the left width, the width of 30 percent, as shown in the following code:

> These percentages are just a part of the example.

```
/* desktop */
@media only screen and (min-width: 768px) {
  #site-nav ul {
    width: 70%;
    float: right;
  }
  #logo {
    float: left;
    width: 30%;
    clear: none;
  }
}
```

> It is very simple to implement, but take care when you have more than three lines of menu items because it will consume much of the important area.

Footer anchor

Footer anchor is a smart solution for which the main objective is to keep more useful space to the content, without penalizing the mobile users seeing our site in a small area. To do this, it is necessary to reallocate the main menu to the footer and just keep an anchor link in the header that will focus on the menu whenever the user clicks on it.

Building Responsive Navigation Menu

The following screenshot represents this navigation pattern being applied only to smartphones where the free space is short:

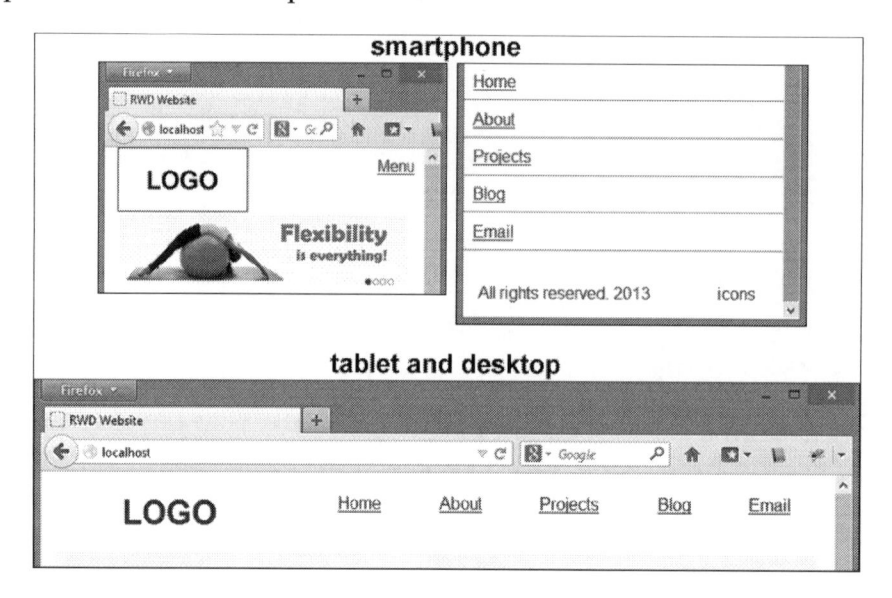

[smartphone and tablet and desktop screenshots]

How to do it

Let's start using the same HTML code from the first navigation pattern. But now we will move the menu to the bottom of the DOM, just before the `</body>` tag and insert the following link in the beginning of the code after the `<body>` tag, because when the user clicks on it, the website will focus on the navigation menu:

```
<a id="link-to-menu" href="#site-nav">&#9776; Menu</a>
```

> The decimal code `&#9776` is a symbol to represent menus because it shows a symbol with three lines.

In the CSS code for smartphones, we need to:

- Create a style for the menu items from menu. Some developers prefer to list these items showing one per line (facilitating touch), but it is up to you.
- Create a style for the button from the header (that will drive the user to the menu).

The CSS code is as follows:

```
/* mobile-first */
#site-nav ul {
  list-style: none;
  text-align: center;
  padding: 0;
}
#site-nav li a {
  display: block;
  border-top: 1px solid #CCC;
  padding: 3%;
}
#site-nav li:last-child a {
  border-bottom: 1px solid #CCC;
}
#link-to-menu {
  position: absolute;
  top: 10px;
  right: 10px;
}
```

For tablets and desktops (devices with screen widths higher than 768 px) the best approach is hiding this header button. Now, we need to show the menu on header without changing anything on the HTML (we just have moved it to the footer area).

Let's implement the following code by setting the menu position on the top and hiding the header button:

```
/* tablet and desktop */
@media only screen and (min-width: 768px) {
  #site-nav {
    position: absolute;
    top: 0;
    left: 30%;
    width: 70%;
  }
  #link-to-menu {
    display: none;
  }
  #site-nav li {
    display: inline-block;
    margin: 0 5%;
    padding: 0;
    width: 18%;
```

```
    border: none;
    line-height: 1.5;
}
#site-nav li a {
    display: inline;
    border: none;
    padding: 0;
}
#site-nav li a,
#site-nav li:last-child a {
    border: none;
  }
}
```

The toggle menu

The toggle navigation pattern has almost the same behavior when compared to the previous pattern. The real difference is shown when the user clicks on the link from the header, and instead of driving the user to the anchored menu, the menu slides down just after the header, thereby providing the user an impressive effect and quick access to the main links. Its implementation is relatively easy, as we will soon see.

> In order to improve the performance of animation, try to use the `max-height` property

The Responsive Nav plugin

The Responsive Nav plugin, `http://responsive-nav.com/`, is a lightweight solution to create the toggle navigation for small screens. We are fond of three main features, which are:

- Using the touch events (we will understand it better later) and CSS3 transitions
- Building this plugin with accessibility in mind and also working with disabled JavaScript. The plugin does not require any external libraries
- Working in all major desktop and mobile browsers, including IE 6 and higher

How to do it

After downloading the files for of this solution, let's insert this code in the `<head>` tag of our HTML:

```
<link rel="stylesheet" href="css/responsive-nav.css">
<script src="js/responsive-nav.js"></script>
```

We will also use the same HTML code of the first example, but right before the `</body>` closing tag of DOM, we need to insert the function that executes the script:

```
<script>
var navigation = responsiveNav("#site-nav");
</script>
```

For now, let's insert the same menu style from the footer anchor pattern:

```
nav ul {
  list-style: none;
  text-align: center;
  padding: 0;
}
.menu-item a {
  display: block;
  border-top: 1px solid #CCC;
  padding: 3%;
}
.menu-item:last-child a {
  border-bottom: 1px solid #CCC;
}
```

And that is it. We are done. There are some customizable options that will power up our feature implementation. Feel free to test other options, but by default it is already set to CSS3 animation in 400 ms showing up before the toggle button that is created automatically, or you can define yours this way:

```
<script>
var navigation = responsiveNav("#site-nav", {
  customToggle: "#mybutton"
});
</script>
```

Building Responsive Navigation Menu

In the following screenshot, we will see the **Responsive Nav** window in action, changing the menu style on smartphones and displaying an unobtrusive way to show the menu:

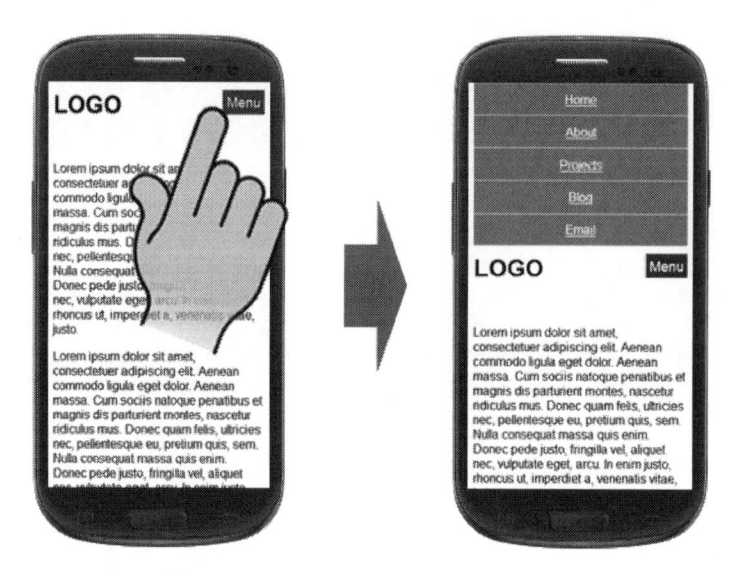

> The customization of toggle button and the orange color from the menu do not display by default. This is just a suggestion made by the creator's plugin in one of its demos.

The select menu

One way of drastically reducing the space occupied by the menu is to use this pattern, where all the menu items are wrapped into a `<select>` tag. It avoids some alignment issues and ensures the cross-browser solution.

However, there are problems with this approach that affect usability, accessibility, and SEO. At first glance, a select menu for the main navigation does not look right because it does not blend in with the design. Maybe the user will think it is awkward or may get confused with the `select` form element.

The TinyNav.js jQuery plugin

The TinyNav.js jQuery plugin, `http://tinynav.viljamis.com/`, is very useful for converting the `<ul>` or `<ol>` navigations to a select dropdown for small screens, and when the user selects one option, it navigates to the correct page with no extra effort. It may also select the current page and add `selected="selected"` for that item automatically.

How to do it

Let's start using the same HTML code from the first navigation pattern. After downloading the TinyNav plugin, we will include the following code in the `<head>` tag:

```
<script src="http://code.jquery.com/jquery-1.9.1.min.js"></script>
<script src="js/tinynav.min.js"></script>
```

And include the following code right before the `</body>` closing tag:

```
<script>
$(function () {
  $("#site-nav ul").tinyNav()
});
</script>
```

Add the following code in our CSS file which is hiding this navigation pattern and setting the common menu style in tablets and desktops. Also, it is exclusively showing the solution for devices with width less than 767 px (smartphones):

```
/* styles for desktop */
.tinynav {
  display: none;
}
#site-nav {
  float: right;
  width: 80%;
  padding: 0;
}
#site-nav li {
  display: inline-block;
  margin: 0 2%;
  padding: 0;
  width: 15%;
  text-align: center;
  line-height: 1.5;
}
/* styles for mobile */
@media screen and (max-width: 767px) {
  .tinynav {
    display: block;
  }
  #site-nav {
    display: none;
  }
}
```

TinyNav also provides some options such as inserting a label before the `<select>` element, setting the menu option from the current page to `active`, as I mentioned before, and defining the starter value from `<select>` if another option was not selected before. Here we can see how to use these three options:

```
$('#site-nav ul').tinyNav({
  active: 'selected',
  label: 'Menu',
  header: 'Navigation'
});
```

This navigation pattern could be implemented for all devices with no extra work. In the example shown in the following screenshot, look at the plugin affecting only small devices:

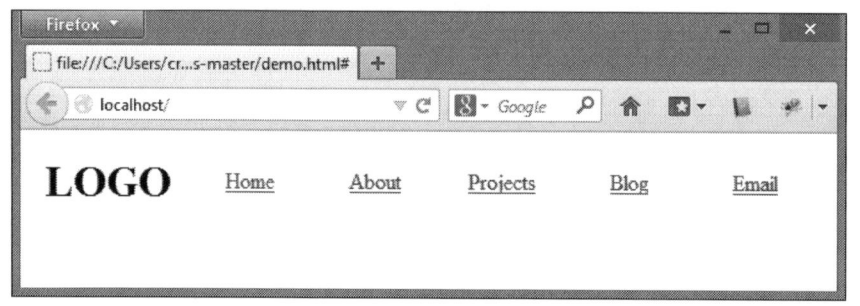

Footer-only

The footer-only navigation is similar to the footer anchor approach, except for the `link` anchor in the `header` section.

Take care while using this navigation pattern because the users may not find the menu on the footer and they may have to scroll to the end whenever they want to access other menu options. This navigation pattern may well adapt for sites with small amount of content and those that require less user's effort for scrolling.

How to do it

Simply move the menu to the bottom of DOM.

> Remember, if we change the code like this, it will directly affect the visual positioning of the menu for all devices. Make sure that your website is not too long before applying this technique because most users expect it at the top of the website.

Multi toggle

The multi toggle pattern is almost the same as the toggle menu because it also slides down just after the header, but it was crafted for complex menus, where there is at least one nested submenu. It works when the user clicks on the header button and a menu pops over the content. If the user clicks on the parent category, the children submenu will slide down displaying its subitems.

How to do it

This is the HTML code that will be used in this example. We will use the `<input type="checkbox">` element as a status controller of menu (opened or closed) and it will not be visible to users. I will explain in more detail about this technique later.

```html
<h1 id="logo">LOGO</h1>
<label class="link-to-menu" for="toggle" onclick>&#9776; Menu</label>
<input id="toggle" type="checkbox" />
<nav>
 <ul id="site-nav">
   <li><a href="" id="back" class="before"> Back</a></li>
   <li><a href="#">Home</a></li>
   <li><a href="#">About</a></li>
   <li class="current">
     <a href="#" class="contains-sub after">Projects</a>
   <ul class="submenu">
     <li><a href="#">Project 1</a></li>
     <li><a href="#">Project 2</a></li>
     <li><a href="#">Project 3</a></li>
   </ul></li>

   <li><a href="#">Blog</a></li>
   <li><a href="#">Email</a></li>
 </ul>
</nav>
```

The next step is customizing the menu style. Since it requires a lot of code, I highly recommend downloading the entire CSS source code provided by this book as suggestion for this pattern.

Let me explain two piece of code that may confuse you. In the beginning of CSS file there are properties with values " \0025Bc" (down arrow) and " \0025C0" (before arrow) that may render as arrow character instead of this code. Also, the `#toggle` checkbox should then be kept in the page (we cannot just set it as display:none), but not in the visible area:

```css
.after:after {
  content: " \0025Bc";
  font-size: 0.5em;
}
.before:before {
  content: " \0025C0";
  font-size: 0.5em;
}
.link-to-menu {
  display: block;
  position: absolute;
  right: 0;
  top: 0;
  z-index: 100;
}
#toggle {
  left: -9999px;
  position: absolute;
  top: -9999px;
}
#site-nav ul {
  left: 0;
  list-style: none;
  position: absolute;
  right: 0;
  top: 4em;
  z-index: 10;
}
#site-nav a {
  display: block;
  height: 0;
  line-height: 0;
  overflow: hidden;
  text-decoration: none;
  transition: all 0.5s ease 0s;
}
```

Just a little interruption in the CSS code, as I want to explain a little bit more about the functionality of the `#toggle` checkbox for submenus.

When the label `link-to-menu` is clicked, the `<a>` tag sets its height to `3em`. Also, we need to prepare the style to increase the height of links because jQuery will input the `open` class in the `<li>` element with `submenu` inside:

```
#toggle:checked ~ nav #site-nav a {
  line-height: 3em; height: 3em; border-bottom: 1px solid #999;
  position: relative; z-index: 1; }
#toggle:checked ~ nav #site-nav .submenu li,
#toggle:checked ~ nav #site-nav .submenu a {
  height: 0; line-height: 0; transition: 0.5s; }
#toggle:checked ~ nav #site-nav .submenu a {
  padding-left: 7%; background: #555; }
#toggle:checked ~ nav #site-nav .submenu.open li,
#toggle:checked ~ nav #site-nav .submenu.open a {
  height: 3em; line-height: 3em; }
```

Also, do not forget to include the `jquery` library in the `<head>` tag:

```
<script src="http://code.jquery.com/jquery-1.9.1.min.js"></script>
```

Almost in the end of DOM (right before the `</body>` closing tag), we will execute the following script to manage the insertion of the `open` class only for submenus controlling which submenu will be shown:

```
<script>
$(document).ready(function() {
  $('a.contains-sub').click(function() {
    if($(this).siblings('ul').hasClass('open')){
      $(this).siblings('ul').removeClass('open');
    } else {
      $(this).siblings('ul').addClass('open');
    }
  return false;
  });
});
</script>
```

The expected visual result is demonstrated in the following screenshot:

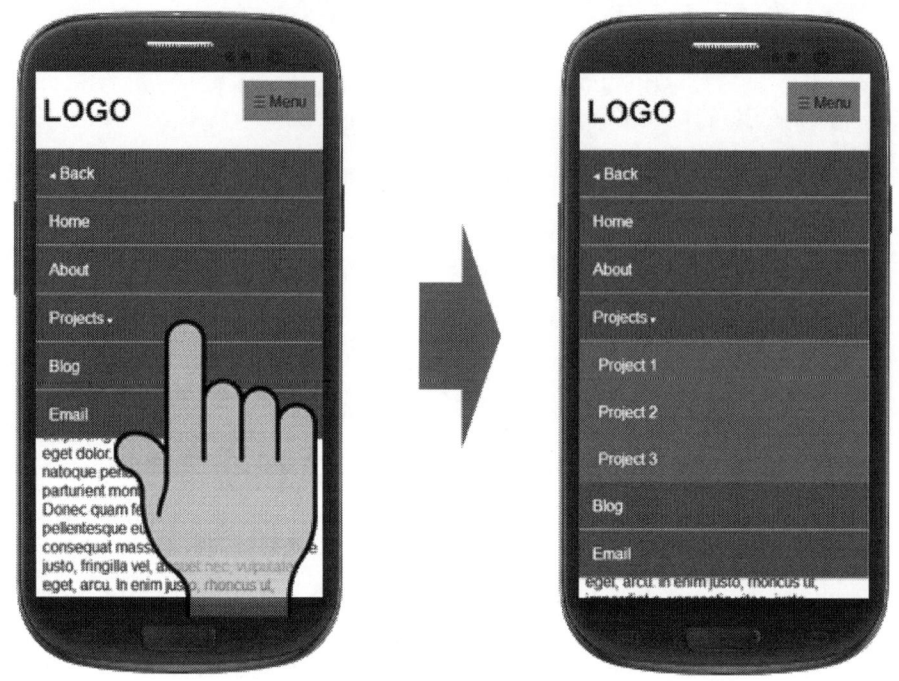

Toggle and slide

This pattern is similar to the multi toggle pattern, but instead of just toggling the submenu, the submenu slides from left to right when the top-level link is clicked. There is a `back` link to facilitate the user's navigation. I really appreciate this interaction effect and it certainly may impress the users.

How to do it

Let's use exactly the same HTML code from the multi toggle pattern for this example (including the call of jQuery script from the `<head>` tag).

About the CSS code, we will use the same code from the multi toggle pattern, but inserting the following code at the end of file. The main difference between toggle and slide and multi toggle pattern is the new arrow character for submenu (the right arrow); the submenu is displayed, but not on the visible area:

```
.after:after {
  content: " \0025B6";
```

```
    font-size: 0.5em;
}
.submenu {
  position: absolute;
  left: -100%;
  top: 0;
  height: 100%;
  overflow: hidden;
  width: 100%;
  transition: all 0.75s ease 0s;
  z-index: 10;
}
.submenu.open {
  left: 0;
}
```

Using the same suggestion, the following screenshot shows the exact moment before and after clicking on the **Projects** link (in this case, implemented only on smartphones):

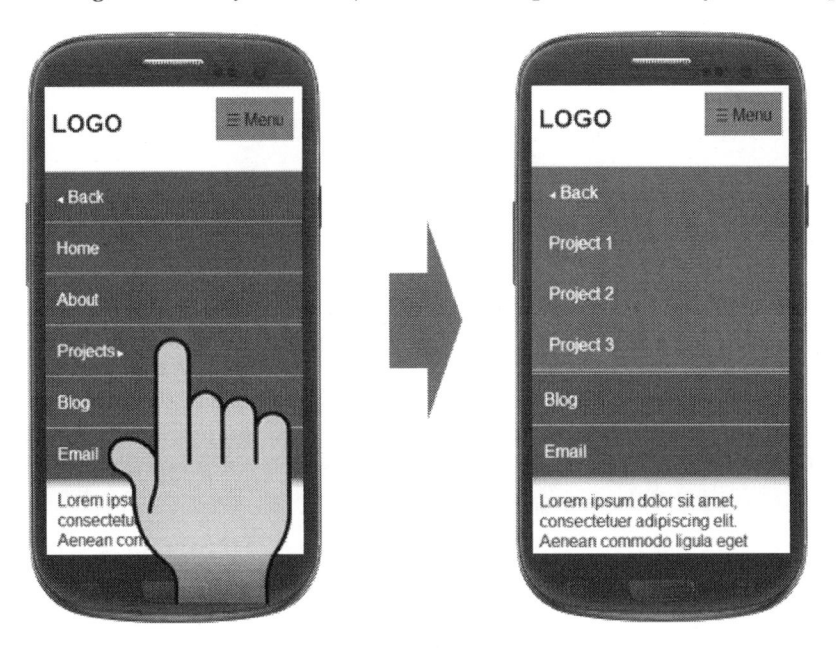

Almost at the end of DOM (right before the `</body>` closing tag), we will execute almost the same script we had seen before, but one more functionality is added now.

The following is the same code we used in previous example, which was added for the menu displaying control

```
<script>
$(document).ready(function() {
  $('a.contains-sub').click(function() {
    if($(this).siblings('ul').hasClass('open')){
      $(this).siblings('ul').removeClass('open');
    } else {
      $(this).siblings('ul').addClass('open');
    }
    return false;
  });
```

The following part of the code handles the function that adds/removes the `open` class for submenus. Whenever this class is set in the element by clicking on the parent element, the submenu may slide horizontally on the screen.

```
  $('ul.submenu a.contains-sub').click(function() {
    if($(this).offsetParent('ul').hasClass('open')){
      $(this).offsetParent('ul').removeClass('open');
    } else {
      $(this).offsetParent('ul').addClass('open');
    }
    return false;
  });
});
</script>
```

The off-canvas menu

If you have used Facebook from the iPhone app or any other apps that now follow the off-canvas menu convention, you have seen an off-canvas panel on a native app. If you hit a menu button, a panel will slide and occupy part of the useful device area.

The jPanelMenu jQuery plugin

The jPanelMenu plugin, http://jpanelmenu.com/, is a lightweight JavaScript solution which hides the menu that you specified and displays it when we click on a header button triggering the action. jPanelMenu has some interesting options to append, such as animation with duration and effects, keyboard shortcut, and choosing the direction. We will see an example with these features soon.

So, the following screenshot is a suggestion for the off-canvas menu style implemented only for smartphones. As usual, we keep the original top menu for tablet and desktop:

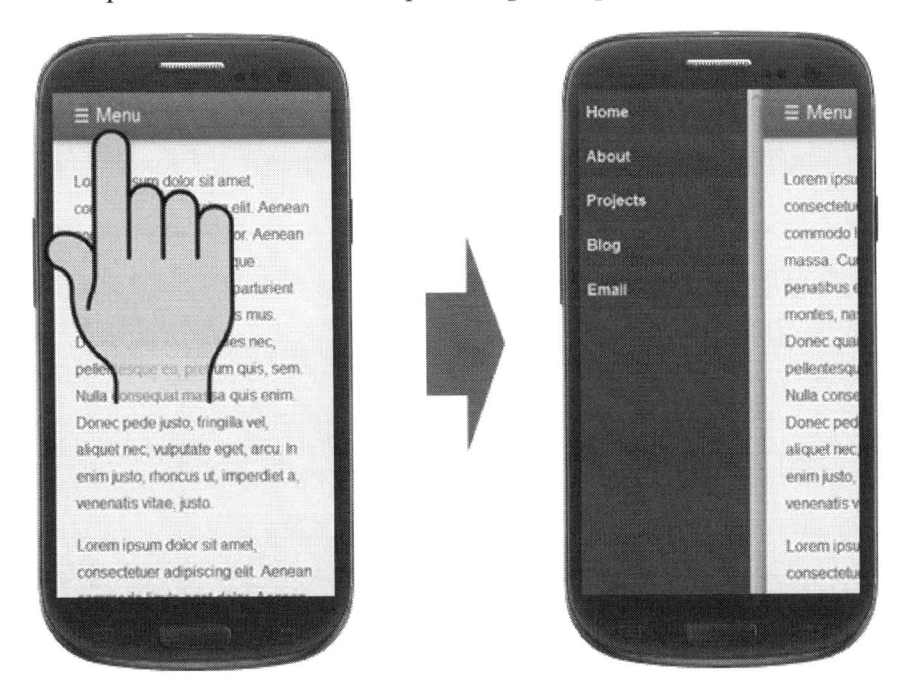

How to do it

Let's start including the following CSS in the <head> tag:

```
<link rel="stylesheet" href="css/style.css">
```

Then, we will use almost the same HTML code from the footer navigation pattern, where we moved the menu to the final part of the HTML structure (footer area) and inserted the following link in the header of the page, because when the user clicks on it, the website will focus on the navigation menu:

```
<header class="main">
  <a id="link-to-menu" href="#menu">&#9776; Menu</a>
  <nav id="site-nav">
    <ul>
      <li><a href="#">Home</a></li>
      <li><a href="#">About</a></li>
      <li><a href="#">Projects</a></li>
      <li><a href="#">Blog</a></li>
```

```
            <li><a href="#">Email</a></li>
        </ul>
    </nav>
</header>
```

After downloading the jPanelMenu, let's include the following code in the `<head>` tag:

```
<script src="http://code.jquery.com/jquery-1.9.1.min.js"></script>
<script src="js/jquery.jpanelmenu.min.js"></script>
```

Include the following code right before the `</body>` closing tag too. Also, this plugin offers some cool options, such as defining which effect will be used, direction and duration used when the menu appears, keyboard shortcuts, and some callbacks:

```
<script>
$(document).ready(function() {
  var jPM = $.jPanelMenu({
    menu: '#site-nav',
    openPosition: '33%',
    duration: '300',
    direction: 'left',
    openEasing: 'easy-in',
    trigger: '#link-to-menu'
  });
  jPM.on();
});
</script>
```

There is no specific CSS code required for this pattern, but it still requires creating our CSS style for the menu to be shown beautifully.

Exercise 3 – customizing menu using the toggle menu solution

After seeing eight types of responsive menus and how to implement each one of them, let's choose the toggle menu to implement in our site.

If you are building your own site, feel free to analyze the best option considering all the features from each menu navigation pattern.

Summary

In this chapter, we learned how the top and left navigation work better depending on each situation. We also learned eight different navigation patterns by using CSS3 or JavaScript plugins.

In the next chapter, we will cover a way to handle the responsive font size of the text. Also, we will customize the font family by using CSS3 and three good JavaScript plugins, giving more creativity to heading titles.

4
Designing Responsive Text

When talking about responsive titles, we talk about flexibility. So, the use of fixed measures in font sizes should also be dynamic. The difference between how it have been implemented in the past years and the present is that earlier we only thought of two ways to show our content: print and screen. Although times change, worries about text adaptation remain.

We think typography is the base of our design and the backbone of our CSS because the main objective of our site is to inform the users by answering their questions. It is good practice to avoid creating ten different subtitle styles, and in order to do this, we must plan a few distinct headings according to our website theme.

In this chapter we will learn:

- Understanding and converting the text to relative units
- Box-sizing and paragraph spacing
- Customizing the font family for beautiful responsive titles
- Managing the font size automatically

Understanding and converting the text to relative units

One of the main advantages of using relative units is the cascade effect generated when the user modifies the font size of the base element (from the browser) and all font sizes increase/decrease proportionally.

These days, almost every browser has the default settings of this base element `<html>` at 16 px. However, this value can be modified on the user side if the user wants to increase the browser font size making it easier to read.

Before talking about the most commonly used measuring units, there are two units we would emphasize because their popularity has grown impressively, and they are: **vw (viewport width)** and **vh (viewport height)**.

These viewport units still do not have much acceptance for most used browsers, but I suggest you check either `http://www.w3.org/TR/css3-values/` or `http://caniuse.com/viewport-units` to stay tuned because these units make the scale of the font size proportionally easier depending on the size of the browser.

So, the most used relative units recently are given in the following section.

Relative unit – percentage

Percentage is relative to the container element and it is more used to create structures as we learned in *Chapter 2, Designing Responsive Layouts/Grids*. However, there is no problem to use it for setting up our font size. The sample code is as follows:

```
body {
   font-size: 100%;   /* base 16px /*
}
p {
   font-size: 87.5%; /* 14px ÷ 16 */
}
```

Some developers prefer to define the font size of the body fixed to 62.5 percent (10 px) to facilitate the calculation. In this case, we may define the child elements to 150 percent representing 15 px, 190 percent representing 19 px, and so on. Although this method makes the identification of the correspondent value easier, it may only help in the first level of the cascade from the font sizing.

Relative unit – em

The em unit is relative to the computed font size of its parent. In the following example, we want to convert the font size of a child element to `20px`:

```
body {
   font-size: 1em; /* base 16px /*
}
p {
   font-size: 1.25em; /* 20px ÷ 16 */
}
```

There is a really good site helping us with this calculation, `http://pxtoem.com`. Let's see how to use this tool on the components in the following screenshot; in the left column, we define the base font and the result is in the column at the center. Also, for different sizes from 6 px to 24 px, we may convert it using the right column.

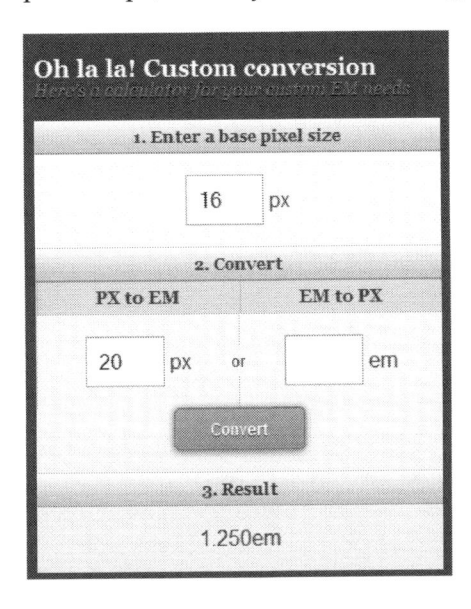

Oh la la! Custom conversion
Here's a calculator for your custom EM needs

1. Enter a base pixel size

   16 px

2. Convert

PX to EM	EM to PX
20 px	or __ em

   Convert

3. Result

   1.250em

So remember, always include the px value (when we are converting) in front of the final value (as we recommended in *Chapter 2, Designing Responsive Layouts/Grids*). We are reinforcing this tip because when handling font sizes, there are a lot of cascading styles. For example, consider the following figure:

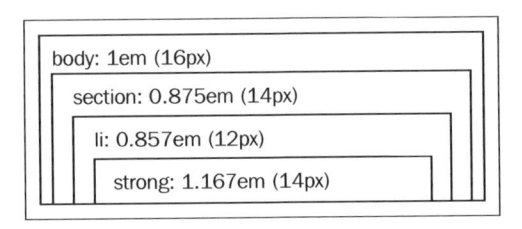

- body: 1em (16px)
  - section: 0.875em (14px)
    - li: 0.857em (12px)
      - strong: 1.167em (14px)

Relative unit – rem

rem came from CSS3 which stands for **root em** and is relative to the root (or the HTML) element. In other words, redefining a font size on the `<html>` element and all rem units may scale a proportion of this base element, and not its parent. This is the only difference when compared with em.

Let's see how these sizes from the previous figure were converted to rem:

```
body {
   font-size: 1em; /* base 16px /*
}
section,
section li strong {
   font-size: 14px; /*  fallback for IE8 or earlier   */
   font-size: 0.875rem; /* 14px ÷ 16 */
}
section li {
   font-size: 12px; /* fallback for IE8 or earlier   */
   font-size: 0.750rem; /* 12px ÷ 16 */
}
```

The following practice may save a good amount of time and help analyze if the page requires more blank space depending on the density of the content.

Try to begin projects by coding the text typography right before all the main structure has been developed. We do this by producing a template document that contains all the major HTML elements with the correct stylesheet that is based on the website design.

Improving your element dimensioning using the box-sizing property

The model known as **box-model**, illustrated in the following screenshot, which requires a calculation to find out the total width of the element including borders and padding, is getting outdated:

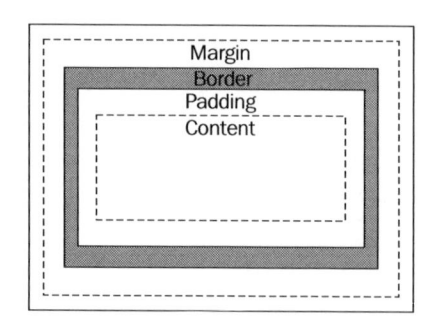

The following example shows the concept of box-model that divides the useful area between two divs with padding of five percent on each side of these containers and a 2 px border which will make the width calculation more difficult:

```
div.splitted {
  padding: 0 5%;
  border: 2px solid black;
  float: left;
  width: ?; /* real value= 50% - 10% - 4px */
}
```

With CSS3, we have the `box-sizing` property which receives the value `border-box`, meaning this width value already considers the padding and border dimensions. Although it works well in Versions 8 and higher of Internet Explorer browser, this property does not work purely on IE6 and IE7. If you need to grant support for these browsers, there is a polyfill which does this complementary task and may be found at `https://github.com/Schepp/box-sizing-polyfill`.

Let's see how it may facilitate the entire calculation to work on this sample:

```
div.splitted {
  padding: 0 5%;
  width: 50%;
  border: 2px solid black;
  float: left;
}
```

We can see in the following code that we may have less difficulty in performing the calculation and analyzing clean or blank spaces from the screen. In addition, many people relate this `padding` spacing to the size of the font based on em because it may avoid the calculation of proportion in some cases.

```
div.splitted {
  padding: 0 0.5em;
  width: 50%;
  border: 2px solid black;
  float: left;
  -webkit-box-sizing: border-box;
  -moz-box-sizing: border-box;
  box-sizing: border-box;
}
```

Currently, some browsers require the prefixes above, but by using them this way, we are covering them. Also, the same padding may be done for the vertical spacing; for example, consider the following code:

```
div.splitted {
  padding-top: 1em;
}
```

Customizing the font family for beautiful responsive titles

Fonts allow you to create a more engaging site for your users, and consistently maintain the theme style without having to produce a lot of heading images, one for each title.

> It is important to choose the font carefully because it may influence the content assimilation by the user or may not contribute to show more than a page or two of our work.

`@font-face` is a CSS rule that allows designers to use non-standard web fonts that are not installed in their users' machines and helps a lot to change all headings faster. The great benefit of the `@font-face` method is that it does not replace your regular fonts with images and also gives the required flexibility to the responsive web design.

> `@font-face` only supports IE8 or earlier if we are using EOT fonts. Also, Safari iOS 4.1 and lower only support SVG font. We will see in the next topic how to provide this support easily.

We really recommend the site http://www.google.com/fonts to check a variety of fonts and especially the font's authorship. Please read the license on each font before using it to be sure it can be used commercially.

The basic usage of the property `@font-face` is to define this rule style, `font-family` is the label used to call the font later, `src` is where it can be found, and `font-weight` (not needed for normal ones, but required by everything else, such as bold and thin). For example, consider the following code:

```
@font-face {
  font-family: "Kite One";
  src: url(/fonts/KiteOne-Regular.ttf);
}
```

Then just use it as any other font in any other style rule:

```
p {
  font-family: "Kite One", Helvetica, Arial, sans-serif;
}
```

However, there are other better ways to do it. We are going to see clearly how to use Font Squirrel, Fit Text, Slabtext, Lettering, and Responsive Measure.

Using Font Squirrel tool generating

Font Squirrel has an awesome tool which allows us to take a desktop font file and generate its web counterparts. Also, the service of generating the correct code and files for our specific font is 100 percent free*.

*Only the service is free. Remember that each font family has its own license. It is highly recommended that the user reads the font license before using them.

On the website `http://www.fontsquirrel.com/tools/webfont-generator`, we may find further information about its main features, which are:

- Font Squirrel does not require a lot of CSS skills
- It offers an extra area to improve the loading performance (the **Expert** mode)
- Generated code/files support users with old browsers
- Resource kits are absolutely free

How to do it

It starts by accessing the Font Squirrel site and clicking on **Add fonts** to choose your personal font or the one for which you already have the right license. Then, select the **Basic** option (for now) and download your kit.

After unzipping the downloaded file, we should add the following code at the beginning of the CSS file. The following code will allow the CSS file to access the font files and provide the correct one depending on the situation:

```
@font-face{
  font-family: 'kite_oneregular';
  src: url('kiteone-regular-webfont.eot');
  src: url('kiteone-regular-webfont.eot?#iefix') format('embedded-opentype'),
  url('kiteone-regular-webfont.woff') format('woff'),
```

```
    url('kiteone-regular-webfont.ttf') format('truetype'),
    url('kiteone-regular-webfont.svg#kite_oneregular) format('svg');
    font-weight: normal;
    font-style: normal;
}
```

And whenever we want to use the new font, we just need to call it the same as we do with the `@font-face` rule as shown in the following code:

```
p {
    font-family: 'kite_oneregular', Helvetica, Arial, sans-serif;
}
```

If we go back to the download page, Font Squirrel will also allow you to take a subset of the font, significantly reducing the file size by choosing the **Optimal** and **Export** modes. To show just how significant it is, we added the same Kite One font and tried all the three settings. Summarizing the result, the byte size is directly correlated to the hash of glyphs (characters) in the font file and how many resources we want to append.

The **Basic** setting leaves the characters untouched. The **Optimal** setting reduces the characters to around 256. In specific cases where the Kite One font has less characters than this number, no optimization is done.

We are able to see the greatest savings by selecting the **Expert** mode and only including the **Basic Latin** setting, then manually adding the characters we need.

Let's try to do it together following the steps for the **Expert** Font Squirrel settings:

1. Click on **Add Fonts** and select the font file you want to work with.
2. Under **Rendering**, uncheck **Fix Vertical Metrics**.

3. Under **Font Formats**, check **SVG** as shown in the following screenshot:

4. Under **Subsetting**, check **Custom Subsetting...**.
5. Under **Unicode Tables**, check only **Basic Latin**.

> This assumes that the fonts will only use English characters; for other languages, add only the characters that you need.

In some sites the symbols such as ', ', ", and " are important too, so copy and paste them into the **Single Characters** field, as shown in the following screenshot:

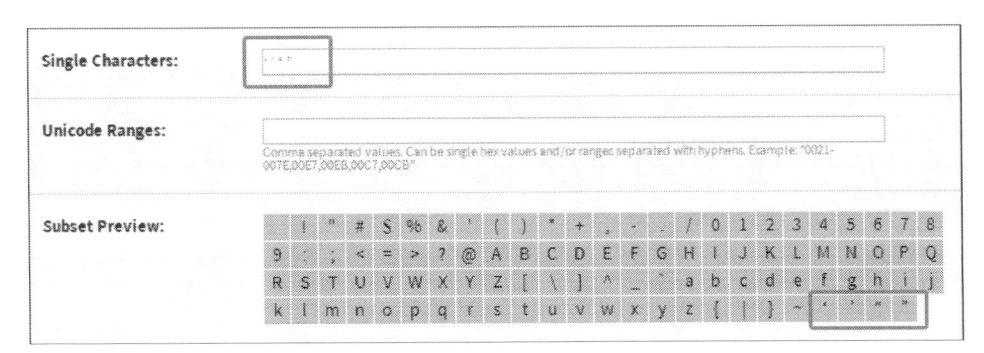

6. Verify the generated image from **Subset Preview** and adjust if needed.
7. After you confirm that you are uploading legally eligible font for web embedding, just click on **DOWNLOAD YOUR KIT**.

The FitText plugin

FitText is a jQuery plugin that makes font sizes flexible and it is a utility that has grown in popularity, making flexible display type much more accessible. It works by scaling the headline text to fill the width of a parent element. If you want to see a quick demonstration of this plugin to analyze how impressive its flexibility is, you can see it in use on plugin's website at http://fittextjs.com/.

How to do it

After downloading the files of this solution on the plugin's Github website https://github.com/davatron5000/FitText.js, let's insert this code in our HTML:

```
<h1 id="responsive_headline">My title using FitText</h1>
```

At the bottom of the HTML (before the `</body>` closing tag), we will need to add jQuery and Fittext libraries. Then you have to execute the plugin applying it to your headline:

```
<script src="http://code.jquery.com/jquery-1.9.1.min.js"></script>
<script src="jquery.fittext.js"></script>
<script>
  $("#responsive_headline").fitText();
</script>
```

By plugin's default, it will set the font size as 1/10th of the element's width. There are two ways to modify this standard font size control: configure the compressor, and define minimum and maximum sizes.

By using the compressor, you will need to specify the compress value, for example, `1.2` to resize the text more gradually or `0.8` to resize it less gradually, as shown in the following code:

```
<script>
$("#responsive_headline").fitText(1.2);
</script>
```

We can also modify this standard font size control by defining the minimum and maximum font size, in order to provide more control over the situations in which you wish to preserve the hierarchy, as shown in the following code:

```
<script>
$("#responsive_headline").fitText(1,{ minFontSize: '20px',
maxFontSize: '40px' });
</script>
```

The SlabText plugin

SlabText is a plugin that lets you build big, beautiful, and completely responsive headlines making it easier for anyone to produce big, bold, and responsive headlines. The script splits headlines into rows before resizing each row to fill the available horizontal space. The ideal number of characters to set on each row is automatically calculated by dividing the available width by the pixel font size.

The following are its features:

- The SlabText plugin is fully responsive and built for mobiles with a completely responsive nature
- **Color Control** chooses the section's background color, text, and text shadow color
- **Extra Options** sets some padding, and determines the length of the text shadow and **Image Overlay** uploads an image and has it superimposed onto the text using CSS3 background clip
- **Font Control** chooses your own font and has ultimate control over fonts
- **Clonable** clones the section as many times as you want and creates a whole bunch of clones
- The SlabText plugin allows you to break the line manually
- Its minified version weighs just 4 KB
- It has headlines with a lot of horizontal space to fill the display better across browsers
- Be sure to call the script after all the `@font-face` fonts are downloaded

So, let's download this plugin from `https://github.com/freqDec/slabText/` and experiment.

How to do it

First, we need to add an ID to a `header` tag that we can select in the JavaScript and then insert the `<script>` tag before the closing `</body>` tag in our HTML code. Consider the following example:

```
<header>
  <h1 class="page-title">Linux commands: New users adds new users...
fast & furious!</h1>
</header>
```

The following is the script to come up with the solution:

```
<script>
$(".page-title").slabText();
</script>
```

However, instead of keeping it automatic, let's break the line into different parts, modifying the communication between the user perception and our website:

```
<header>
  <h1 id="specific-title"></h1>
</header>
```

The script is as follows:

```
<script src="http://code.jquery.com/jquery-1.9.1.min.js"></script>
<script src="js/jquery.slabtext.min.js"></script>
<script>
var stS = "<span class='slabtext'>",
    stE = "</span>",
    txt = [
       "Linux commands:",
       "Newusers",
       "adds new users...",
       "fast & furious!"];
$("#specific-title").html(stS + txt.join(stE + stS) + stE).slabText();
</script>
```

The following screenshot shows two states, before (on the left) and after (on the right) running the code that forces the manual line to break:

For more options, please check the creator's page at `http://freqdec.github.io/slabText/`.

Lettering

Lettering offers a complete down-to-the-letter control by wrapping each character, word, or line, and adding a class (creating a manageable code) for a quick access to the character inside the CSS file. It is a jQuery-based plugin that makes the adjustment of the spacing between characters easier, creating an editorial design, and so on.

There are two quite impressive websites that show good design and a lot of creativity by using customized letters. Take a look at the following examples, courtesy of `http://lostworldsfairs.com/moon/` and `http://lostworldsfairs.com/eldorado/`:

How to do it

After downloading the zip file from https://github.com/davatron5000/Lettering.js, let's practice this usage by inserting the following simple HTML code with class which will be used later:

```
<h1 class="fancy-title">Page Title</h1>
```

Then, remember to include the jQuery library in the `<head>` tag as shown in the following code:

```
<script src="http://code.jquery.com/jquery-1.9.1.min.js"></script>
<script src="js/jquery.lettering.js"></script>
```

At the bottom of the HTML (before the `</body>` closing tag), we will need to call this script for action specifying which class this plugin will affect:

```
<script>
  $(document).ready(function() {
    $(".fancy-title").lettering();
  });
</script>
```

The previous code will give the following output. Look at the spans and imagine you are building it without this plugin:

```
<h1 class="fancy-title">
  <span class="char1">P</span>
  <span class="char2">a</span>
  <span class="char3">g</span>
  <span class="char4">e</span>
  <span class="char5"> </span>
  <span class="char6">T</span>
  <span class="char7">i</span>
  <span class="char8">t</span>
  <span class="char9">l</span>
  <span class="char10">e</span>
</h1>
```

Now, the structure is ready to receive a style like this:

```
<style type="text/css">
  h1 { font-family: 'Impact'; font-size:50px;
    text-transform:uppercase; text-shadow: 1px 1px 2px #666; }
  .char1, .word1, .line1 { color: purple; }
  .char2, .word2, .line2 { color: orange; }
  .char3, .word3, .line3 { color: yellow; }
  .char4, .line4 { color: blue; }
  .char5 { color: green; }
  .char6 { color: indigo; }
  .char7 { color: violet; }
  .char8 { color: gold; }
  .char9 { color: cyan; }
  .char10 { color: lime; }
</style>
```

Furthermore, if the title has a distinct style for each word (not character), this plugin may handle it by defining the parameter "words", as shown in the following code:

```
<script>
  $(document).ready(function() {
    $(".fancy-title").lettering("words");
  });
</script>
```

Consider the case of a different style for each line being split by using <br /> as follows:

```
<h1 class="fancy-title">Page Title <br /> with long text</h1>
```

For the previous scenario, the only difference in the script will be the parameter `"lines"`:

```
<script>
  $(document).ready(function() {
    $(".fancy-title").lettering("lines");
  });
</script>
```

So, now we think you are wondering about the big effort to create a style, to measure distances, and to know how much is necessary to increase the font for each element. We strongly suggest using the online tool Kern.js.

The Kern.js tool

Kern.js is an online tool that matches perfectly with Lettering.js because it offers a great interface between clicking-and-dragging, adjusting the letter kerning, line height, and letter placement. And when you finish this task, just copy the generated CSS and use it in our stylesheet.

How to use it

After entering the tool's website, `http://www.kernjs.com/`, there is a link at the bottom of the page: **drag to bookmarks bar to install**. Dragging it to the bookmark will make the activation of the Kern.js tool on our website easier.

The requirements of its usage are including jQuery in specific 1.7.2 Version and the Kern.js libraries in the `<head>` tag of our website. The Kern.js script may be found at `https://github.com/bstro/kern.js` to download.

```
<script src="http://code.jquery.com/jquery-1.7.2.min.js"></script>
<script src="js/kern.min.js"></script>
```

Here are five options that may show at the top of the page whenever a website is opened by clicking on the **Kernjs.com** link from the bookmarks bar:

- Adjustment of the kerning (horizontal spacing)
- Increase or decrease in font size
- Adjustment of the line height (vertical spacing)
- Full letter placement adjustment
- Adjustment of the angle rotation

The following screenshot shows these options:

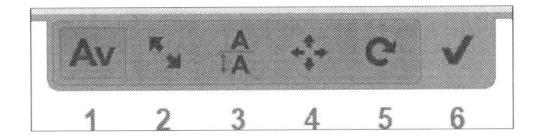

As soon as you finish the adjustments, just click on the check button to convert this visual change into code ready to be copied and performed on the site.

Be careful when there is more than one customized element because this code may overwrite the previous one. However, there is an easy way to avoid further issues: defining a class to the element specification. The following code is an example of this:

```
<h1 class="fancy-title">Page Title</h1>
```

Responsive Measure

Responsive Measure is a simple script that allows you to pass in a selector (ideally the container where your primary content will go) that generates the ideal font size required to produce the ideal measure for your text. Does it sound like magic? We will see in the following section how to customize this solution and its usage.

How to do it

After downloading the files of this solution from `https://github.com/jbrewer/Responsive-Measure`, let's insert this code in the `<head>` tag in the beginning of DOM:

```
<script src="http://code.jquery.com/jquery-1.9.1.min.js"></script>
<script src="js/jquery.rm.js"></script>
```

At the bottom of the HTML (before the `</body>` closing tag), we need to call the Responsive Measure script to action. However, before executing the script, we will clarify the following two ways to control the text size:

- **idealLineLength**: Its default value is `66`, but we may define our specific value to represent how many characters and spaces will fit in the line. Also, the minimum font size was set to `16px` and the maximum set to `300px`. The parameter `sampleText` may help calculate the number of characters that have average character width.

> Keep in mind that a range of 45-75 characters per line is generally accepted as safe for comfortable reading.

Here comes the preceding mentioned code:

```
<script>
$('section').responsiveMeasure({
  idealLineLength: 45,
  minimumFontSize: 16,
  maximumFontSize: 300,
  sampleText: "n"
});
</script>
```

- **minimumFontSize and maximumFontSize**: This is where the handling of the font size is improved by defining 13 to minimum and 30 to maximum, for example. Also, the default value of `idealLineLength` may influence sometimes a little on the result. If it happens, define your own value and fix it, as we have just seen in the previous code.

So, the following is the code:

```
<script>
$('section').responsiveMeasure({
  minimumFontSize: 13,
  maximumFontSize: 30,
  sampleText: "n"
});
</script>
```

Exercise 4 – customizing the homepage title

Let's do this exercise in three steps. The second and third steps are just complementary of the first step:

1. Use Font Squirrel generator to create your font face kit. Then, implement it on the `<h1>` tag of your site. If you do not have any idea of which font to use, I would recommend to download Kite One font from GoogleFont site.

2. Use the Lettering plugin to have more control over each letter, word, or line of your title. After that, increase the color of the first letter, changing the `color` property of the `.char1` class from your CSS file.

3. Use the Kern.js tool by clicking on the link from your bookmarks bar. After that, click on the second button from toolbar and select the first letter to increase its font size. Then, click on the last button to generate a code and include it in your CSS file

Summary

In this chapter, we have seen the responsive font size of the text. Also, we have learned different ways of customizing the font family by using solutions such as the Font Squirrel, FitText, SlabText, Lettering, and Responsive Measure. These solutions create a support and independence to image that is required when building our responsive website.

In the next chapter, we will talk about images and videos and learn how to convert them into responsive and adaptive media for different devices. Also, we will see how to work well with videos considering different player technologies and devices.

5
Preparing Images and Videos

The image preparation to be used in responsive sites has been one of the most discussed issues recently because there is no technique approved by W3C yet. Meanwhile, the community has created some techniques, each one with its advantages, trying to resolve this issue.

We will begin this chapter by looking at basic image resizing. This technique may be incorporated into the code with no difficulty, but mobile users are waiting for better experiences.

However, only resizing the image is not so effective when it comes to smaller devices such as smartphones and tablets, because loading images with high quality in those devices may take a long time. Later, we will see the importance of image breakpoints and its benefits.

Also, we will focus our attention on videos, since they had been inserted into our code before HTML5, avoiding issues on site conversions from fixed to responsive ones.

Furthermore, we will talk about some available jQuery plugins and how to use each one of them, by saving development time and bringing improvements to our interface.

In this chapter, we will learn:

- Basic image resizing only using CSS
- Why to use image breakpoints
- How the picture tag will work
- Controlling the image art direction
- Using image breakpoints with jQuery plugins

- Creating a responsive background with jQuery plugins
- Dealing with high-density displays
- Making the video elements responsive

Basic image resizing only using CSS

The following code may be used to give freedom to the image to scale whenever its parent container had been resized. The maximum width was set to 100 percent of the original size and its height may follow the same image proportion automatically:

```
img {
  max-width: 100%;
  height: auto;
}
```

Although, to use this effectively, the image must be large enough to scale up to whatever size we may reasonably expect on the largest possible display. However, images that are optimized for desktop sites are still quite heavy for a mobile Internet speed.

> If you are using the `max-width` or `height` tags to resize JPG images in your DOM, you will probably see pixelated images only on browser IE7 or older versions. However, there is a simple code for solving this problem:
> ```
> img {
>   -ms-interpolation-mode: bicubic;
> }
> ```
> This specific problem was fixed in IE8 and became obsolete in IE9.

Using image breakpoints

Adaptive images are not just about the issue of scaling images. It is about dealing with other issues, and variables to be kept in mind when delivering the best user experience. Variables such as the following:

- Screen resolution
- Bandwidth
- Browser width window

The problem of trying to determine the best image to be sent to the browser may be independent of each variable. And that is the problem. For instance, knowing only the value of the screen resolution does not mean the user has a good bandwidth to receive a high-definition picture.

So, based on these facts, how will we make a picture in our web application that needs to be displayed with good quality on a bunch of devices, without causing a huge waste of bandwidth?

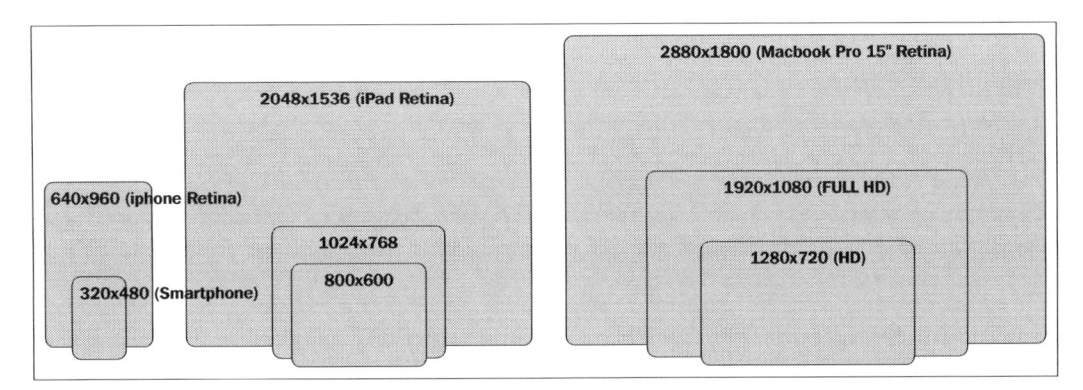

When we are dealing with bitmap images (non-vectorized images such as SVG), the ideal solution seems simple: to serve an image of a different size for each group of resolutions, where each of these images would be suitable for certain types of devices.

Usually, we consider three different screen sizes to cover the diversity of devices:

- **480 px**: Smartphones with standard resolution (mobile-first)
- **1024 px**: iPhone retina (smartphones with high image density), tablets, and desktops with normal resolution
- **1600 px**: iPad Retina (tablets with high image density) and desktops with high resolution

There are many techniques that have already been trying to deal with this problem and to bring solutions that will help us serve the correct image for each occasion. They all work in a way slightly different from each other, and depending on your requirements, you will make the choice that best meets your project needs. We will see some of them soon.

How the picture tag works

The W3C, facing this need of providing the correct image to the user, is working hard to finish studying them. There is an unofficial draft of this initiative, which includes the `<picture>` tag and different sources inside it, in its standards, in order to make adaptation of the image easier.

> Without this standard, browser developers cannot prepare their browsers to render it well. Today, the frontend community is using CSS and JavaScript trying to do this same task.

This is the definition of the `<picture>` tag by W3C:

> "This specification provides developers with a means to declare multiple sources for an image, and, through CSS Media Queries, it gives developers control as to when those images are to be presented to a user."

They also thought of older browsers, which will show a simple image as a fallback content. The following is an example of how the tag will be used:

```
<picture width="500" height="500">
  <source media="(min-width:45em)" srcset="large1.jpg 1x, large2.jpg 2x">
  <source media="(min-width:18em)" srcset="medium1.jpg 1x, medium2.jpg 2x">
  <source srcset="small1.jpg 1x, small2.jpg 2x">
  <img src="small1.jpg" alt="">
  <p>Accessible text for all image versions</p>
</picture>
```

I would recommend checking the updated information about this specification at http://picture.responsiveimages.org/.

Control of art direction for responsive images

This topic has been discussed a lot recently. Authors should provide different sources for images in different sizes, and based on their visual judgment, they will focus the main element of the image for that particular breakpoint. This is art direction.

Let me clarify it by showing this case here. When the image is displayed in larger sizes, it makes sense for the image to show the couple on the boat and the river in the background. The background helps explain where they are but, in general, it gives no relevant information. Now, look what happens when we scale the image down to fit a smaller screen. It is not art direction.

Reducing to that size, you can barely recognize the couple. Instead of simply resizing the image, it may make sense to crop it to get rid of some of the background and focus on it. The end result is an image that works better in a smaller size. Let's compare the left picture (art direction) and the right picture as follows:

Focal Point CSS framework

The Focal Point improves the focus on the most important part of the image before scaling it down. This way it allows users to see the main part of the image in a larger size on smartphones. All this without the use of JavaScript or jQuery.

With Focal Point, you may define an area that represents the parts you do not want to miss out due to smaller resolutions. Parts covered by the Focal Point stay visible no matter how far down you scale them.

The following classnames allow you to crop and resize into a general area of the image. Note that X in the class names represents a number between one and six:

- **left-X/right-X**: These define how many units the image will focus on horizontally
- **up-X/down-X**: These define how many units the image will focus on vertically
- **portrait**: By default, the value is set to landscape. But if an image has height more than its width, add the class portrait too

How to do it

After downloading the CSS file from `https://github.com/adamdbradley/focal-point`, let's insert this code in the `<head>` tag of our DOM:

```
<link rel="stylesheet" href="/css/focal-point.min.css">
```

Later, we may see it in the action demonstrated as follows:

Chapter 5

The principle of Focal Point is simple: Imagine a grid of 12 x 12 units put upon the picture:

Now, we suppose the head of this individual is the most important part of the picture and we need to define it as the Focal Point. Even though the face of this individual is on the right side of the picture, it will stay in focus when being scaled down to smaller resolutions.

To define the Focal Point technically, we just need to set two classes of an image. These classes may position the Focal Point inside the grid, horizontally and vertically. It will start from the center of the grid as shown in the following picture:

The following is the code to focus on the person's face:

```
<div class="focal-point right-3 up-3">
  <div><img src="guy.jpg" alt=""></div>
</div>
```

In this example, the Focal Point is defined to focus three grid units from the center to the left and then to two units up. The `focal-point` class is as mandatory as the surrounding div around the image.

Alternative solutions for the <picture> tag

We have just seen that W3C is working hard to set a standard to tag the picture as soon as possible, which will enable you to provide visual contents that are more appropriate for the device you are using to view our site.

Because of the great necessity of this functionality, the community has created two JavaScript plugins leading to the expected result accepted by most used browsers. They are Foresight and Picturefill.

Foresight – selecting the right image to display depending on the screen size

Foresight provides web pages the ability to inform whether a user device is capable of viewing high-resolution images (such as retina display devices), before the image has been requested from the server.

Additionally, Foresight judges if the user device currently has a fast enough network connection for high-resolution images. Depending on the device display and the network connectivity, foresight.js will request the appropriate image for the webpage.

By customizing the `img source` attribute, using methods such as URI templates, or finding and replacing values within the URI, it is possible to form requests, which were built for your image's resolution variants, and specifically use a hybrid implementation of the new CSS `image-set()` function.

The basic format is that the `image-set ()` function may have one or many image-set variants, each one separated by a comma. Each image-set variant may have up to three arguments:

- **URL**: This is similar to `background-image:url()`.
- **Scale factor**: The scale factor argument is used as a multiplier for the image's dimensions applied to identify the image density. Some mobile devices have a pixel ratio of 1.5 or 2.
- **Bandwidth**: This can be defined as low-bandwidth or high-bandwidth.

Foresight also performs a quick network speed test to make sure the user device can handle high resolution images, without making users with slow connectivity wait for a long time to download images.

How to do it

Let's access the website https://github.com/adamdbradley/foresight.js and download the files. Then, we will insert the following code in the <head> tag of our DOM:

```
<script src="js/foresight.js "></script>
```

Let's see a real example of the following code, where we are using the mobile-first concept:

```
.fs-img {
  width:100%;
  font-family: 'image-set( url(-small|-small-2x) 2x high-bandwidth )';
  display:none;
}
```

Then, for windows, the width is at least 600 px and 800 px:

```
@media (min-width:600px) {
  .fs-img {
    font-family: 'image-set( url(-small|-medium), url(-small|-medium-2x) 2x high-bandwidth )';
  }
}
@media (min-width:800px) {
  .fs-img {
    font-family: 'image-set( url(-small|-large), url(-small|-large-2x) 2x high-bandwidth )';
    max-width:100%;
  }
}
```

Preparing Images and Videos

So, we highlighted some words to explain better how it works. The code will find the fragment of a name inside the source of the `<img>` tag and will replace it by another one. After that, the site will search for the changed name in its files, verifying if the required code is there:

```
<img data-src="/castle-small.jpg" data-width="240" data-height="157"
class="fs-img" src="/castle-small.jpg">
```

> This engine is used to change the suffix of the filename, making it well scalable, and it is really good because it avoids a lot of interventions on code when creating new responsive images.

If we compare images in this example for the difference in KB, we will have the larger image with 44 KB, the medium image with 20 KB, and the small image with 12 KB. That is not a huge difference for just one image. However, by applying it to the entire site, there may be great reduction on the loading of unnecessary images.

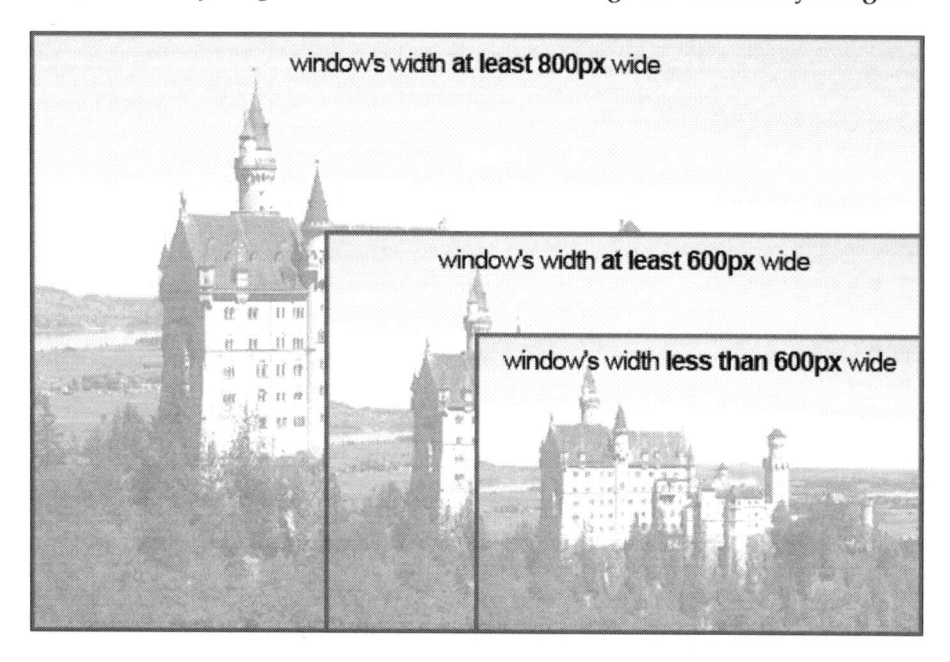

Picturefill – the solution that most closely resembles the picture tag

Picturefill is a JavaScript plugin for responsive images, similar to the future `picture` element that is ready to be used today. This very lightweight solution uses the `span` tag instead of `picture` or `image` for the sake of its own safety.

Picturefill natively supports HD (Retina) image replacement. Picturefill also has the benefit of good performance, selecting the correct image depending on the screen size without downloading the other ones.

For more information about this plugin, you can visit `https://github.com/scottjehl/picturefill`.

How to do it

After downloading the files of this solution, let's insert this code in the `<head>` tag of your DOM:

```html
<script src="js/matchmedia.js"></script>
<script src="js/picturefill.js"></script>
```

This is the code to be used in HTML. Note that it requires that you specify the source of each image and their variations. See the following example:

```html
<span data-picture="" data-alt="Picture alternative text">
  <span data-src="imgs/small.jpg"></span>
  <span data-src="imgs/medium.jpg" data-media="(min-width: 400px)"></span>
  <span data-src="imgs/large.jpg" data-media="(min-width: 800px)"></span>
  <span data-src="imgs/extralarge.jpg" data-media="(min-width: 1000px)"></span>
  <!-- Fallback content for non-JS browsers -->
  <noscript>&lt;img src="imgs/small.jpg" alt="Picture alternative text"&gt;</noscript>
  <img alt="Picture alternative text" src="imgs/extralarge.jpg">
</span>
```

Maybe some projects need it as a solution (the entire specification inside the HTML code and also their image variations), but we should bring scalability issues if we have many images on the site and problems for site maintenance.

Responsive background images by using jQuery plugins

Positioning a background image is not always an easy task for responsive sites because its correct visualization depends on the behavior of its contents.

Just to clarify, let me show you a sample of this problem:

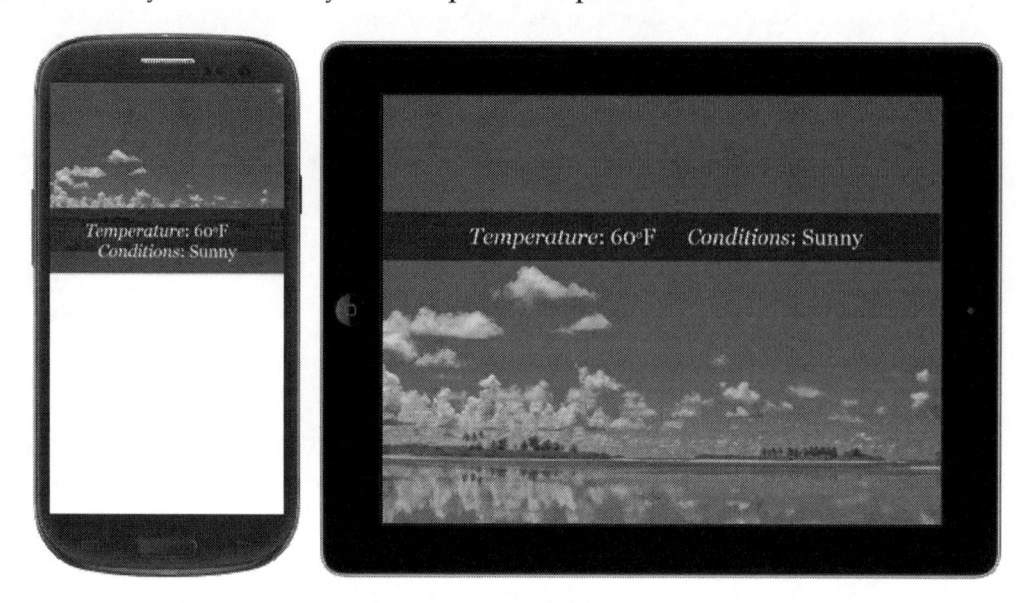

The problem is that sometimes we fix the content to keep the background still correct and it needs to change. There are two plugins that help a lot in positioning this background: Anystretch and Backstretch.

Anystretch – stretching your background easily

Anystretch is a jQuery plugin that allows you to add a dynamically-resized background image to any page or block-level element. Originally, Anystretch was forked from Backstretch.

The image will stretch to fit the page/element and will be automatically resized as the window size changes. There are some options to configure it such as horizontal positioning, vertical positioning, speed, positioning of the element, and data name.

Another advantage of this plugin is if we want to change the image after Anystretch has been loaded, we will only need to come up with it again, informing the new path.

> Yes, we can use it together with the Breakpoints.js plugin as we have seen in *Chapter 2, Designing Responsive Layouts/Grids*, making it possible to change the image path and coming up with Anystretch again, if it is necessary.

How to do it

After downloading the files from `https://github.com/danmillar/jquery-anystretch`, let's use the following HTML code just to clarify how it works:

```
<div class="div-home stretchMe" data-stretch="img/bg-home.jpg">
  <p>main content</p>
</div>
<div class="div-footer stretchMe" data-stretch="img/bg-footer.jpg">
  <p>footer content</p>
</div>
```

For this structure, there are two highlighted words:

- `stretchMe`: This is used to identify that those elements will be handled by the plugin
- `data-stretch`: This will inform the plugin what image may become a background

At the bottom of the DOM (before the `</body>` closing tag), we will need to include the jQuery code and the Anystretch script. Then, we will execute the plugin for all elements that were set by the classname `stretchMe` (just a suggested name).

```
<script src="http://code.jquery.com/jquery-1.9.1.min.js"></script>
<script src="js/jquery.anystretch.min.js"></script>
<script>
$(".stretchMe").anystretch();
</script>
```

And this is the visual result of the plugin applied to a div element:

Preparing Images and Videos

Good so far, but this method, if used will apply the same behavior for all responsive backgrounds. In other words, if we want to change the characteristics, we need to call the function separately.

> If we call the `anystretch` method twice for the same element, it will replace the existing image and stop the previous processing.

If we look at the previous HTML code, there is a class named `div-home`, which may be executed with different options, for example:

```
<script>
$(".div-home").anystretch('',{speed:300, positionX:'right',
positionY:'bottom'});
</script>
```

> The `speed` parameter will configure the time to fade in the image after downloading it. By default, `positionX` and `positionY` are aligned in the center, but the plugin permits us to change it.

Backstretch – creating a responsive background slideshow

Backstretch is a jQuery plugin that allows users to add a dynamically resized background image to any page or element and it was the basis of the Anystretch plugin.

However, Backstretch evolved and now also offers to resize the background images from the slideshow element dynamically. All of these background images will stretch to fit the page/element and will be automatically resized as the window/element size changes.

Another good improvement is the fetch of images that will be used after the page is loaded, this way the users will not have to wait too long to complete the download of the image.

You can find the files to be downloaded at `https://github.com/srobbin/jquery-backstretch`.

How to do it

At the bottom of the DOM (before the `</body>` closing tag), we will include the jQuery and the Backstretch libraries. Then we will execute the plugin attaching the Backstrech to the element's background:

```
<script src="http://code.jquery.com/jquery-1.9.1.min.js"></script>
<script src="js/jquery.backstretch.min.js"></script>
<script>
$.backstretch("path/bgimage.jpg");
</script>
```

And the following is the visual result:

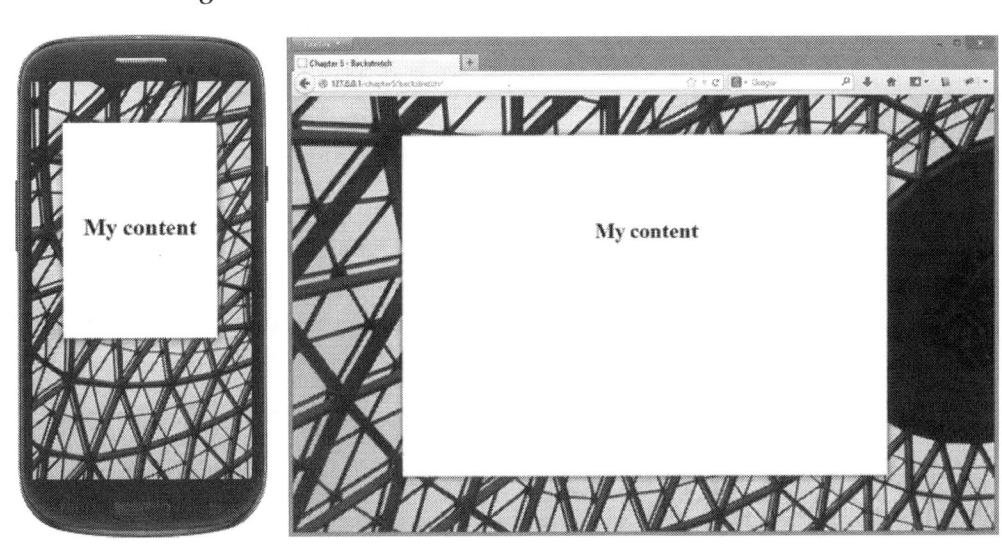

By default, the image alignment (vertical and horizontal) is set to the center because it is more usual for people who are using this solution, but we can turn it off, if necessary. The other option included is the `fade` parameter to configure the time to fade in the image. The `parameter` duration is used for slideshows and it is related to the amount of time (in milliseconds) each slide will be displayed before switching it.

We may also attach the Backstretch to any block-level element. By default, the `<body>` tag will receive this responsive background. To do this, a better way is by defining a class to receive this action using the following code instead of the previous one:

```
<script>
$(".div-home").backstretch("path/bgimage.jpg");
</script>
```

Or, to start a slideshow, just inform an array of images and the amount of time between slides:

```
<script>
  $(".div-home").backstretch([
    "path/bgimage1.jpg",
    "path/bgimage2.jpg",
    "path/bgimage3.jpg"
  ], {duration: 5000});
</script>
```

This plugin was well documented and provides a slideshow API for better handling. It can be found at `https://github.com/srobbin/jquery-backstretch#slideshow-api`.

Dealing with high-density displays

Screen density refers to the number of device pixels on a physical surface. It is often measured in **pixels per inch** (**PPI**). Apple has coined the marketing term **Retina** for its double-density displays. According to Apple's official website:

> *"Retina display's pixel density is so high your eye is unable to distinguish individual pixels."*

In other words, the retina display has a high enough pixel density to prevent pixelation to be noticeable to the human eye. But, because these displays are being widely implemented and used, it is more important than ever to create websites and apps that support these displays.

In the following figure, we compared the pixels between Retina and a standard definition display. In Retina display, there are double the pixels in the same amount of space as you would have with a traditional display:

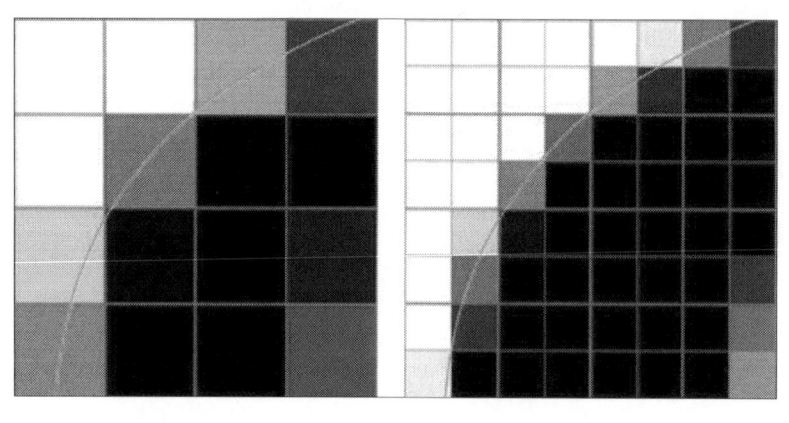

> The word double is not exactly the value that is used for all devices that support high-density images. Currently, there are other screen densities in the market whose density values are 1.5 and 2.25.

How to do it

The common value for retina images is twice the value of the normal images. So, by using media queries, we can test if the browser supports high-density images. Let's check it in the following example:

```
/* normal sprite image has dimension of 100x100 pixels */
span.bigicon-success {
  background: url(sprite.png) no-repeat -50px 0;
}
@media only screen and (-webkit-min-device-pixel-ratio: 2), only
screen and (min-device-pixel-ratio: 2) {
  span.bigicon-success {
    background-image: url(sprite@2x.png);
    /* retina sprite image has dimension of 200x200 pixels */
    background-size: 200px 200px;
  }
}
```

If the browser accepts, we make a request for another image to be displayed. However, this usage makes two image requests: one before the check and the other inside of media queries.

Now, let's see how we can make only one request using Foresight.

How to do it using Foresight

This plugin has the ability to detect which screen density the device is showing, before displaying any image to the user.

Let's see it in the following example:

```
.fs-img {
  font-family: 'image-set(url(-small | -small-2x) 2x high-bandwidth)';
}
```

In this example, the browser checks which image element has the class `fs-img` and before showing any image (default behavior of Foresight), it checks if it has support for retina images; in addition, it can check if the user is in a high bandwidth.

Note that before requesting the `castle-small.jpg` file, for example, it will find the suffix `-small` and replace it with `-small-2x` and then request for the file `castle-small-2x.jpg`.

There is an online tool that helps calculating the size that the image should have if viewed with retina. It is available at `http://teehanlax.com.s3.amazonaws.com/files/teehanlax_density_converter.html`.

Making responsive video elements

Before using HTML5 in our website development, the use of videos was restricted to the acceptance of Adobe Flash Player on devices. However, that obligation does not exist anymore because of the great effort in the development of `<video>` in HTML5, and also very powered by the positioning of Apple to deny Adobe Flash Player on their devices.

Currently, this element `<video>` is very well accepted in the existing devices and modern browsers (IE9 and later), making its handling and especially its flexibility on responsive websites much easier. Just to clarify, the following is how the video tag is commonly seen on DOM:

```
<video id="highlight-video" poster="snapshot.jpg" controls>
   <source src="video.m4v" type="video/mp4" /> <!-- for Safari -->
   <source src="video.ogg" type="video/ogg" /> <!-- for Firefox -->
</video>
```

The CSS code which makes the video fluid is quite simple:

```
video, iframe {
   max-width: 100%;
   height: auto;
}
```

However, there are operational differences between the old and new browsers and to increase the accessibility of the content. It is usually preferable to use a safer way. This path would be to keep using embedded videos or the `<iframe>` tags. We will soon see how to make those videos a little more responsive and flexible.

Now, let's focus on the current technology. The good news is that video providers such as YouTube or Vimeo have already been supporting the `<video>` tag, but it is still not the default behavior. This differently used code, depending on the device, may also become a problem because we need to adapt the code to each situation.

To solve this problem of adaptation, they created the FitVids plugin.

FitVids – a quick win solution for responsive videos

FitVids is a lightweight jQuery plugin that automates the job of making the video width fluid in our responsive web design by creating a wrapper around the iframe to preserve the ratio, otherwise the ratio of iframed videos will look like this:

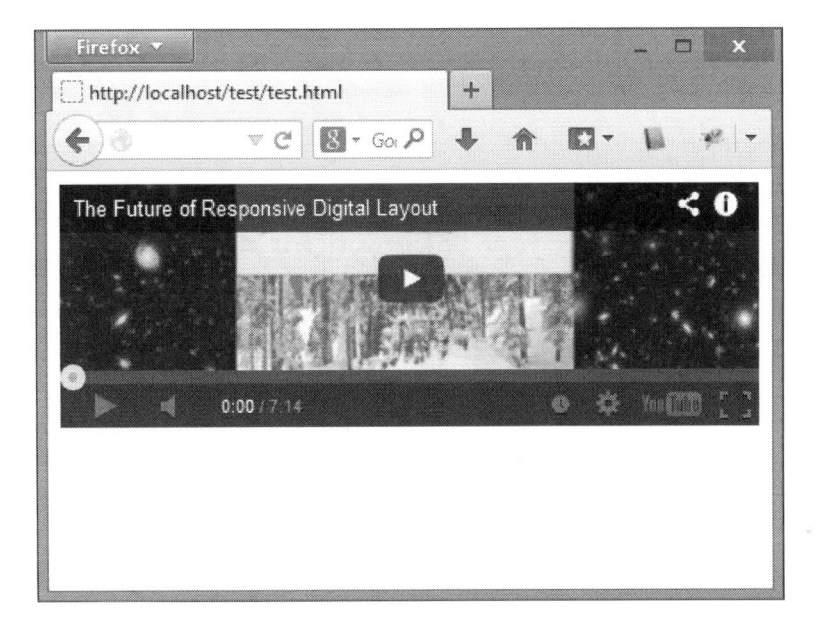

The currently supported players are YouTube, Vimeo, Blip.tv, Viddler, and Kickstarter. But if it is necessary to use our own player, there is an option to specify this custom player.

How to do it

At the bottom of DOM (before the `</body>` closing tag), we will need to include the jQuery code and the FitVids script. Then, we only need to attach its execution into a class or ID of the element, as follows:

```
<script src="http://code.jquery.com/jquery-1.9.1.min.js"></script>
<script src="jquery.fitvids.js"></script>
<script>
$(function () {
  $(".video-wrapper").fitVids();
});
</script>
```

After that, let's use this HTML code just as a sample to see how it works:

```
<div class="video-wrapper ">
  <iframe width="560" height="315" frameborder="0" allowfullscreen src="http://www.youtube.com/embed/UM0Cl3wWys0"></iframe>
</div>
```

The following screenshot shows a sample of YouTube, Vimeo, and Viddler videos using FitVids:

Exercise – creating different image versions for featured homepage images

As we have just seen, loading the correct image for each device is very important for our responsive site. So, let's practice this technique in our design showing different images in the following breakpoints:

- Maximum width = 480
- Maximum width = 1024
- Minimum width = 1025

The following screenshot shows the site along with the photos I'm referring to, as we saw in *Chapter 2*, *Designing Responsive Layouts/Grids*. For this exercise, I'm referring to the highlighted images inside the boxes:

For this activity, I recommend using the Foresight plugin because it provides a better visualization of the image sources and breakpoints.

> Do not forget to check if the specific device you are using supports to show high-density images.

Summary

In this chapter, we have learned to perform a simple conversion from a fixed image to a flexible image, only to understand it is not enough to make them adaptable to different devices. Also, we have learned other ways to provide the right image to the user by using the Foresight and Picturefill plugins. We have also controlled the art direction, focusing on the main element in the picture when the image is being resized using the FocalPoint framework. Further, we have learned to make the video dimensions fluid by using the FitVids plugin with no stress.

In the next chapter, we will know which slider plugins are prepared for responsive sites, learn how to build them, change some options and effects, and create a good impression on the users. In addition, we will understand which gestures are commonly used and implemented on mobile sites.

6
Building Responsive Image Sliders

The image slider has been used a lot and has become a very popular web element. On a website, with beautiful transitions and animations, captions and descriptions, and the use of custom timings, an attractive business presentation is delivered online. Also, a good image slider can display a product showcase, catches the user's attention, and improves its sale.

In this chapter we will learn about:

- Different types of responsive image sliders
- Introducing touch gestures in user experience
- Implementing touch events with JavaScript plugins

Responsive image sliders

Opening a website and seeing an image slider in the header area is common nowadays. Image sliders display highlighted content, which are really useful, within a limited space. Although the free space is more limited when a site is viewed through mobile devices, the slider element still catches the client's attention.

The difference between how much area can be used to display a highlighted content and the resource available to render it is really big if compared with desktop, where we generally do not have problems with script performance, and the interaction of each transition is performed through the use of arrow signs to switch images.

When the responsive era started, the way that people normally interacted with image sliders was observed, and changes, such as the way to change each slide, were identified, based on the progressive enhancement concept. The solution was to provide a similar experience to the users of mobile devices: the adoption of gestures and touches on image slider elements for devices that accept them instead of displaying fallbacks.

With the constant evolution of browsers and technologies, there are many image slider plugins with responsive characteristics. My personal favorite plugins are Elastislide, FlexSlider2, ResponsiveSlides, Slicebox, and Swiper. There are plenty available, and the only way to find one you truly like is to try them!

Let's look in detail at how each of them works.

Elastislide plugin

Elastislide is a responsive image slider that will adapt its size and behavior in order to work on any screen size based on jQuery. This jQuery plugin handles the slider's structure, including images with percentage-based width inside, displaying it horizontally or vertically with a predefined minimum number of shown images.

Elastislide is licensed under the MIT license and can be downloaded from `https://github.com/codrops/Elastislide`.

When we are implementing an image slider, simply decreasing the container size and displaying a horizontal scrollbar will not solve the problem for small devices gracefully. The recommendation is to resize the internal items too. Elastislide fixes this resizing issue very well and defines the minimum elements we want to show instead of simply hiding those using CSS.

Also, Elastislide uses a complementary and customized version of jQuery library named jQuery++. jQuery++ is another JavaScript library very useful to deal with DOM and special events. In this case, Elastislide has a custom version of jQuery++, which enables the plugin working with **swipe events** on touch devices.

How to do it

As we will see four different applications of this plugin for the same carousel, we will use the same HTML carousel's structure and may modify only the JavaScript before executing the plugin, specifying the parameters:

```
<ul id="carousel" class="elastislide-list">
  <li><a href="#"><img src="image-photo.jpg" /></a></li>
  <li><a href="#"><img src="image-sky.jpg" /></a></li>
```

```
    <li><a href="#"><img src="image-gardem.jpg" /></a></li>
    <li><a href="#"><img src="image-flower.jpg" /></a></li>
    <li><a href="#"><img src="image-belt.jpg" /></a></li>
    <li><a href="#"><img src="image-wall.jpg" /></a></li>
    <li><a href="#"><img src="image-street.jpg" /></a></li>
</ul>
```

At the bottom of the DOM (before the `</body>` closing tag), we will need to include the jQuery and jQuery++ libraries (required for this solution), and then the ElastiSlide script:

```
<script src="http://code.jquery.com/jquery-1.9.1.min.js"></script>
<script src="js/jquerypp.custom.js"></script>
<script src="js/modernizr.custom.17475.js"></script>
<script src="js/jquery.elastislide.js"></script>
```

Then, include the CSS stylesheet inside the `<head>` tag:

```
<link rel="stylesheet" type="text/css" href="css/elastislide.css" />
```

Alright, now we already have the basis to show four different examples. For each example, you must add different parameters when executing the plugin script, in order to get different rendering, depending on the project need.

Example 1 – minimum of three visible images (default)

In this first example, we will see the default visual and behavior, and whether we will put the following code right after it, including the ElastiSlide plugin:

```
<script type="text/javascript">
$('#carousel').elastislide();
</script>
```

The default options that come with this solution are:

- Minimum three items will be shown
- Speed of scroll effect is 0.5 seconds
- Horizontal orientation
- Easing effect is defined as ease-in-out
- The carousel will start to show the first image on the list

The following screenshot represents what the implementation of this code will look like. Look at the difference between its versions shown on tablets and smartphones:

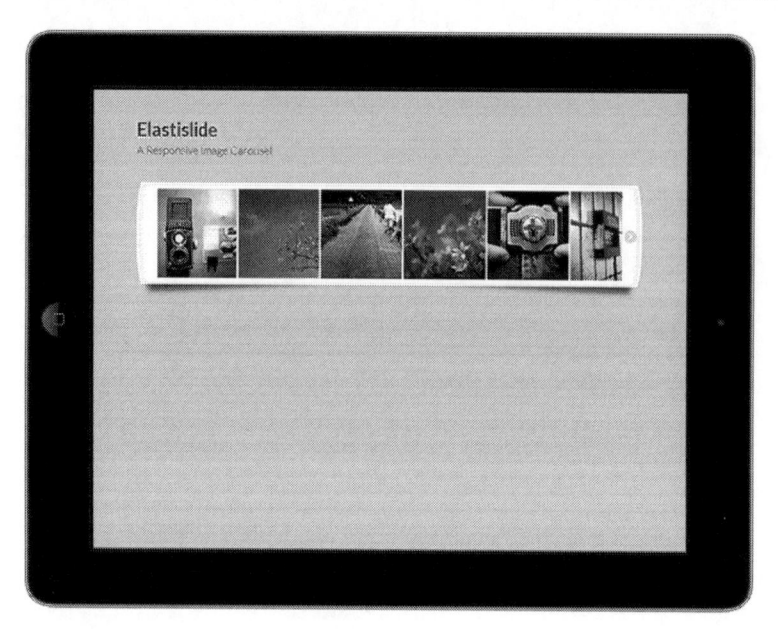

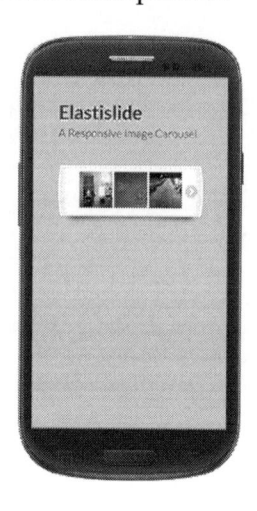

Example 2 – vertical with a minimum of three visible images

There is an option to render the carousel vertically, just by changing one parameter. Furthermore, we may speed up the scrolling effect. Remember to include the same files used in Example 1, and then insert the following code into the DOM:

```
<script type="text/javascript">
$('#carousel').elastislide({
  orientation: 'vertical',
  speed: 250
});
</script>
```

By default, three images are displayed as a minimum. But this minimum value can be modified as we will see in our next example:

Example 3 – fixed wrapper with a minimum of two visible images

In this example, we will define the minimum visible items in the carousel, the difference may be noticed when the carousel is viewed on small screens and the images will not reduce too much. Also, we may define the image to be shown starting from the third one.

Remember to include the same files that were used in Example 1, and then execute the scripts informing the following parameters and positioning them after including the ElastiSlide plugin:

```
<script>
$('#carousel').elastislide({
  minItems: 2,
  start: 2
});
</script>
```

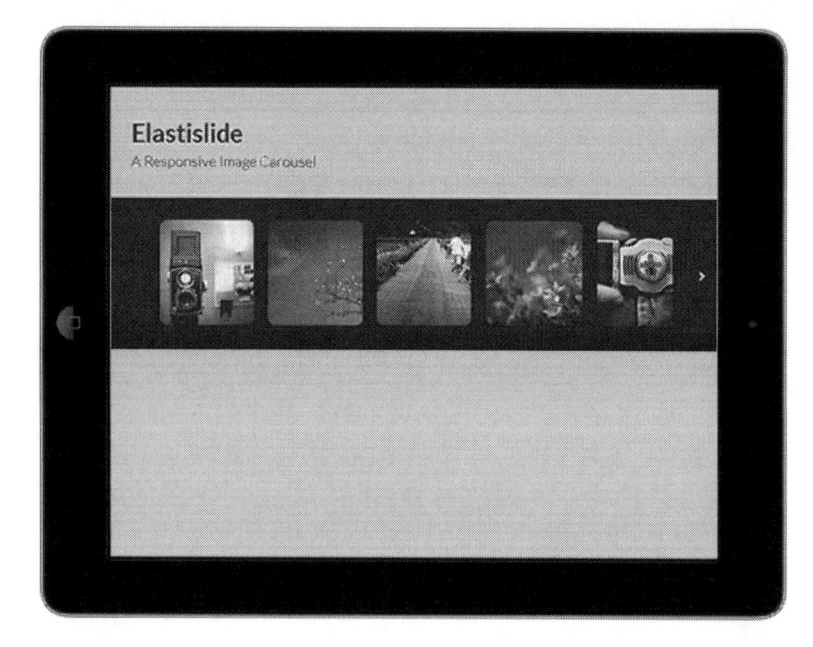

Example 4 – minimum of four images visible in an image gallery

In the fourth example, we can see many JavaScript implementations. However, the main objective of this example is to show the possibility which this plugin provides to us. Through the use of plugin callback functions and private functions we may track the click and the current image, and then handle this image change on demand by creating an image gallery:

```
<script>
var current = 0;
var $preview = $('#preview');
var $carouselEl = $('#carousel');
var $carouselItems = $carouselEl.children();
var carousel = $carouselEl.elastislide({
```

```
    current: current,
    minItems: 4,
    onClick: function(el, pos, evt){
      changeImage(el, pos);
      evt.preventDefault();
    },
    onReady: function(){
      changeImage($carouselItems.eq(current), current);
    }
});
function changeImage(el, pos) {
    $preview.attr('src', el.data('preview'));
    $carouselItems.removeClass('current-img');
    el.addClass('current-img');
    carousel.setCurrent(pos);
}
</script>
```

For this purpose, ElastiSlide may not have big advantages if compared with other plugins because it depends on our extra development to finalize this gallery. So, let's see what the next plugin offers to solve this problem.

FlexSlider2 – a fully responsive slider

FlexSlider2 is a lightweight jQuery plugin for image slider which includes fade and slide animations, touch gestures for mobile devices, and a bunch of customizable options.

FlexSlider2 is demonstrating a constant confidence in the developers' community, and some of the known **CMS (Content Management Systems)**, such as Drupal and WordPress, have already imported this plugin to be used on their systems since the plugin was released in 2011.

The stable Version 2.0 also supports users with old browsers since Safari 4, Chrome 4, Firefox 3.6, Opera 10, and IE7. Android and iOS devices are supported as well.

How to do it

To see the wide variety of options which this plugin provides, we will see the following three application examples of the most-used plugin options. We will start by showing the default layout of the slider. Then, we will see a slider using a navigation to support a situation where we have a high quantity of images to be shown, and in the last example we will see another way to configure a carousel of images provided by FlexSlider2.

You may find the downloadable files at `https://github.com/woothemes/FlexSlider`; for the additional plugin options, we recommend you to read the well-done documentation on the official website of the plugin at `http://www.woothemes.com/flexslider/`.

Example 1 – basic slider (default)

Let's start by including the CSS stylesheet inside the `<head>` tag:

```
<link rel="stylesheet" href="css/flexslider.css" type="text/css">
```

At the bottom of the DOM (before the `</body>` closing tag), we will need to include two files: jQuery library and FlexSlider2 script.

```
<script src="http://code.jquery.com/jquery-1.9.1.min.js"></script>
<script src="js/jquery.flexslider.js"></script>
```

Good so far, the first example starts here, when we are defining the carousel structure using a simple unordered list. There are only two requirements for it, which are, defining a `flexslider` class to the wrapping `<div>` and the `slides` class to `<ul>`.

```
<div class="flexslider">
  <ul class="slides">
    <li><img src="slide-img1.jpg" /></li>
    <li><img src="slide-img2.jpg" /></li>
    <li><img src="slide-img3.jpg" /></li>
    <li><img src="slide-img4.jpg" /></li>
  </ul>
</div>
```

After including the FlexSlider2 library, let's add this following code to execute the script. We will see the default visual and behavior of this plugin only displaying the common slide of image elements inside the carousel:

```
$(document).ready(function() {
  $('.flexslider').flexslider({
    animation: "slide"
  });
});
```

The style that comes with this plugin seems beautiful on smartphones and desktop versions:

Example 2 – slider with carousel slider as navigation control

The initial HTML structure is almost the same, but now we have to duplicate the slides structure for carousel. By executing the JavaScript function, the relationship between these two elements is identified and connected to the expected behavior.

Remember to include the same files used in Example 1, and then insert the following code into the HTML code.

```html
<div id="slider" class="flexslider">
  <ul class="slides">
    <li><img src="slide-img1.jpg" /></li>
    <li><img src="slide-img2.jpg" /></li>
    <li><img src="slide-img3.jpg" /></li>
    <li><img src="slide-img4.jpg" /></li>
  </ul>
</div>
<div id="carousel" class="flexslider">
  <ul class="slides">
    <li><img src="slide-img1.jpg" /></li>
    <li><img src="slide-img2.jpg" /></li>
    <li><img src="slide-img3.jpg" /></li>
    <li><img src="slide-img4.jpg" /></li>
  </ul>
</div>
```

To create this image gallery, we must identify the elements which the plugins will affect by using IDs, avoiding any kind of behavior conflicts. Comparing this example with Example 1, where FlexSlider2 was instantiated only once, we have two calls to the plugin script.

In the first part of the following code, the slideshow of pictures is being created, and in addition some other options that the plugin offers, such as `animation`, `itemWidth`, `itemMargin`, and `asNavFor`, are being complemented.

In the second part of this code, the navigation control is being created:

```javascript
$(document).ready(function() {
  $('#carousel').flexslider({
    animation: 'slide',
    controlNav: false,
    animationLoop: false,
    slideshow: false,
    itemWidth: 210,
    itemMargin: 5,
```

```
    asNavFor: '#slider'
  });
  $('#slider').flexslider({
    animation: "slide",
    controlNav: false,
    animationLoop: false,
    slideshow: false,
    sync: "#carousel"
  });
});
```

> The `asNavFor` option transforms `#slider` in a thumbnail navigation for #carousel. And the `sync` option creates a mirror of actions performed on `#slider` to `#carousel`. For example, if the user navigates through the slider, the carousel items will follow the actions showing the same active slider and vice versa.

Very simple, professional, and useful! So, let's see this responsive slider visual with navigation control on small devices and a desktop:

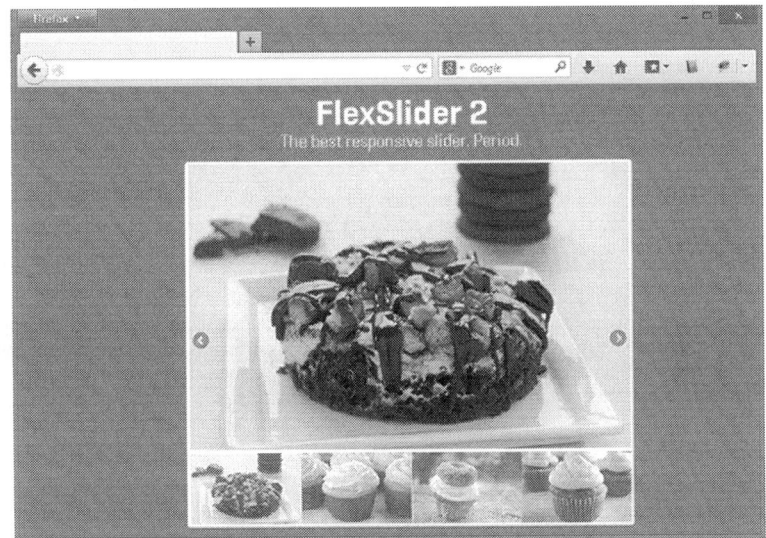

Example 3 – carousel setting minimum and maximum range

Remember to include the same files used in Example 1, and then insert the following code into the HTML code. Notice that it uses the same HTML structure as the first example:

```html
<div id="slider" class="flexslider">
  <ul class="slides">
    <li><img src="slide-img1.jpg" /></li>
    <li><img src="slide-img2.jpg" /></li>
    <li><img src="slide-img3.jpg" /></li>
    <li><img src="slide-img4.jpg" /></li>
  </ul>
</div>
```

However, to build it we need to change the JavaScript code, where we inform different parameters such as `itemWidth`, `itemMargin`, `minItems`, and `maxItems`, as we will see in the following code:

```javascript
$(document).ready(function() {
  $('.flexslider').flexslider({
    animation: "slide",
    animationLoop: false,
    itemWidth: 210,
    itemMargin: 5,
    minItems: 2,
    maxItems: 4
  });
});
```

> The options `itemWidth` and `itemMargin` should be measured and defined in pixels, but do not worry, the plugin will handle this fixed unit very well.

Also, `minItems` and `maxItems` are being used to define the values of minimum/maximum elements displayed on the screen depending on the device width. In the following screenshot, we will see the preceding code in practice in both versions, mobile and desktop:

ResponsiveSlides – the best of basic slides

ResponsiveSlides is a jQuery plugin, which is a very lightweight solution that basically acts in two different modes. Also, it just automatically fades the images, or operates as a responsive image container with pagination and/or navigation to fade between the slides.

ResponsiveSlides performs on a wide range of browsers including the older versions of IE and the Android Version 2.3 and above. It also adds the CSS `max-width` support for IE6 and other browsers that do not natively support it. This property helps to keep it responsive for small screens.

This plugin has two dependencies which are the jQuery library and that all of the images must have the same dimensions.

You will find the downloadable files and more details about plugin options at `https://github.com/viljamis/ResponsiveSlides.js`.

How do to it

In the following sections, you will find three examples where we can see the main features which this plugin offers. In the first example, we will see which files are necessary for working it out and what are the default options of ResponsiveSlides.

Building Responsive Image Sliders

In the second example, we will add various parameters to check how this plugin can be customized and meet the needs of our projects.

In the third example, we will implement an additional navigation through images, facilitating the user access to go to the specific slide they want to view.

Example 1

So, we will start by including the CSS file responsible for ResponsiveSlides theme inside the `<head>` tag:

```
<link rel="stylesheet" href="responsiveslides.css">
```

After that, the plugin supports the use of a simple HTML unordered list to craft our slideshow. However, we need to define a classname for this `<ul>`, making sure the plugin will detect which `<ul>` must be transformed:

```
<ul class="rslides">
  <li><img src="slide-img1.jpg" /></li>
  <li><img src="slide-img2.jpg" /></li>
  <li><img src="slide-img3.jpg" /></li>
  <li><img src="slide-img4.jpg" /></li>
</ul>
```

Then, at the bottom of the DOM (before the `</body>` closing tag), we should include the jQuery library and ResponsiveSlides script.

```
<script src="http://code.jquery.com/jquery-1.9.1.min.js"></script>
<script src="js/responsiveslides.min.js"></script>
```

Now, we will just have to execute the ResponsiveSlides script for `<ul>` with the `rslides` class when the site has loaded. Let's put this code after the inclusion of ResponsiveSlides:

```
<script>
$(function() {
  $(".rslides").responsiveSlides();
});
</script>
```

> Inside the `demo.css` file (that comes with plugin files), there is a bunch of CSS stylesheets, which may help us customize the slideshow. This file is not required, but it makes a lot of difference on the visual and may be useful for further references.

This is the default visual of the plugin:

Example 2

So, we will start the same way as we did with the previous example by including the CSS file inside the `<head>` tag, then at the bottom of the DOM code (before the `</body>` closing tag), we will include the jQuery library and ResponsiveSlides script.

For this example, we added a div wrapping to the slideshow `slider_container`, helping us to position the arrows and the caption text for each slide. If some projects need this caption text to explain the slide, ResponsiveSlides may handle this feature very well.

So, let's test it on this next slideshow:

```
<div class="slider_container">
  <ul class="rslides" id="slider-example2">
    <li><img src="images/slide-img1.jpg" />
      <p class="caption">This is a caption</p>
    </li>
    <li><img src="images/slide-img2.jpg" />
      <p class="caption"><strong>Other</strong> caption here</p>
    </li>
    <li><img src="images/slide-img3.jpg" />
      <p class="caption">The <u>third</u> caption</p>
```

```
        </li>
        <li><img src="images/slide-img4.jpg" />
            <p class="caption">The fourth caption</p>
        </li>
    </ul>
</div>
```

Then, remember to execute the ResponsiveSlides script for `<div>` with the `slider-example2` ID when the site has loaded, by putting this code after the inclusion of ResponsiveSlides:

```
<script>
    $(function() {
        $('#slider-example2').responsiveSlides({
            auto: false,
            pager: false,
            nav: true,
            maxwidth: 540,
            speed: 500,
            namespace: "callbacks",
            before: function () {
                /* before event fired */
            },
            after: function () {
                /* after event fired */
            }
        });
    });
</script>
```

> It is also possible to inform the plugin to render only next/previous arrows with no pager navigation by setting `false` for the `pager` option and `true` for the `nav` option.

In the following screenshot, we will see this example with the caption and navigation arrows styles from `demo.css`, which come with the plugin:

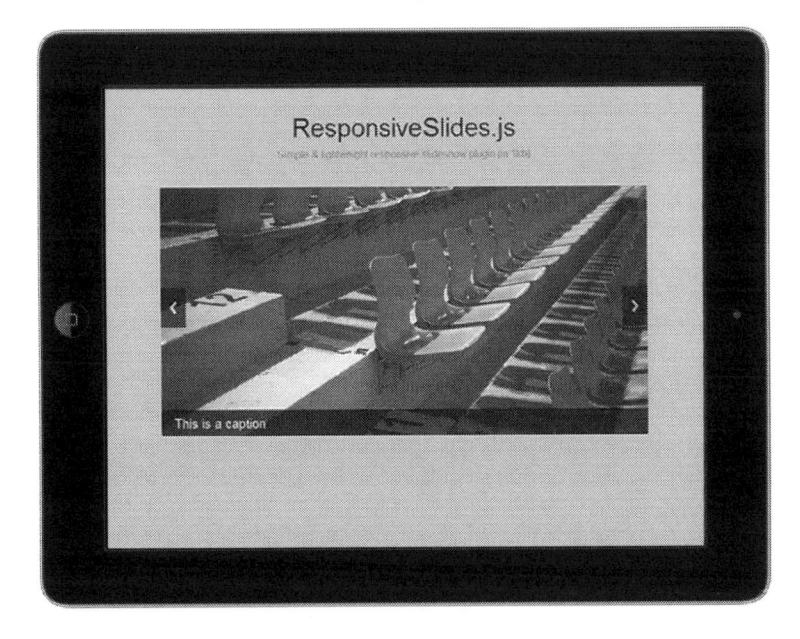

Example 3

This example is focused on creating a custom navigation, based on thumbnail images and images created by us previously, offering another way to the user to display a slideshow gallery. In order to build it, we will insert other simple unordered lists showing thumbnail images and setting an ID to inform to the plugin later:

```
<ul class="rslides" id="slider-example3">
  <li><img src="slide-img1.jpg" /></li>
  <li><img src="slide-img2.jpg" /></li>
  <li><img src="slide-img3.jpg" /></li>
  <li><img src="slide-img4.jpg" /></li>
</ul>
<ul id="pager-example3">
  <li><a href="#"><img src="thumb-img1.jpg" /></a></li>
  <li><a href="#"><img src="thumb-img2.jpg" /></a></li>
  <li><a href="#"><img src="thumb-img3.jpg" /></a></li>
  <li><a href="#"><img src="thumb-img4.jpg" /></a></li>
</ul>
```

Again, we must ensure that the CSS file will be included inside the `<head>` tag, then include the jQuery library and ResponsiveSlides script at the bottom of the HTML code. When we execute ResponsiveSlides for `#slider-example3`, we will set the `manualControls` option and specify our custom pager navigation ID for that thumbnail image structure, as follows:

```
<script>
$("#slider-example3").responsiveSlides({
  manualControls: '#pager-example3'
});
</script>
```

The following screenshot depicts the visual of this navigation feature implemented:

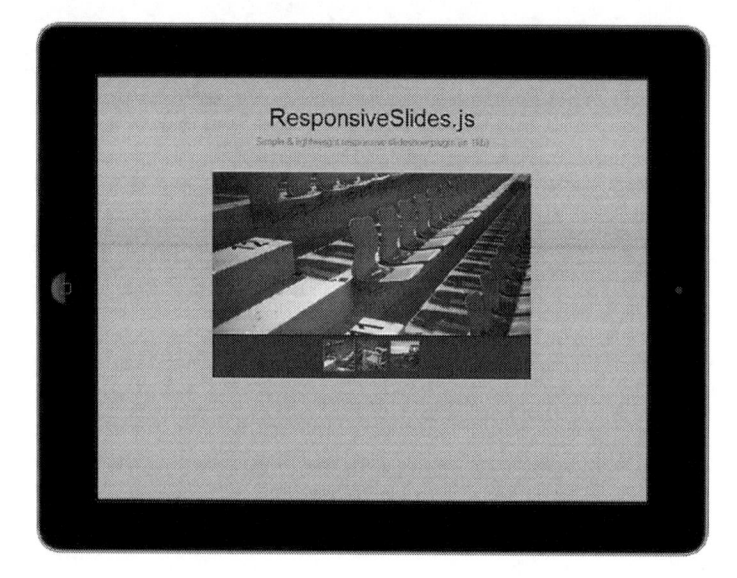

Swiper – performatic touch image slider

Swiper is a lightweight mobile touch slider with hardware-accelerated transitions (where supported) and amazing native behavior. It is intended to be used on mobile websites, but also works great on modern desktop browsers.

There are two reasons why this plugin is my favorite: its performance is really good, especially on smartphones, and it also allows a desktop user to feel almost the same touch gestures experienced when navigating through the slider content.

You can download this solution from `https://github.com/nolimits4web/Swiper/`. For more information about plugin options, visit `http://www.idangero.us/sliders/swiper/api.php`.

How to do it

So, we will start by including the JS and CSS files inside the `<head>` tag:

```
<script src="http://code.jquery.com/jquery-1.9.1.min.js"></script>
<script src="js/idangerous.swiper-2.2.min.js"></script>
<link rel="stylesheet" href=" css/idangerous.swiper.css">
```

Now, we will execute the Swiper script, informing the `container` and `pagination` classes:

```
<script>
$(function(){
  var mySwiper = $('.swiper-container').swiper({
    pagination: '.pager',
    paginationClickable: true
  });
});
</script>
```

Note that this CSS file only customizes the slide animation. Even so, we need to add the following code to customize the slide structure as we want, complementing the styles that come with Swiper:

```
<style>
.swiper-container {
  width: 70%;
  height: 300px;
}
.pager {
  position: absolute;
  z-index: 20;
  left: 10px;
  bottom: 10px;
}
.swiper-pagination-switch {
  display: inline-block;
  width: 1em;
  height: 1em;
  background: #222;
```

[125]

```
        margin-right: 5px;
    }
</style>
```

After that, the plugin supports the use of a simple HTML unordered list to craft our slideshow. Also, we need to define some class names for this structure in order to ensure the plugin performs:

```
<div class="swiper-container">
  <div class="swiper-wrapper">
    <div class="swiper-slide slide-1">
      <p>Slide 1</p>
    </div>
    <div class="swiper-slide slide-2">
      <p>Slide 2</p>
    </div>
    <div class="swiper-slide slide-3">
      <img src="img/slide-img3.jpg" />
    </div>
    <div class="swiper-slide slide-4">
      <img src="img/slide-img3.jpg" />
    </div>
  </div>
  <div class="pager"></div>
</div>
```

The `swiper-container` and `swiper-wrapper` classes are wrapped by all the slider structure. Also, the `swiper-slide` class defines the div as a slide item and the `pager` class specifies the div which will display the slide pagination.

The visual adopted on the site demonstration provided by the plugin developers is beautiful; however, those styles are not inside `idangerous.swiper.css`. It still depends on our entire slide customization, as we will see in the following screenshot:

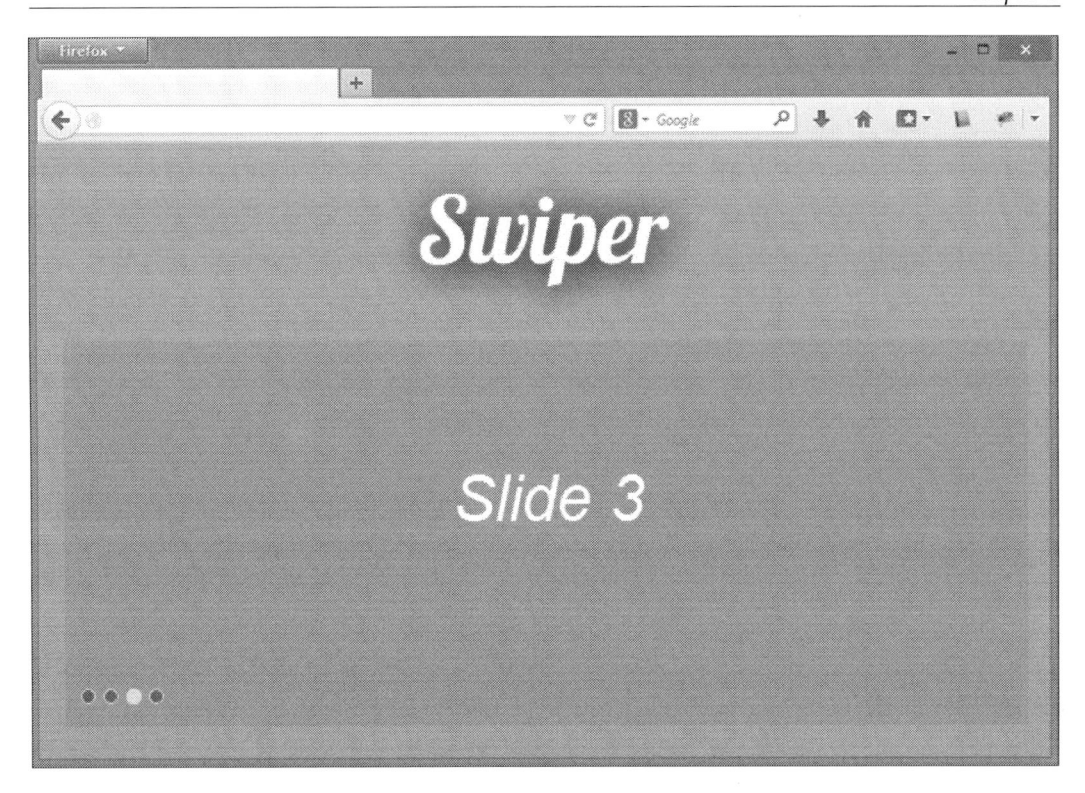

Featured options

By analyzing the code, this plugin seems very clever and provides a fast rendering to the browser. Another important consideration is the constant update by the community, fixing major and minor mistakes. Its current differences from other plugins are:

- Vertical/horizontal sliding
- Rich API
- Flexible configuration
- Nested Swipers
- 3D flow

In the plugin Version 1.8.5, they introduced the 3D flow complement to the Swiper. It simply provides an amazing realistic 3D gallery with dynamic shadows, providing a big advantage compared to other slider plugins. Let's see how to implement it.

Using the 3D flow style on Swiper

Since it is a complement of Swiper, we need to include the same files of the previous example, starting by the CSS on `<head>`. Also, append these following new JS and CSS files referred to the 3D flow styles:

```
<script src="js/idangerous.swiper.3dflow-2.0.js"></script>
<link rel="stylesheet" href="css/idangerous.swiper.3dflow.css">
```

Now, let's change the code we have used to execute Swiper previously. The following one has many parameters, which come with it by default, and it will execute our 3D-flow script:

```
<script>
$(function(){
  var mySwiper = $('.swiper-container').swiper({
    slidesPerView: 3,
    loop: true,
      tdFlow: {
      rotate: 10,
      stretch: -50,
      depth: 400,
      modifier: 1,
      shadows: true
    }
  });
});
</script>
```

Alright, look at the big difference this complement may bring to the slider visual. Just by using the CSS3 Transform, the Swiper plugin may provide us an automatic way to display a different slideshow effect:

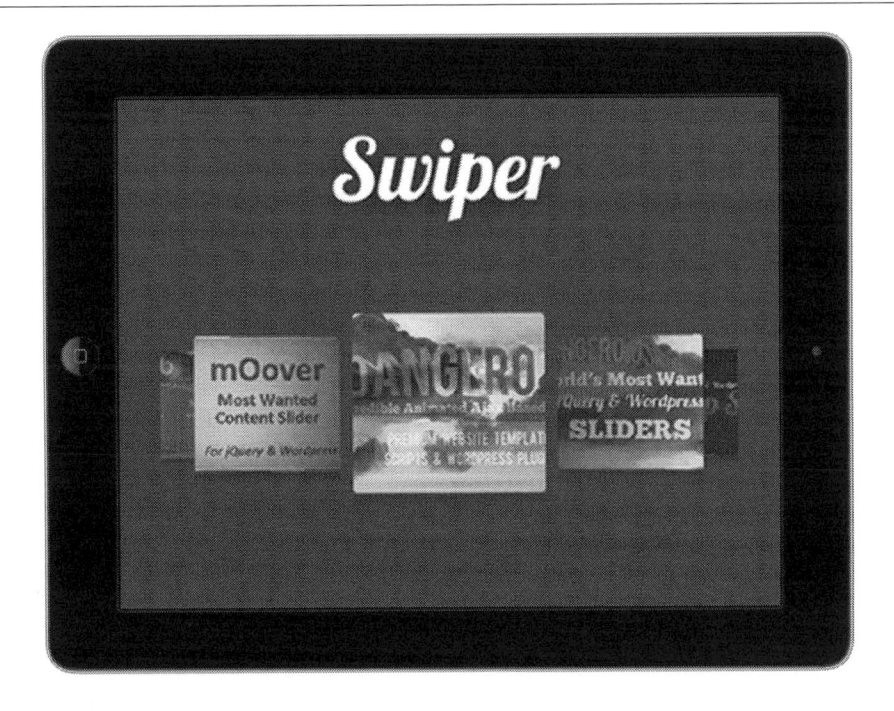

By visiting the site `http://www.idangero.us/sliders/swiper/plugins/3dflow.php`, we will find more examples and other usage options for 3D flow.

Slicebox – a slice animation when using slide images

The Slicebox is a jQuery plugin for responsive 3D image sliders with a graceful fallback (for older browsers that do not support the new CSS properties).

The visual effect of this plugin is really cool. Once the slide is changed, the image is sliced in three or five pieces of image and it is rotated, showing an incredible effect.

How to do it

So, after downloading the plugin from `https://github.com/codrops/Slicebox`, we will start by including the CSS file inside the `<head>` tag:

```
<link rel="stylesheet" type="text/css" href="css/slicebox.css" />
<link rel="stylesheet" type="text/css" href="css/custom.css" />
```

However, there is a wrapping configuration missing in CSS that comes with the plugin and should be made by us:

```
<style>
.wrapper {
  position: relative;
  max-width: 840px;
  width: 100%;
  padding: 0 50px;
  margin: 0 auto;
}
</style>
```

After that, we will make use of a simple HTML-unordered list to craft our slideshow, and define some required IDs for this structure, such as `sb-slider`, `shadow`, `nav-arrows`, and `nav-dots`, and name code sections for the plugin reading:

```
<div class="wrapper">
  <ul id="sb-slider" class="sb-slider">
  <li>
    <a href="#"><img src="images/slide-img1.jpg" /></a>
    <div class="sb-description"><h3>Creative Lifesaver</h3></div>
  </li>
  <li>
    <a href="#"><img src="images/slide-img2.jpg" /></a>
    <div class="sb-description"><h3>Honest Entertainer</h3></div>
  </li>
  <li>
    <a href="#"><img src="images/slide-img3.jpg" /></a>
    <div class="sb-description"><h3>Brave Astronaut</h3></div>
  </li>
  <li>
    <a href="#"><img src="images/slide-img4.jpg" /></a>
    <div class="sb-description"><h3>Faithful Investor</h3></div>
  </li>
  </ul>
  <div id="shadow" class="shadow"></div>
  <div id="nav-arrows" class="nav-arrows">
    <a href="#">Next</a>
    <a href="#">Previous</a>
  </div>
  <div id="nav-dots" class="nav-dots">
```

```
        <span class="nav-dot-current"></span>
        <span></span>
        <span></span>
        <span></span>
    </div>
</div>
```

Also, there are some utility classes complementing the code such as `wrapper` (for slider wrapping) and `sb-description` (to display the content as the slider description).

At the bottom of DOM (before the `</body>` closing tag), include the jQuery and Slicebox libraries:

```
<script src="http://code.jquery.com/jquery-1.9.1.min.js"></script>
<script src="js/jquery.slicebox.js"></script>
```

After that, we will execute the Slicebox script by inserting the next code.

> However, in my opinion, this is the major problem of this plugin because there are many lines of code exposed to us.

The following code is too extensive and avoiding typos, you will find the code to be downloaded from `http://www.packtpub.com/support`.

This is a screenshot of the effect on mobile devices and desktops:

Introducing touch gestures to user experience

Touchscreen devices are ruling the mobile platform nowadays. Most of the smartphones and tablets have many elements using touch gestures and now it's coming to our desktop development. In his article *Optimizing for Touch Across Devices*, Luke Wroblewski says:

> "So what does it mean to consider touch across all screen sizes? Two things: touch target sizes and placement of controls."

Luke Wroblewski highlights two of the most important points to consider with responsive touch design: touch target sizes and placement of controls:

- **Touch target sizes**: They are relatively easy to implement and any navigation system that needs to work with touch needs to have menu options that can be comfortably used by people with imprecise fingers to prevent accidental taps and errors. Some articles mentioning the minimum measure of touchable area should be 44 px.
- **Placement of controls**: Controls need to be positioned in a way that aligns with how people hold and use touch-enabled devices. The bottom area of a smartphone screen is where we want to put an application's most common and important interactions so that they may be reached quickly and easily, as shown in the following website example:

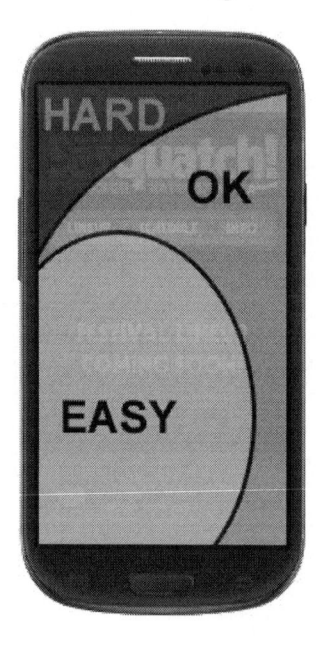

Similarly, we can look at tablet postures or at how people typically hold tablet computers. People hold them with their two hands along the sides, or just type over the screen on their lap:

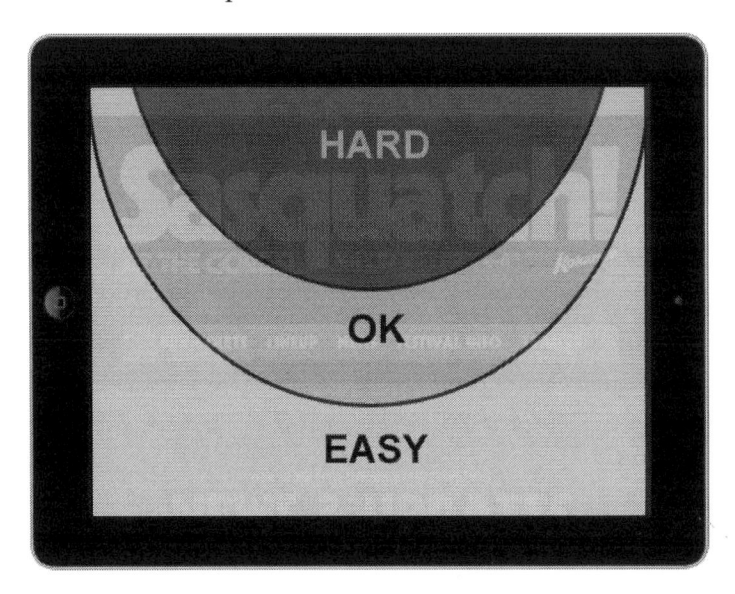

Implementing touch events with JavaScript plugins

There are some important JavaScript extensions and plugins that allow us to integrate touch gestures into our responsive website, improving the user interaction experience. Some examples are QuoJS and Hammer.

QuoJS – simple touch interaction library

It is a micro, modular, object-oriented, and concise JavaScript library that simplifies the HTML document traversing, event handling, and Ajax interactions for rapid mobile web development.

Note that QuoJS does not require jQuery for its working; however, it is a simple and good plugin.

This lightweight plugin, with 5-6 KB when gzipped, allows us to have powerful writing, flexibility, and adapted code. You will find the downloadable files at https://github.com/soyjavi/QuoJS and further details about some extra options at http://quojs.tapquo.com/.

QuoJS have these gestures to help us:

- Single tap
- Hold (650ms+)
- Double tap

And different types of Swipe, Pinch, and Rotate are included in its code package too.

How to do it

At the bottom of the DOM (before the `</body>` closing tag), include the QuoJS script; only then will we be able to execute the script by creating event listeners.

In the following example, we will implement an action if users hold their finger over the element with the ID equal to the toolbox:

```
<script src="js/quo.js"></script>
<script src="http://code.jquery.com/jquery-1.9.1.min.js"></script>
<script>
$(document).ready(function() {
  $('#toolbox').hold(function() {
    $(this).toggleClass('open-box');
  });
});
</script>
```

QuoJS uses the `$$` symbol in the syntax, avoiding conflicts with the `$` jQuery symbol which we are probably using on websites.

Hammer – a nice multitouch library

Hammer is a jQuery lightweight library for multitouch gestures with only 3 KB when gzipped.

Hammer supports these gestures:

- Tap
- DoubleTap
- Swipe
- Drag
- Pinch
- Rotate

Each gesture triggers useful events and event data that comes with the plugin.

How to do it

First of all, let's download the library from `https://github.com/EightMedia/hammer.js`. At the bottom of the DOM (before the `</body>` closing tag), include the Hammer script and then we will be able to execute the script by creating event listeners:

```
<script src="http://code.jquery.com/jquery-1.9.1.min.js"></script>
<script src="js/jquery.hammer.min.js"></script>
```

> Sometimes the version that does not require jQuery seems faster, but it might not work in all browsers. To switch the versions, we just need to replace the `jquery.hammer.min.js` file with `hammer.min.js`.

Let's see an example:

```
<script>
$(document).ready(function() {
  var hammertime = $(".toucharea").hammer();
  hammertime.on("touch", "#toolbox", function(ev) {
    $(this).toggleClass('open-box');
  });
});
</script>
```

In this example, it captures the touch interaction and applies the `open-box` class on objects. However, there are many other touch events to work on and further details on its usage may be found at `https://github.com/EightMedia/hammer.js/wiki`.

Exercise 6 – creating an image slider using the Swiper plugin

Just to remind us, this is a screenshot of our initial design:

> This image is just a suggestion. You can find any image to replace this one. The main focus here is the creation of a responsive image slider within a responsive label.

Now, just select one image per slide, and by using the Swiper solution, insert a slogan on each slider:

- Flexibility is everything
- A few well-designed movements
- Muscle control develops the body uniformly
- Physical fitness is the first requisite of happiness

As we saw in *Chapter 4*, *Designing Responsive Text*, the use of `@font-face` is highly recommended for responsive websites. So, complementing this exercise, use the free font Titan One from Google Fonts for customizing the slogans.

> Remember to use the FontSquirrel kit if necessary.

Summary

In this chapter, we have learned about slider plugins prepared for responsive sites such as the Elastislide, FlexSlider, ResponsiveSlides, Swiper, and Slicebox. We have also learned how to build them, their advantages, and effect characteristics. Although many of these slider plugins have already implemented gesture touches, as we saw in this chapter, we have also shown you how to incorporate touch functions by using the QuoJS and Hammer libraries.

In the next chapter, we will see how to deal with tables in small width devices. We will see how to implement each technique that has often been used, such as horizontal scrolling, reducing visible columns, and converting into stack table.

7
Designing Responsive Tables

The HTML element table can be quite wide to be able to show a structured content. Sometimes the entire row of data needs to be kept along to make sense in a table. Tables can flex by default, but if they get too narrow, cell content will begin to wrap; this is often not very cleanly done!

Garrett Dimon mentioned an interesting topic about the difficulty of adjusting table width accommodating different screen sizes and ensuring the sense in content of the table:

> *"Data tables don't do so well with responsive design. Just sayin'."*

In this chapter, we will learn four different approaches to create responsive tables:

- Expandable responsive tables
- Stacked tables
- Horizontal overflow
- Link to full-table

Responsive tables

The following screenshot shows the most common problems found about responsive table, which are: the minimum table width exceeds the screen size and the decrease in the size of the whole table (text size included):

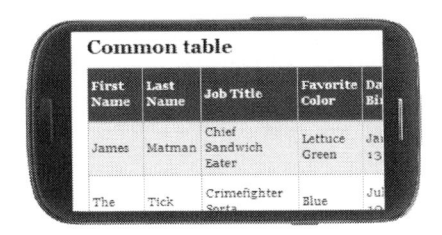

However, let's see the different ways to solve this responsive problem.

Expandable responsive tables

Through FooTable we can transform our HTML tables into expandable responsive tables, allowing devices with small screen sizes to keep the same content, and the only change is you will have to prioritize the content that will be displayed. Its function is to hide the columns you consider less important when viewed for the first time depending on the breakpoint. So, the hidden data will appear when clicking/touching the row only.

If we look more deeply into this jQuery plugin, we will notice two big features that have contributed for a good code and ease of development: **out of the box customization** (via data attributes from DOM) and **breakpoint settings** (which may be set different from breakpoints which have already been used on a website).

Let's see in the next example how to define it on DOM.

How to do it

After downloading the plugin from `https://github.com/bradvin/FooTable/`, we will include the CSS stylesheet inside the `<head>` tag:

```
<link href="css/themes/footable.metro.css" rel="stylesheet" type="text/css" />
```

By default, there are only two breakpoints that FooTable uses: `phone` set to `480 px` and `tablet` to `1024 px`. These breakpoint values need not be the same as the ones you are probably using because it depends on how much space the table needs. Also, we will see later how to change it if necessary.

Let's insert the following code as a sample into the HTML code just to practice the plugin resources:

```
<table class="expandable-table">
  <thead>
    <tr>
      <th data-class="expand-icon">Contact name</th>
      <th data-hide="phone">Phone</th>
      <th data-hide="phone,tablet">Email</th>
      <th data-hide="phone" data-ignore="true">Picture</th>
    </tr>
  </thead>
  <tbody>
    <tr>
```

```
        <td>Bob Builder</td>
        <td>555-12345</td>
        <td>bob@home.com</td>
        <td><img src="http://fpoimg.com/30x30" alt="Profile image" />
        </td>
      </tr>
      <tr>
        <td>Bridget Jones</td>
        <td>544-776655</td>
        <td>bjones@mysite.com</td>
        <td><img src="http://fpoimg.com/30x30" alt="Profile image" />
        </td>
      </tr>
      <tr>
        <td>Tom Cruise</td>
        <td>555-99911</td>
        <td>cruise1@crazy.com</td>
        <td><img src="http://fpoimg.com/30x30" alt="Profile image" />
        </td>
      </tr>
    </tbody>
</table>
```

Data attributes facilitate the understanding of the functioning of FooTable, knowing which columns will be hidden in phones or tablets by only looking at the DOM.

The following are the basic data attributes used by FooTable and their functions:

- `data-class`: This specifies a CSS class to be applied to all cells in a column.
- `data-hide`: This defines which breakpoints will be hidden in a column. It is possible to specify more than one breakpoint by separating them using a comma.
- `data-ignore`: This hides the content only when the detailed information is seen. It is normally used along with the `data-hide` class and the acceptable values for this option may be `true` or `false`.

For further information about a list of all data attributes, you may visit `http://fooplugins.com/footable/demos/data-attributes.htm`.

> If we use these data attributes, we should apply them on the `<th>` element and the plugin will reflect its changes in the internal cells.

Designing Responsive Tables

At the bottom of DOM (before the `</body>` closing tag), we will need to include two files: jQuery and FooTable libraries. After that, insert the following code executing the script:

```
<script src="http://code.jquery.com/jquery-1.9.1.min.js"></script>
<script src="js/footable.min.js"></script>
<script>
  $(function() {
    $(".expandable-table").footable();
  });
</script>
```

If we want to change the breakpoints of FooTable, we will only need to specify our own values when executing the previous script, as is shown in the following code:

```
<script>
  $(function() {
    $(".expandable-table").footable({
      breakpoints: {
        tablet: 768,
        smartphone: 480,
        mini: 320
      }
    });
  });
</script>
```

In the following screenshot, we will see what happens if we click on Bob's table row. Let's compare our responsive tables on a Smartphone and a tablet:

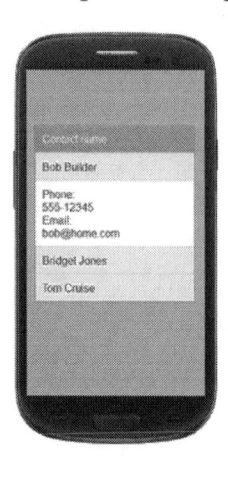

[140]

In this example, on each device there are some fields that are visible only if you are clicking for more details of a specific contact. Although this approach avoids massive data, it may be difficult to find a contact, for example, by e-mail, as it requires clicking on all contacts to display the information.

There are some plugin extensions that solve this. Let's check them.

Extending the plugin

Another advantage of using the FooTable as a solution is its extensibility. The plugin is modular, which allows you to include additional functionality such as sorting, filtering, and pagination through the use of add-ons.

The sorting add-on provides the capability of sorting the data contained within your table columns. To do this, we will include this script file:

```
<script src=" js/footable.sort.js"></script>
```

Then we will set `data-sort-initial="true"` for items for which we want to enable the sorting and `data-sort-ignore="true"` for items for which sorting does not make sense, such as images and phones:

```
<th data-sort-initial="true">Contact name</th>
<th data-sort-ignore="true">Phone</th>
```

In the following screenshot we can see the insertion of arrow icons, which the plugin uses to order that specific table header:

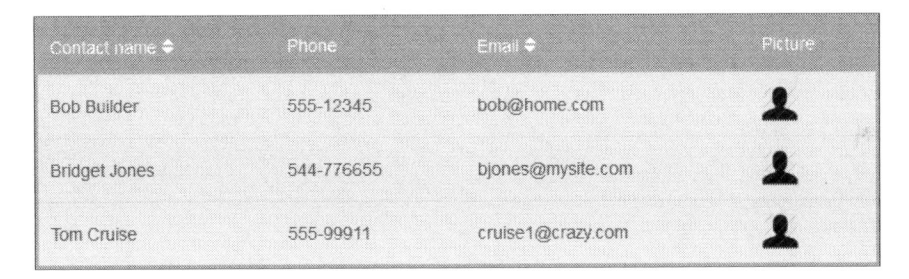

Contact name ⇕	Phone	Email ⇕	Picture
Bob Builder	555-12345	bob@home.com	👤
Bridget Jones	544-776655	bjones@mysite.com	👤
Tom Cruise	555-99911	cruise1@crazy.com	👤

The filtering add-on adds a search field allowing users to locate the data they are looking for. The search result brings the correct data to us even if it is hidden from viewers. To do so, let's include the following in the script file:

```
<script src=" js/footable.filter.js"></script>
```

Designing Responsive Tables

Add a text input field to your page (before or after the table) with the `#filter` ID, and then specify it on the `data-filter=#filter` data attribute of your table element. The following is the code of this filter:

```
Filter by: <input id="filter" type="text">
```

In the following screenshot the content was filtered showing just one item, even the value found is hidden:

Also, the pagination add-on helps displaying part of the total content creating a pagination of 10 items by default. To do this, we must include the following code in the script file:

```
<script src="js/footable.paginate.js"></script>
```

So, in the previous table example, after `</tbody>` we will add the following code which will receive the pagination. The `pagination` class in the following div is required and other classes such as `pagination-centered` and `hide-if-no-paging` are only complementary:

```
<tfoot>
<tr>
  <td colspan="4">
    <div class="pagination-centered hide-if-no-paging pagination">
    </div>
  </td>
</tr>
</tfoot>
```

Also, for this example let's limit two items per page, to see the pagination in use, by adding `data-page-size="2"` on `table` element. And this is how it looks:

For further information about these add-ons and more plugin options, the complete documentation can be found at `http://fooplugins.com/footable-demos/`.

Although this plugin looks very complete, there are some situations where the content demands an other interface. Let's take a look at the stackedtable solution.

Stackedtables

Stackedtable is a jQuery plugin that offers another option for our responsive table which is available to download from `http://johnpolacek.github.io/stacktable.js/`.

This solution creates a copy of the table and converts wide tables into a two-column key/value format that works better on small screens.

> This solution is recommended for tables with few rows only because it increases a lot of the vertical content.

By using a simple media query, we can hide the original table and show the stacked table. Let's take a look and see how we can put this into action.

How to do it using the table from the previous example

We will start by including the CSS stylesheet inside the `<head>` tag:

```
<link href="stacktable.css" rel="stylesheet" />
```

Designing Responsive Tables

If we want to change the breakpoint, aiming to use this solution for Smartphones, we only need to go inside the `stacktable.css` file and change the `max-width` property:

```css
@media (max-width: 480px) {
  .large-only { display: none; }
  .stacktable.small-only { display: table; }
}
```

After that, we will add the base of the table that we saw in the previous solution, just adding an ID and class:

```html
<table id="stack-table" class="large-only">
  <thead>
    <tr>
      <th>Contact name</th>
      <th>Phone</th>
      <th>Email</th>
      <th>Picture</th>
    </tr>
  </thead>
  <tbody>
    <tr>
      <td>Bob Builder</td>
      <td>555-12345</td>
      <td>bob@home.com</td>
      <td><img src="http://fpoimg.com/30x30" alt="Profile image" />
      </td>
    </tr>
    <tr>
      <td>Bridget Jones</td>
      <td>544-776655</td>
      <td>bjones@mysite.com</td>
      <td><img src="http://fpoimg.com/30x30" alt="Profile image" />
      </td>
    </tr>
    <tr>
      <td>Tom Cruise</td>
      <td>555-99911</td>
      <td>cruise1@crazy.com</td>
      <td><img src="http://fpoimg.com/30x30" alt="Profile image" />
      </td>
    </tr>
  </tbody>
</table>
```

At the bottom of DOM (before the `</body>` closing tag), we will need to include two files: the `jquery` and `stacktable` libraries. After that, insert the following code executing the script and inform the table ID and a class to restrict the stacked table only for Smartphones as we want:

```
<script src="http://code.jquery.com/jquery-1.9.1.min.js"></script>
<script src="js/stacktable.js"></script>
<script>
$('#stack-table').stacktable({myClass:'stacktable small-only'});
</script>
```

The following is a screenshot of the two views—for small device and desktop:

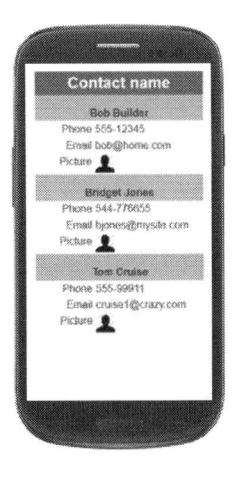

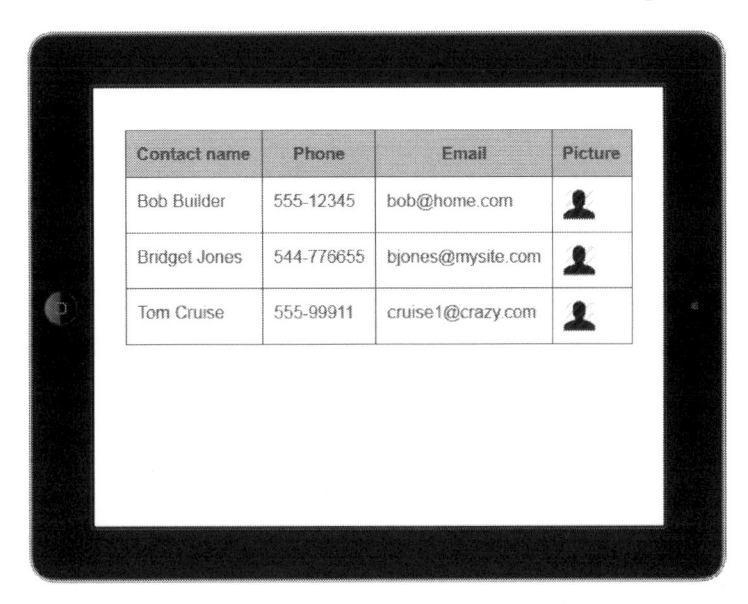

Horizontal overflow

This technique works by freezing the first column, allowing you to scroll down the other columns under it. This way we keep seeing the first column content for each row, which permits left scrolling, to see the remaining content in order to make data comparison easier.

This table is recommended for tables that have a greater number of columns and the content of the first column is more important than others. Let's clarify how it will look by practicing it in the next example.

How to do it

We will start by downloading the solution from `http://zurb.com/playground/responsive-tables`. After that, let's create a new HTML file and include the CSS stylesheet inside the `<head>` tag:

```
<link rel="stylesheet" href="css/responsive-tables.css">
```

Now insert the following HTML table code using more columns than the previous one and with a class named `responsive`:

```
<table class="responsive">
<tr>
  <th>Header 1</th>
  <th>Header 2</th>
  <th>Header 3</th>
  <th>Header 4</th>
  <th>Header 5</th>
  <th>Header 6</th>
</tr>
<tr>
  <td>first column important data</td>
  <td>row 1, cell 2</td>
  <td>row 1, cell 3</td>
  <td>row 1, cell 4</td>
  <td>row 1, cell 5</td>
  <td>row 1, cell 6</td>
</tr>
<tr>
  <td>first column important data</td>
  <td>row 2, cell 2</td>
  <td>row 2, cell 3</td>
  <td>row 2, cell 4</td>
  <td>row 2, cell 5</td>
  <td>row 2, cell 6</td>
</tr>
</table>
```

At the bottom of DOM (before the `</body>` closing tag), we will only need to include jQuery and Responsive-Tables libraries:

```
<script src="http://code.jquery.com/jquery-1.9.1.min.js"></script>
<script src="js/responsive-tables.js"></script>
```

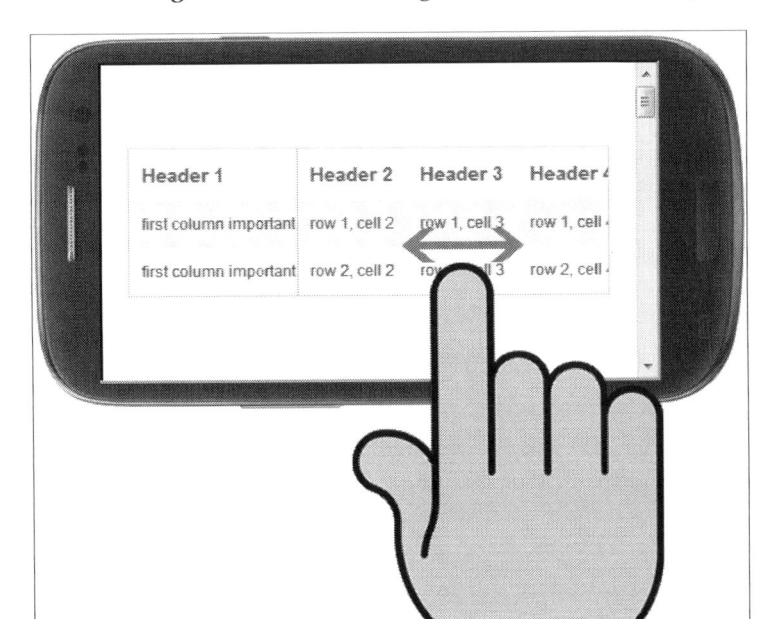

Let's look at the following screenshot showing this table on a Smartphone and tablet:

> When the available screen width is over 767 px, changes start to occur on our table. If we want to modify this default value, we need to open the `responsive-tables.js` file, look for the value 767, and change it.

It is technically simple to do. However, we cannot underestimate its efficiency on responsive websites, since it helps a lot to understand the table information, especially on small devices.

Header orientation flip

If you find that the header row of our table is more important than the first column and that you need to keep displaying the header row when using small devices, *David Bushell* has created an interesting solution by using only the CSS code.

This CSS solution swaps places with the first column and does not require any JavaScript library, just CSS3.

Designing Responsive Tables

Let's start by including the CSS stylesheet inside the `<head>` tag:

```css
<style>
@media only screen and (max-width: 767px) {
  .responsive {
    display: block; position: relative;
  }
  .responsive thead {
    display: block; float: left;
  }
  .responsive tbody {
    display: block; width: auto; position: relative;
    overflow-x: auto; white-space: nowrap;
  }
  .responsive thead tr {
    display: block;
  }
  .responsive th {
    display: block; border: 0; border-top: 1px solid #AAA;
    background: #CCC; border-right: 1px solid #ccc;
    padding: 8px 10px !important;
  }
  .responsive tbody tr {
    display: inline-block; vertical-align: top;
    border-right: 1px solid #ccc;
  }
  .responsive td {
    display: block; min-height: 1.25em; border: 0;
  }
  table.responsive th:first-child, table.responsive td:first-child,
  table.responsive td:first-child, table.responsive.pinned td {
    display: block;
  }
}
</style>
```

Using a more realistic content, let's create this table on our HTML code:

```html
<table class="responsive" cellspacing="0" border="1">
  <thead>
    <tr>
      <th>Doctor names</th>
      <th>Values</th>
      <th>Dates</th>
      <th>Cash Money</th>
      <th>Message</th>
```

```
            <th>City</th>
            <th>State</th>
        </tr>
    </thead>
    <tbody>
        <tr>
            <td>Dr. Jayhawk</td>
            <td>102</td>
            <td>03/30/1940</td>
            <td>$60.42</td>
            <td>PAID</td>
            <td>Atlanta</td>
            <td>Georgia</td>
        </tr>
        <tr>
            <td>Dr. John Smith</td>
            <td>137</td>
            <td>03/18/1953</td>
            <td>$69.68</td>
            <td>PAID</td>
            <td>Orlando</td>
            <td>Florida</td>
        </tr>
        <tr>
            <td>Dr. Wolverine</td>
            <td>154</td>
            <td>03/29/1976</td>
            <td>$86.68</td>
            <td>PAID</td>
            <td>New Orleans</td>
            <td>Louisiana</td>
        </tr>
        <tr>
            <td>Dr. Tarheel</td>
            <td>113</td>
            <td>03/30/1981</td>
            <td>$63.50</td>
            <td>PAID</td>
            <td>San Antonio</td>
            <td>Texas</td>
        </tr>
    </tbody>
</table>
```

Let's see the result on Smartphone and tablet:

Doctor names	Values	Dates	Cash Money	Message	City	State
Dr. Jayhawk	102	03/30/1940	$60.42	PAID	Atlanta	Georgia
Dr. John Smith	137	03/18/1953	$69.68	PAID	Orlando	Florida
Dr. Wolverine	154	03/29/1976	$86.68	PAID	New Orleans	Louisiana
Dr. Tarheel	113	03/30/1981	$63.50	PAID	San Antonio	Texas

Link to full-table

Linking to full-table is a technique less used because it does not solve the situation completely. It works by replacing the table with a small mock table and creating only a link to view the full table.

The problem persists, but this time, the user can swipe the screen to the left/right in order to see all the content. There is a media query to handle this mechanism for showing it only on small screens.

How to do it

First of all, let's begin by downloading the `full-table.css` file, which is available in the downloadable code files that accompany this book. Then insert it inside the `<head>` tag of the HTML code. Although we are dealing with a CSS solution, this code is too extensive and it increases the chances of typo mistakes.

Let's re-use a copy of the table code from the previous example but with alterations in the table element, which is as follows:

```
<table id="responsive" class="full-table">
```

At the bottom of DOM (before the `</body>` closing tag), we will need to include the `jquery` library and insert the following code which will display/hide the solution based only on a class name:

```
<script src="http://code.jquery.com/jquery-1.9.1.min.js"></script>
<script>
$(function(){
  $("#responsive").click(function(){
    $("html").toggleClass($(this).attr("class"));
  });
});
</script>
```

In the following screenshot we will see the minified table for small screens, driving the user to the full table visualization on clicking. This effect occurs when the screen size is less than or equal to 520 px (this value can be modified if we need to use the CSS file).

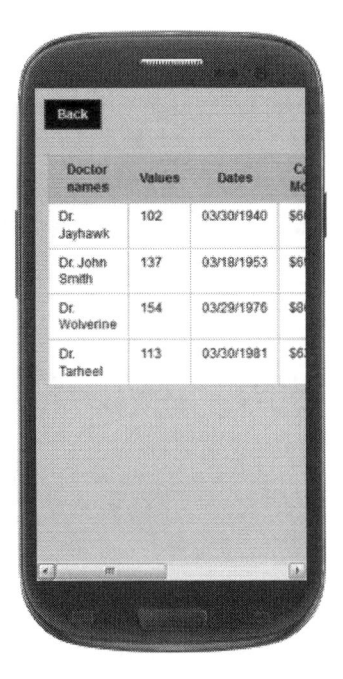

> The plugin generates a horizontal scrollbar after clicking to see the table in full width.

Exercise 6 – creating a responsive table of prices using the FooTable jQuery plugin

Let's create a responsive table using the FooTable jQuery plugin and the contents of the table in the following screenshot.

> The content of this table is not real and we will use it just for practice.

In the following screenshot we can see the table as shown on Smartphone and tablet, each device using a different design:

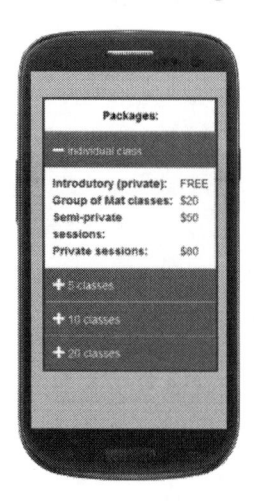

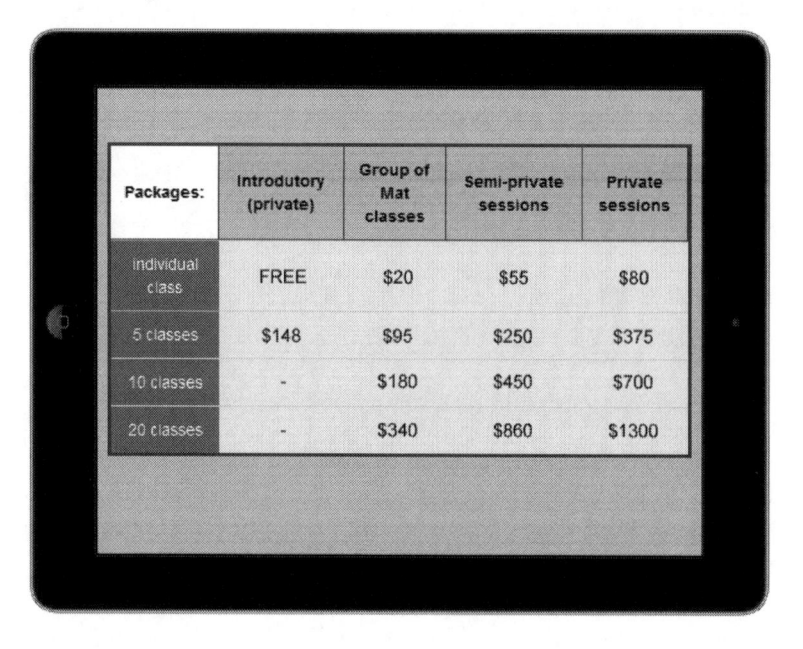

You can start by creating the table structure based on the tablet's design and then implement the FooTable plugin automatizing the compact visual for Smartphones.

Summary

In this chapter, we learned four different ways to deal with wide tables in small devices' widths. We focused on how to implement each technique because its usage depends on the type of table's content. The techniques we just saw are: expandable responsive tables (FooTable), stacked tables, horizontal overflow, and link to full-tables.

In the next chapter, we will take a look at using forms and learn how to implement features such as autocomplete, datepickers, and tooltips.

8
Implementing Responsive Forms

Coding with HTML5 has dramatically changed the landscape within frontend web development. There are more opportunities to build better forms by using the appropriate field type and native validation, which is the best scenario for SEO. All of these features are gradually being adopted in all modern web browsers.

With the use of jQuery, we can enhance the HTML5 experience on our pages, with the addition of complementary features to improve user experience.

In this chapter we will learn about:

- Types and attributes of form inputs
- The `autocomplete` feature
- The `datepicker` feature
- The `tooltips` feature
- Responsive frameworks with IdealForms

Types and attributes of form inputs

The use of HTML5 input types brought two main advantages of developing to the front: reduction of development time and improvement of user experience. Many modern browsers have already adopted these new input types and attributes and the entire web community is benefited from it, facilitating the spread of its usage.

Implementing Responsive Forms

The most frequently used HTML5 input types are `email`, `date`, `tel`, `number`, and `time`. Also, the most common attributes that come with HTML5 are `placeholder`, `required`, `autocomplete`, and `multiple`. We will see in *Chapter 10, Ensuring Browser Support*, that not all web browsers support HTML5 features the same way and require jQuery intervention to provide the proper support.

However, it still depends on jQuery technology to display features such as `autocomplete` and other more complex validation. Normally, jQuery plugins work really well with the new HTML5 input types, being almost mandatory for responsive websites. Before starting the implementation of the feature, let's create a basic form; this is the first step and will be used in further examples. Create an empty HTML site structure with basic tags and then keep the jQuery included, which will be used soon:

```
<!DOCTYPE html>
<html lang="en">
<head>
<meta name="viewport" content="width=device-width, initial-scale=1" />
<title>Responsive form</title>
</head>
<body>
<script src="http://code.jquery.com/jquery-1.9.1.min.js"></script>
</body>
</html>
```

For the sake of progressive learning, each feature will be presented independently; only the previous basic code will be reused.

These plugins we will see are not a replacement for server-side validation; they only make the user experience better, reduce the server requests, and give a better interactive interface.

The autocomplete feature with Magicsuggest

Magicsuggest is a flexible autosuggest combobox that gives suggestions whenever the user starts typing in the field. Using this feature will reduce the necessity of typing, mainly on mobile devices, where the typing in of each letter is cumbersome.

By default, Magicsuggest has some good features, such as holding the *Ctrl* key to select multiple items and allowing the user to add a new input using the *Enter* key after having entered the text.

The JSON data source is used to populate the combobox. There are some options available here:

- **No data source**: When left as `null`, the combobox will not suggest anything. It can still enable the user to enter multiple entries if the allowed FreeEntries are set to `true` (default).
- **Static source**: It uses an array of JSON objects, an array of strings, or even a single CSV string as the data source.
- **URL**: We can pass the URL from which the component will fetch its JSON data. The data will be fetched using a POST AJAX request that will include the entered text as a query parameter.
- **Function**: We can set a function to return an array of JSON objects. Only one callback function or return value is needed for the function to succeed.

How to implement it

Let's start by downloading the files from http://nicolasbize.github.io/magicsuggest/. After downloading, we will include the JavaScript and CSS files inside the `<head>` tag from the already created basic code:

```
<script src="js/magicsuggest-1.3.1.js"></script>
<link rel="stylesheet" href="css/magicsuggest-1.3.1.css">
```

After that, insert the following piece of code to create the JSON data with these cities and then execute the Magicsuggest script, giving some options along with it if necessary:

```
<script type="text/javascript">
$(document).ready(function() {
  var jsonData = [];
  var cities = 'New York,Los Angeles,Chicago,Houston,Paris,Marseille,Toulouse,Lyon,Bordeaux, Philadelphia,Phoenix,San Antonio,San Diego,Dallas'.split(',');
  for(var i=0;i<cities.length;i++) jsonData.push({id:i,name:cities[i]});
  var city = $('#field-city').magicSuggest({
    data: jsonData,
    resultAsString: true,
    maxSelection: 1,
    maxSelectionRenderer: function(){}
  })
});
</script>
```

Implementing Responsive Forms

The next step is to add the `city` field inside the `<body>` tag.

```
<label for="field-city">City: </label>
<input id="field-city" type="text"/>
```

As seen in the following screenshot, when the select field is clicked on, we will see the suggestion feature appear instantly:

In the previous example, we implemented only the basic usage. However, this plugin has other interesting implementations that may fit your needs in the future, such as:

- Tag selection on the right
- Gmail-style combo
- Column-filter combo
- Custom template combobox using images

The date and time pickers feature

Mobile users already have an interface for entering dates and time, which they are very familiar with. However, we will learn about a jQuery plugin that may help in keeping the website's identity by displaying to the user the same features on all devices.

Pickadate – responsive date/time picker

Pickadate is a responsive jQuery plugin that is quite interesting as well as mobile friendly, responsive, and lightweight. It is possible to provide a custom interface regardless of the browser or device.

This is a good way to facilitate the insertion of the correct date when filling in a form because it avoids typing errors and gives better guidance to the user, showing the full calendar of the month.

How to do it

After downloading the files from http://amsul.ca/pickadate.js/, we will start by including JavaScript and CSS files inside the <head> tag from the already created basic code:

```
<script src="lib/picker.js"></script>
<script src="lib/picker.date.js"></script>
<script src="lib/picker.time.js"></script>
<link rel="stylesheet" href="lib/themes/default.css" id="theme_base">
<link rel="stylesheet" href="lib/themes/default.date.css" id="theme_date">
<link rel="stylesheet" href="lib/themes/default.time.css" id="theme_time">
```

> If you need to support old browsers, the inclusion of the legacy.js file is recommended.

After that, we need to execute the scripts for datepicker and timepicker.

```
<script>
$('.js__datepicker').pickadate();
$('.js__timepicker').pickatime();
</script>
```

The next step is to insert a field for date and another one for time inside the <body> tag. The plugin requires the class names to be highlighted.

```
<fieldset class="fieldset js__fieldset">
  <div class="fieldset__wrapper">
    <label>Schedule detail:</label> 
    <input class="fieldset__input js__datepicker" type="text" placeholder="What date?">  
```

```
        <input class="fieldset__input js__timepicker" type="text"
placeholder="What time?">
    </div>
</fieldset>
```

The following is a screenshot of the `datepicker` plugin being activated on a Smartphone and a tablet:

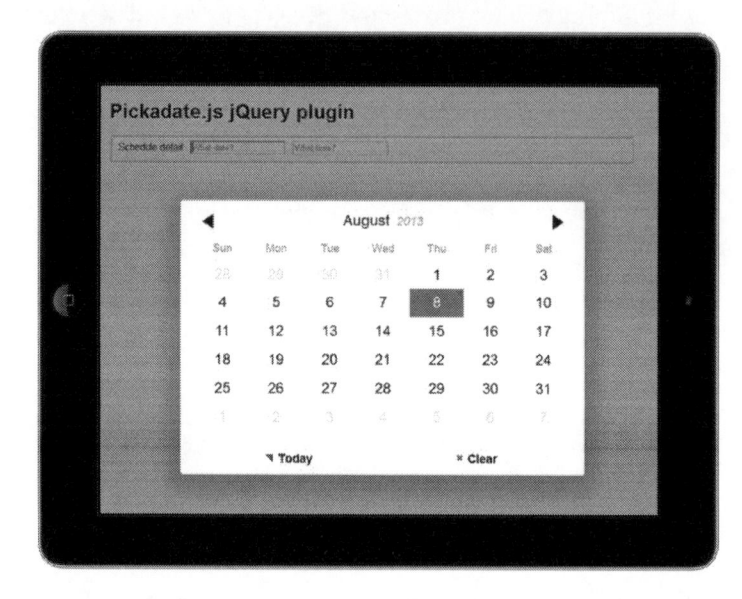

The following is the screenshot from when the user touches on the `time` field:

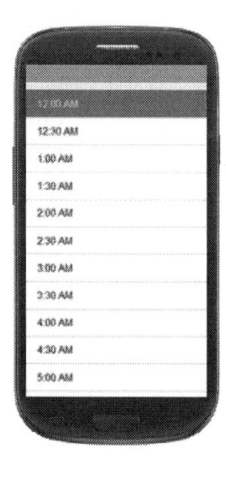

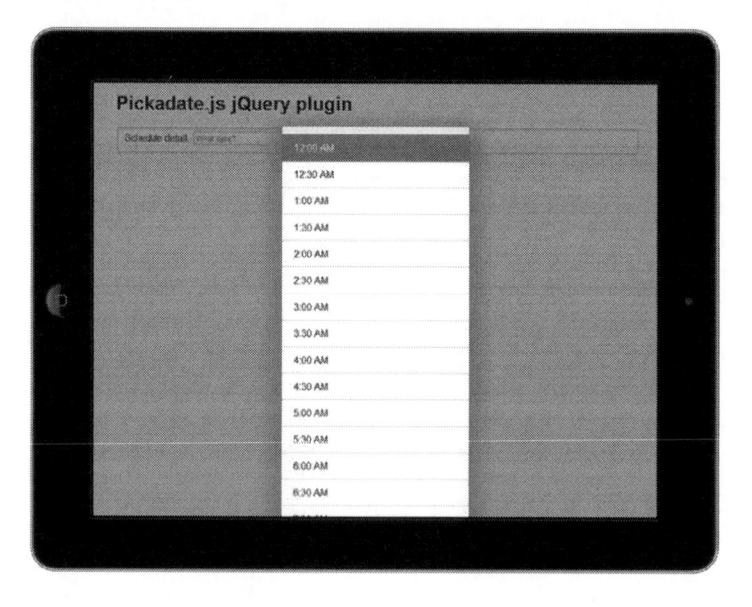

The `pickadate` plugin is very complete, providing its extension to add support for:

- Translations (including right-to-left languages)
- Different formats
- Date/time limits

You will find further information about these extensions at http://amsul.ca/pickadate.js/date.htm#options.

The tooltip feature

`tooltip` is a useful way to present additional, context-sensitive information about an element on a web page, and it is normally found in between a label and an input field. Its job is to provide more information about a particular field.

As tooltips continue to become more common as a means for the users to interact with the web page elements, the necessity for a good tooltip design and interaction has become more important.

Normally, the tooltip can be displayed by putting the pointer of mouse over the element and the message will be displayed. Since most mobile devices do not have a pointer, this issue must be handled by plugins displaying the tooltip on touch.

Tooltipster – modern tooltip feature

Tooltipster is a powerful and flexible jQuery plugin that enables you to easily create semantic and modern tooltips.

How to do it

We will start by downloading the tooltipster files from http://calebjacob.com/tooltipster/ and including the JavaScript and CSS files inside the `<head>` tag from the already created basic code:

```
<script src="js/jquery.tooltipster.min.js"></script>
<link rel="stylesheet" href="css/tooltipster.css" />
```

To activate the plugin, we will add the `tooltipster` library and configure it to execute for all elements that have the `.tooltip` class (in this example, there is only one instance, but you may use more than one in your page):

```
<script>
$(function() {
```

```
    $('.tooltip').tooltipster();
});
</script>
```

After that, we will add a question mark image and define the `tooltip` class on each element where we want to display the tooltip on:

```
<img class="tooltip" title="This is my image's tooltip message!" src="question-mark.png" />
```

The following is a screenshot of the plugin after clicking/touching the element:

We can also modify the default plugin theme by editing the `tooltipster.css` file or override the existing theme by specifying the class in the `script` call.

```
<script>
$(function() {
  $('.tooltip').tooltipster({
    theme: '.my-custom-theme'
  });
});
</script>
```

Responsive form using IdealForms

IdealForms, available at `https://github.com/elclanrs/jq-idealforms`, is a framework used to build and validate responsive HTML5 forms. Also, it has keyboard support, fast validation as soon as the user moves to the next field, and placeholder support for most of the browsers.

The IdealForms framework also has a pagination option that helps a lot to improve the user experience when filling extensive forms. Let's understand its usage by practicing it step by step.

How to implement it

Create a new HTML file and copy the basic code that we already wrote in the beginning of the chapter. Then, we will include the CSS stylesheet inside the `<head>` tag.

```
<link rel="stylesheet" href="css/jquery.idealforms.min.css"/>
```

Let's insert the following sample code into the HTML structure whose interface was divided into two tabs using the `<section>` tag:

```
<form id="form">
  <div><h2>Profile form:</h2></div>
```

In the first tab, we will add the `username`, `password`, and `email` fields:

```
<section name="First tab">
  <div><label>Username:</label>
  <input id="username" name="username" type="text" /></div>
  <div><label>Password:</label>
  <input id="pass" name="password" type="password" /></div>
  <div><label>E-Mail:</label>
  <input id="email" name="email" data-ideal="required email"
  type="email" /></div>
</section>
```

In the second tab, we will add the `file`, `languages`, and `phone` fields.

```
<section name="Second tab">

  <div><label>Image:</label>
  <input id="file" name="file" multiple type="file" /></div>
  <div id="languages">
  <label>Languages:</label>
```

Implementing Responsive Forms

```html
    <label><input type="checkbox" name="langs[]"
value="English"/>English</label>
    <label><input type="checkbox" name="langs[]"
value="Chinese"/>Chinese</label>
    <label><input type="checkbox" name="langs[]"
value="Spanish"/>Spanish</label>
  </div>
  <div><label>Phone:</label>
  <input type="tel" name="phone" data-ideal="phone" /></div>
</section>
```

Finally, we will add a `submit` button.

```html
  <div><hr/></div>
  <div><button type="submit">Submit</button>
</form>
```

At the bottom of DOM (before the `</body>` closing tag), we will need to include the `jquery` and `idealforms` libraries.

```html
<script src="js/jquery.idealforms.js"></script>
```

After that, insert the following code, which will execute the script that starts creating a function that alerts the user when they fill in an incorrect value.

```javascript
<script>
  var options = {
    onFail: function() {
      alert( $myform.getInvalid().length +' invalid fields.' )
    },
```

Here we will set which form element will be inspected by validation.

```javascript
        inputs: {
          'password': {
            filters: 'required pass',
          },
          'username': {
            filters: 'required username',
            data: { //ajax: { url:'validate.php' } }
          },
          'file': {
            filters: 'extension',
            data: { extension: ['jpg'] }
          },     'langs[]': {
            filters: 'min max',
            data: { min: 2, max: 3 },
```

```
          errors: {
            min: 'Check at least <strong>2</strong> options.',
            max: 'No more than <strong>3</strong> options allowed.'
          }
        }
      }
    };
```

After finishing the validation, we will execute the `idealforms` JavaScript, loading all of the validations set before.

```
      var $myform = $('#form').idealforms(options).data('idealforms');
</script>
```

That's it! The client-side validation is already implemented.

The following is a screenshot of the framework in action when viewed on Smartphone devices:

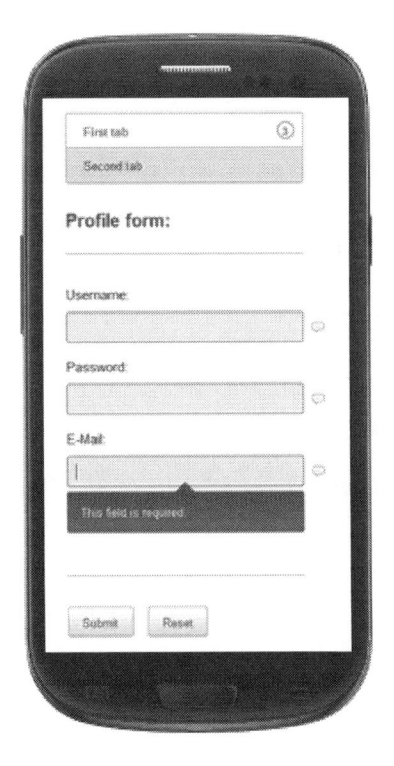

The same page may be viewed on a desktop and the default layout adapts very well.

Exercise 8 – creating a contact form using the IdealForms framework

Let's create a responsive contact form for the project based on the complete step-by-step example seen previously and using the IdealForms framework as a base for this form.

So, as we did before, let's start including the CSS file and the following fields: **Name**, **Email**, **Ideal first class** (date), and **Phone** as the following screenshot shows:

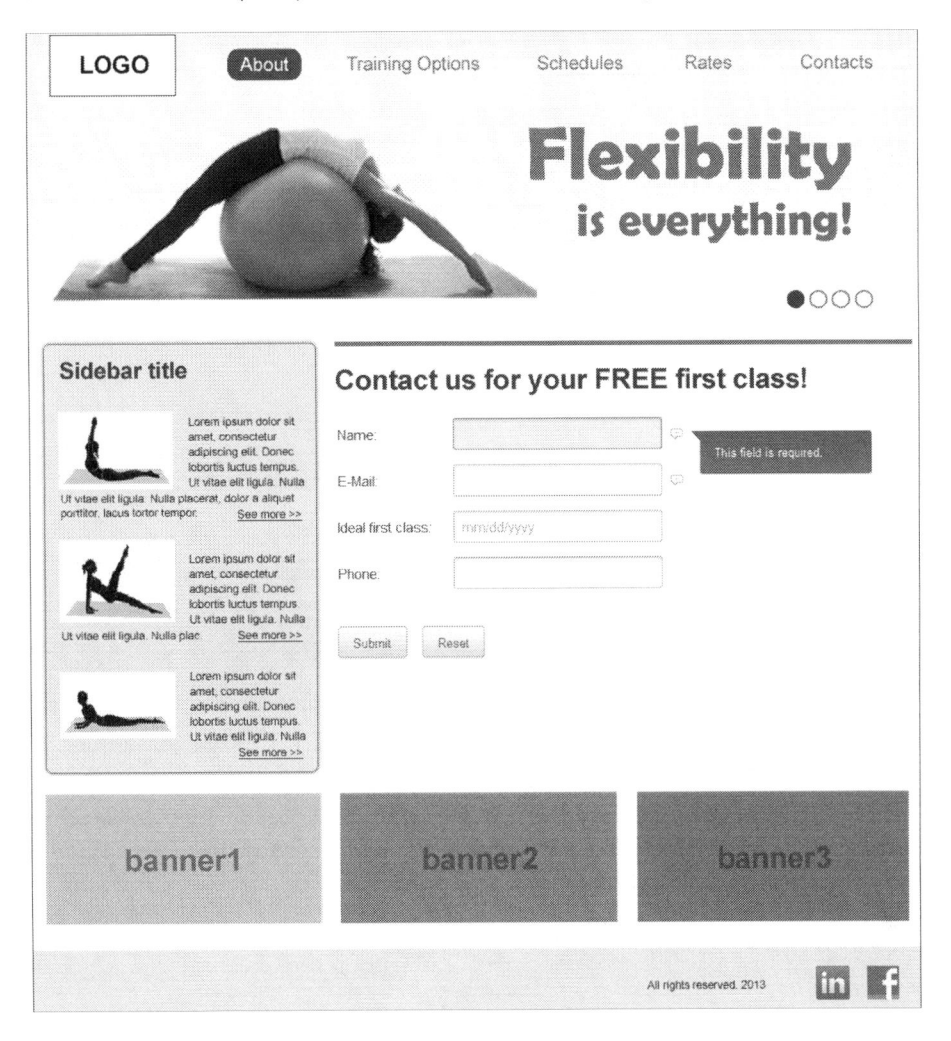

The date field was not mentioned on IdealForms because, by default, it comes with the jQueryUI solution. However, I would recommend to use the Pickadate plugin because it is more lightweight if compared to jQueryUI and it also helps reinforcing the example we have learned before.

Summary

In this chapter, we learned how to work well with HTML5 form elements by complementing the code with some jQuery plugins such as Magicsuggest for `autocomplete`, Pickadate for `datepicker`, and Tooltipster for `tooltips` when necessary. In addition, we have experienced how to work with IdealForms, a responsive form framework, by building a contact form interface.

In the next chapter, we will focus on testing the website by using tools and scripts to ensure its responsivity on all devices. Understanding the next chapter thoroughly is important to check for possible errors on our implementation for old browsers or mobile devices and fix them further. Also, the testing phase is important to avoid future surprises reported by our clients.

9
Testing the Responsiveness

It is a fact that there is no better test than to check your design on the device itself, even though it consumes more time than we expected in our test emulators; browser tools are the solutions found to make testing faster, but will not be able to reproduce a website 100 percent identical to the real thing.

Although they will come very close, we may define this type of test as only the initial testing process, and then test on real devices ensuring that all features are working well.

In this chapter we will learn about:

- Simulating a device using browser tools
- Testing on a device's emulator
- Tips for unit testing on responsive websites

Simulating a device using browser tools

Browser tools will not be able to simulate the same way we usually see on devices, but they help with the CSS breakpoints testing and show how your responsive website will look on the most popular devices such as the iPad, iPhone, or any Android phone based on screen size measures.

Screen resizing does not catch inconsistencies between browsers and their rendering engines. For example, resizing the browser with Chrome does not tell you CSS issues that occur only on Safari mobile browsers.

Let's take a look at a couple of websites, which will help you as a developer to ascertain how well your site will perform on a particular device.

Using the Viewport Resizer website tool

The Viewport Resizer is a website tool that facilitates responsive website testing when developing or after publishing websites.

Among the advantages listed on the tool's website, we would like to highlight some:

- Adding custom screen sizes on the fly
- Visual preview of device metrics (onMouseOver)
- Viewport information (size, aspect ratio, orientation, and user agent)
- Print support: WebKit only (Chrome and Safari)

Unfortunately, this tool still does not work in any version of the Internet Explorer browser, which would be useful to find visual issues on Windows phones.

There is no need to download or install it. You only need to access the website at `http://lab.maltewassermann.com/viewport-resizer` and save the link of the button labeled **Click or Bookmark** in your list of favorite links.

The following is an example of how our site would be rendered on a smartphone if this tool is being used:

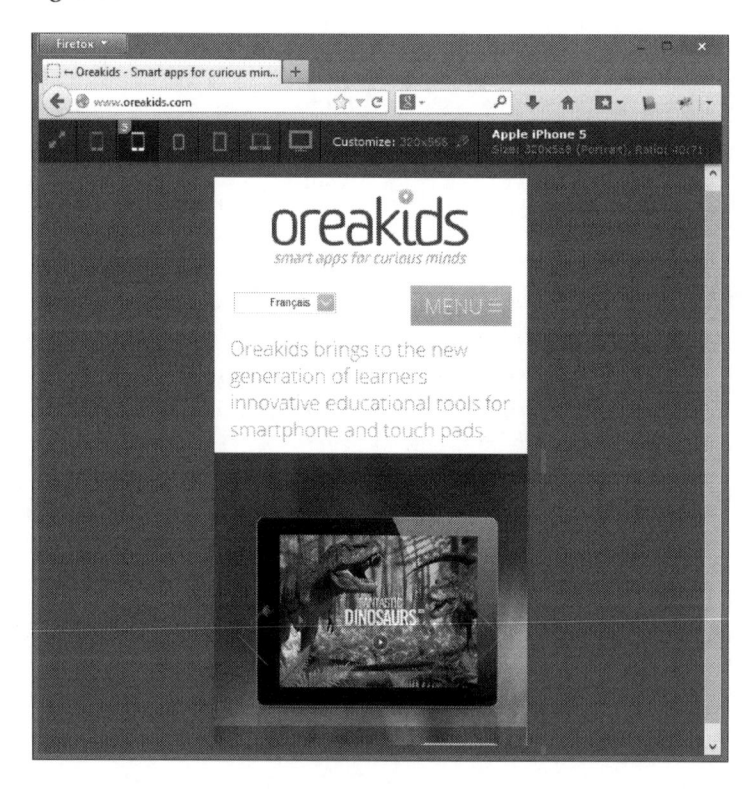

Using the Surveyor website tool

The Surveyor is a website tool that follows the basis of the previous tool and makes it possible to test the responsiveness on both developing sites and the ones that have already been published.

You can test the website by accessing `http://surveyor.io`, and by specifying the URL and the screen size you want to see (no predefined values are displayed to select from).

Then you can test your responsive design at all breakpoints side-by-side, helping you have better sense of design of breakpoints in use, facilitating all the comparisons.

> Sometimes the scrollbar displayed by this browser tool can confuse our website analysis by showing a problem where there is not actually any. In this case, it is worth checking the site and also this next tool.

Look at this site and make the comparison between this site being redimensioned to tablet and smartphone versions:

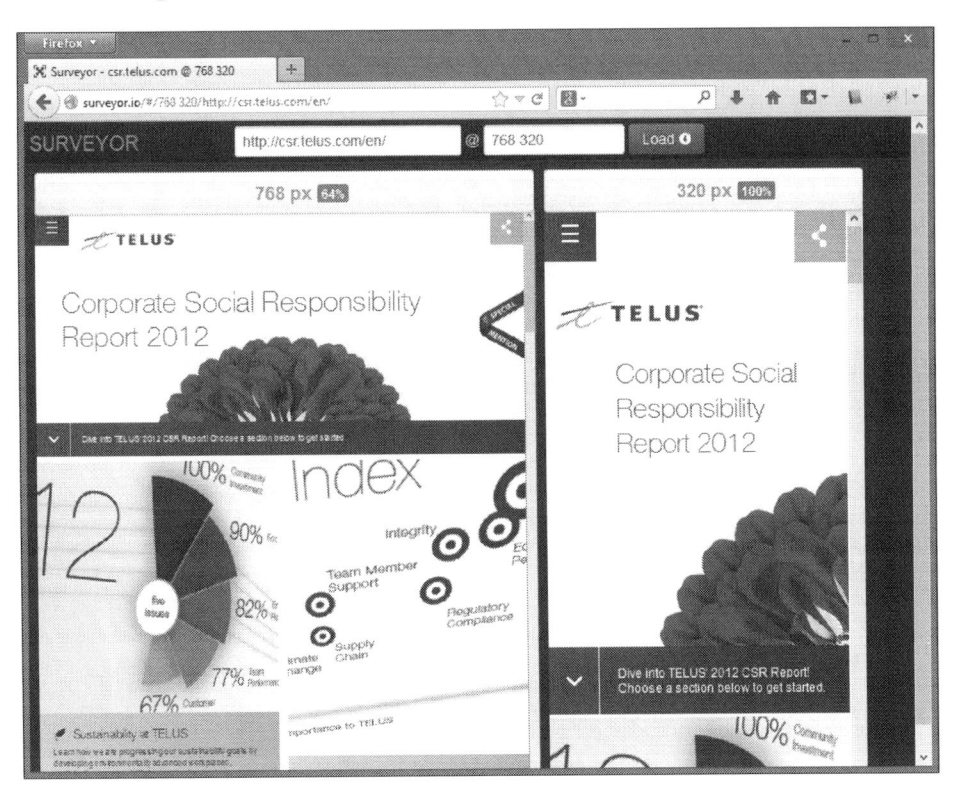

Testing the Responsiveness

Using the ScreenFly website tool

This tool also follows the pattern of resizing the website which we had seen previously, where the developer enters the URL (it also works for developing projects) and chooses which resolution we want to check on the website.

This tool brings to the developer some templates with exact screen sizes to be chosen and the most common device models in the market. And the fact that it does not require memorizing all of them makes it easier. Or if you want to customize your own size, you can perform it just by clicking on the **Custom Screen Size** button.

Accessing the website `https://quirktools.com/screenfly` you can inform the website you want to test. By default, it will show your website in Netbook 10 preview, simulating the device width. You can choose other devices by just clicking on the header buttons and selecting the specific model.

The ScreenFly tool has another interesting feature, which consists of sharing the link, in order to make the communication between customer and developer easier (only for sites that have already been published).

This can be useful to improve communication between customers and developers, showing certain features or issues. In order to do this, simply click on the **Share** button and send the link to someone else. By accessing this link, the person will see a screen similar to this:

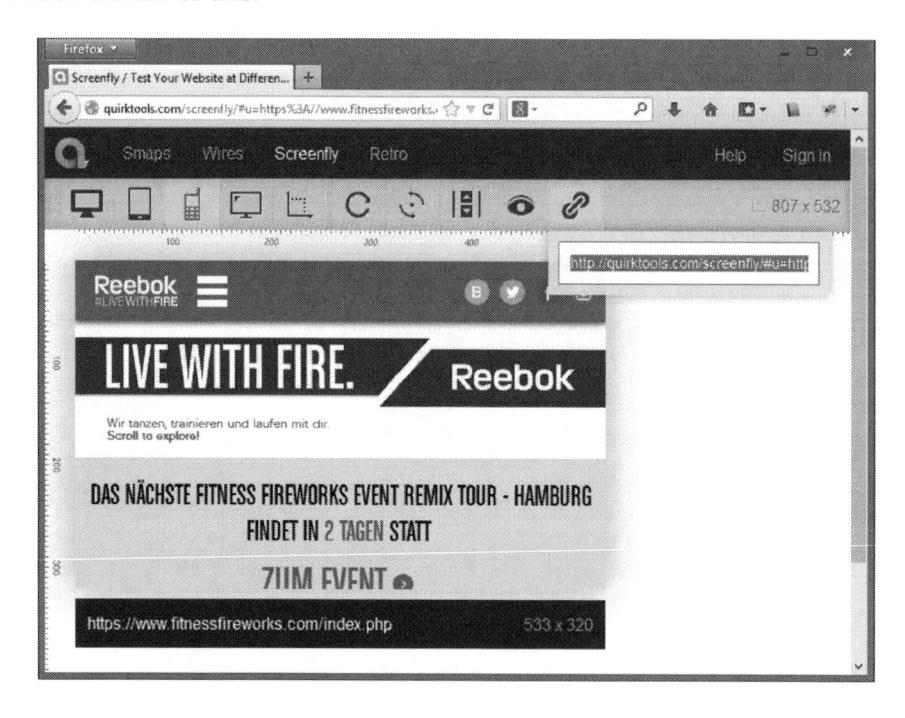

Opera mobile emulator

Even though the Mobile Opera browser is no longer at its peak, it still represents 16.62 percent of accesses by mobile devices only, according to the website `StatCounter.com`. This is the reason it is still important to check at least the main basic features of our site in this mobile browser.

The company Opera Software provides good support to developers by offering an emulator which has Mobile Opera browser inside. Its browser also forms the basis of its emulator, which you can use to test a variety of different mobile devices. You can find the application available for download at `http://www.opera.com/developer/mobile-emulator`.

After getting it installed, simply select the desired device, as shown in the following screenshot, and click on the **Launch** button:

Tips for design testing of responsive websites

With these responsive design tools in our arsenal, we are prepared to create flexible designs ready for any device.

But when we are testing, it is important to pay attention to these following tips:

- Do not finish the entire website without tests. The best way is testing every feature as soon as it is implemented, making it easy to find where the problem is.
- Regression testing is very important to prevent cascading errors. After testing the implemented feature, check if what you did before does not introduce new issues on other parts of the website.

> Regression testing seeks software bugs in existent areas of website after enhancements have been made to them.

- Check the image and icon quality and the fluidity of the website contents over the structure.
- Do performance analysis on responsive websites, especially when they are viewed on mobile devices (we will specifically see this in the next chapter).

Exercise 9 – let's test our website in different screen sizes

We will choose one of the tools that we saw earlier to test our website.

This is a screenshot image simulating smartphone and tablet breakpoints using the Surveyor tool:

When you are testing, first write down all the visual issues found, with your features implemented, and then start fixing them at once. This process ensures that you do not lose concentration and waste your time.

Summary

In this chapter, we have focused on testing the website by using tools and scripts to ensure its responsiveness on all devices. We have understood the importance of checking possible errors in our implementation by using website tools such as Viewport Resizer, Surveyor, and ScreenFly. Also, we have tested the Opera Mobile emulator by opening websites in the native Opera Mobile browser simulating many mobile devices.

In the next chapter, we will ensure that the cross-browser solution is providing fallbacks. We will learn how to handle older browsers and render the correct design by displaying a graceful degradation.

10
Ensuring Browser Support

Different browsers have their own proprietary features and their own subset of the standard features implemented in their own way, bringing a lot of work for us to make these features work for all browsers.

The reason for these differences is that the W3C specifications are constantly updating, and with the constant competition among browsers, they always try promote their products as having better functionality.

However, jQuery has good cross-browser compatibility, and the flexibility to bridge some of these gaps in feature implementation across each browser. These bridges are called **Polyfills**.

Polyfills is the main subject of this chapter and we will also learn about:

- Checking the features the browser supports
- The meaning of polyfill
- Understanding feature detection tools
- Polyfill implementations for HTML5 and CSS3

Checking the features the browser supports

In website development, experience does bring much agility to a programmer. Although this knowledge becomes outdated very fast, we must stay updated with the new features, selectors, and enhancements as soon as they have compatibilities with browsers.

The three main sites to check the compatibility of techniques and features, depending on our browser and device, are: CanIUse.com, MobileHTML5.org, and QuirksMode.org.

CanIUse.com

The `CanIUse.com` website is the best-known site among these reference sites, where we can check the compatibility tables that support HTML5, CSS3, SVG and more, in desktop and mobile browsers.

If you access the website `http://caniuse.com`, you will see that its data is based on statistics collected by StatCounter GlobalStats and it is constantly updated.

It is also important to read the **Notes** and **Known Issues** tab (as we can see in the following screenshot) because we are part of a community that greatly contributes to the evolution of the entire development site. The tabs highlight the exceptions that should be taken into consideration or report problems and the techniques, which they had to use in a specific scenario.

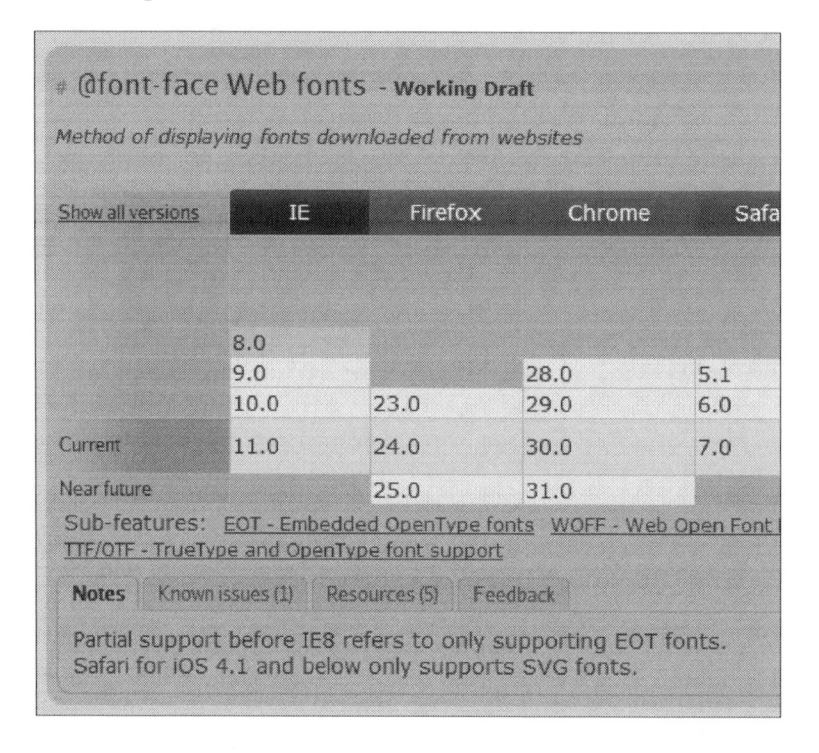

MobileHTML5.org

The `MobileHTML5.org` website focuses on the compatibility of HTML5 features on mobile and tablet browsers with tests on real devices. It makes a difference because, as we have seen in the previous chapter, there are few visual differences between a simulated view from a desktop browser and testing the website on a mobile device.

However, this difference increases considerably when it involves hardware and the operating system of the device, and only if we test the website on real devices, we may detect potential problems.

The variety of devices that are listed is impressive. The following screenshot illustrates part of the capabilities of older devices that no longer hold much of a market share. It even displays the devices with operating systems recently launched, such as FirefoxOS.

Try yourself to access the website `http://mobilehtml5.org`, and check the updated list.

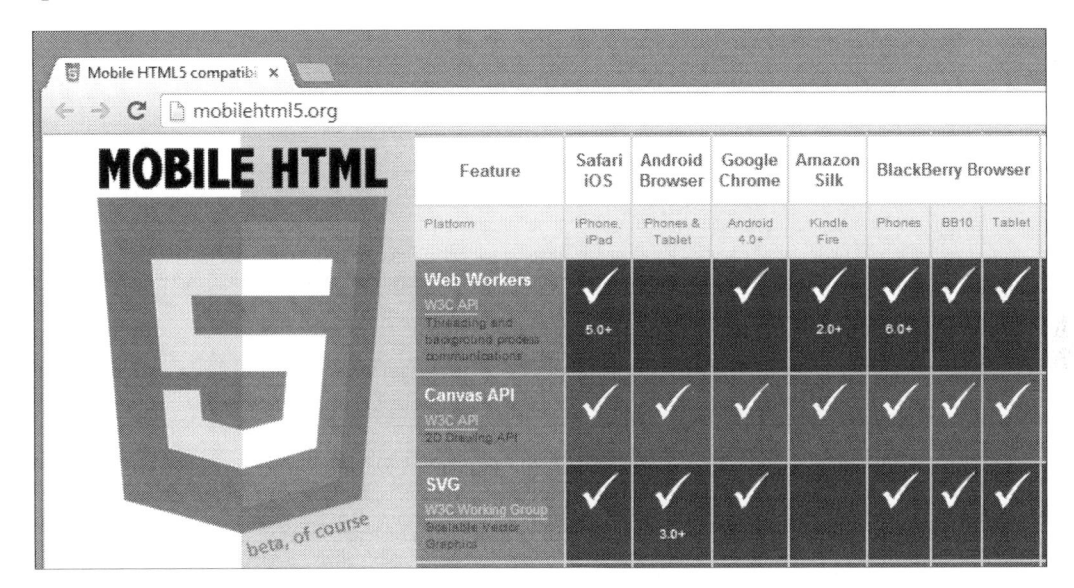

QuirksMode.org

On the `QuirksMode.org` website, we may prevent future bad surprises during our development by checking if a specified selector or pseudo-class is acceptable by the browsers before using it. Otherwise, we must check on each browser we defined in the beginning.

The `QuirksMode.org` website focuses only on storing and keeping updated information about the browser support of almost every CSS selectors and properties. As we can see on `http://www.quirksmode.org/css/selectors`, this information is grouped into the following categories:

- Combinators
- Attribute selectors

- Pseudo-elements
- Pseudo-classes

The following is a part of the `QuirksMode.org` website checking the pseudo-elements technique:

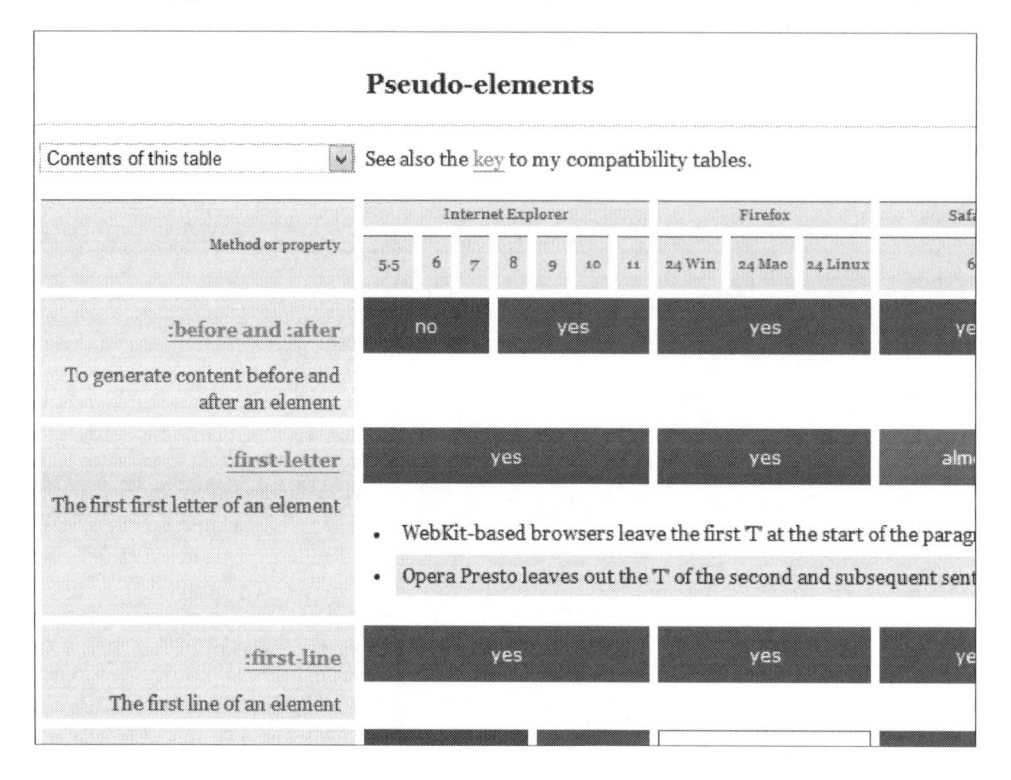

Defining fallback

Fallback is part of a support process when developing a website. Its objective is to provide an alternative to a technology we have applied to a website, but not all browsers support this specific feature.

This term may be split into polyfills and webshims.

A **polyfill** is a specific code that emulates a specific feature for browsers that do not support it natively. Polyfills always try to mimic the original browser feature, but there are a few cases where it may cause slight side effects such as an increase in the loading time or loss of performance.

An example of a polyfill is the html5shiv script that we simply drop in the code and it will act as if nothing changed. We will talk about html5shiv later.

Shims provide a fallback, but often have their own API, and may require an alteration of the code to allow the shim to work. This is why we have libraries such as `yepnope.js` to load these, if required. We will see an example of using `yepnope.js` later.

Let's look at two feature detection tools, which may be useful when we are providing fallbacks.

Feature detection tools

Feature detection is the first step we are able to provide as a progressive enhancement to website users.

Then, we have to test if the given feature is already implemented in the browser. If so, we do not need to reimplement anything that already exists, but if the browser is actually missing the feature, it is recommended to provide the correct support for that.

Sometimes we have to support browsers that have not completely implemented a specific feature yet. However, new features make a difference when your website is being viewed and popularity of the website often increases.

CSS Browser Selector +

A cross-browser responsive design helper is simpler than Modernizr because its only function is detecting features, when the site is loaded and marking it in code, using the class placed in the `<html>` tag.

It has an easy implementation, therefore it allows us to write a specific CSS code and to solve visual problems which are, for instance, restricted to certain operating systems, or browsers, being the end of the CSS hacks!

The main items that this JavaScript library identifies are:

- Browser and browser version
- Rendering engines
- Platforms and operating systems
- Devices

- The `max-width` and `min-width` screen detection
- Browser orientation detection
- Language detection

Try this tool yourself by accessing the website `http://ridjohansen.github.io/css_browser_selector/`, and check the classes by inspecting the `<html>` element.

This way, it is possible to fix the problems of a specific browser or even help to create fallbacks like this one. Consider the following example:

```
.orientation_landscape .div-example {
  border: 2px solid red;
}
```

> The less custom code to create exceptions we have, the better it is to implement future updates and changes. When it is possible, the idea would be to identify the root cause of the error rather than just fixing the visual difference between browsers.

How to do it

After downloading, we just need to include the `css_browser_selector.js` file in our code inside the `<head>` tag:

```
<script src="js/css_browser_selector.js"></script>
```

Through detection it is possible to load up scripts or different features, but this is not included in this solution. To solve this and to have access to more types of feature detections, a more complete solution is recommended: Modernizr.

Modernizr

Modernizr is a JavaScript library that detects HTML5 and CSS3 features in the user's browser, making it easy to write a conditional JavaScript and CSS for each situation, whether a browser supports a feature or not.

It works by adding classes to the `html` element for our future selection on the CSS. Furthermore, it creates a JavaScript object with the results used later to support dozens of tests. When downloading Modernizr from `http://modernizr.com`, we have the option of downloading the full development version or a custom build that includes only the parts we intend to use.

> The Modernizr's website recommends downloading of a custom build version with the features that fit the project instead of using a complete version from CDN, because most times a custom version will be smaller than the fully developed one.

After that, we may include the `modernizr.custom.85330.js` file in our code inside the header section like this:

```
<script src="js/modernizr.custom.85330.js"></script>
```

Let's observe how classes are arranged in the `<html>` tag with all the features detected and ready to use, if viewed on Firefox:

```
<html lang="en" class=" js no-flexbox flexboxlegacy canvas canvastext
webgl no-touch geolocation postmessage no-websqldatabase indexeddb
hashchange history draganddrop websockets rgba hsla multiplebgs
backgroundsize borderimage borderradius boxshadow textshadow opacity
cssanimations csscolumns cssgradients no-cssreflections csstransforms
csstransforms3d csstransitions fontface generatedcontent video
audio localstorage sessionstorage webworkers applicationcache svg
inlinesvg smil svgclippaths">Now, let's look at the features detected,
but this time viewed on Internet Explorer 8:<HTML class="ie8 js
no-flexbox no-flexboxlegacy no-canvas no-canvastext no-webgl no-
touch no-geolocation postmessage no-websqldatabase no-indexeddb
hashchange no-history draganddrop no-websockets no-rgba no-hsla no-
multiplebgs no-backgroundsize no-borderimage no-borderradius no-
boxshadow no-textshadow no-opacity no-cssanimations no-csscolumns
no-cssgradients no-cssreflections no-csstransforms no-csstransforms3d
no-csstransitions fontface generatedcontent no-video no-audio
localstorage sessionstorage no-webworkers no-applicationcache no-svg
no-inlinesvg no-smil no-svgclippaths" lang=en xmlns:html5shiv>
```

This way, we can write this kind of code, where we are guaranteed that if your browser does not support the `boxshadow` property, we can make two borders simulating the shadow effect:

```
.box {
  border:1px solid #DDD;
  border-bottom: 1px solid #AAA;
  border-right: 1px solid #AAA;
}
.boxshadow div.box {
  border: none;
  -webkit-box-shadow: 1px 1px 3px #777;
     -moz-box-shadow: 1px 1px 3px #777;
          box-shadow: 1px 1px 3px #777;
}
```

This simple example of code for shadow on borders will look like the following screenshot:

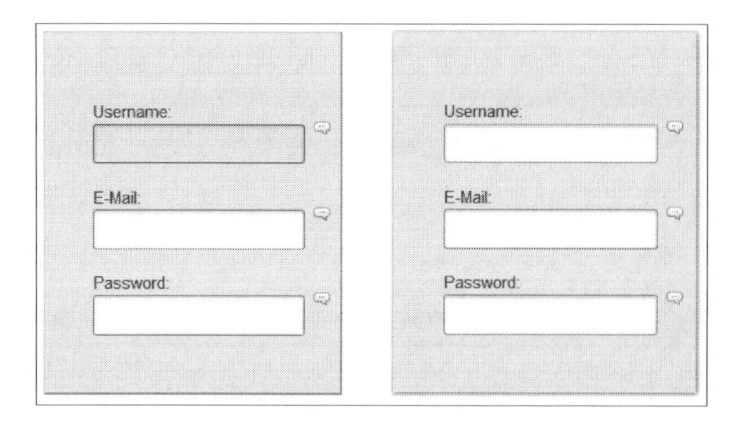

Now, let's see what we can do when the solution requires adding another library to the website in demand with YepNope.js.

YepNope.js

YepNope.js is a JavaScript library for asynchronous conditional loading of external JavaScript and CSS resources.

The following is a sample illustrating how Modernizr has been used to test CSS animations, and where YepNope has been used as a fallback where the browser does not support `CSSTransforms`:

```
<script>
  Modernizr.load({
    test: Modernizr.csstransforms,
    yep : 'css/cssTransform.css',
    nope: ['css/noTransform.css','js/jQuery.pseudoTransforms.js ']
  });
</script>
```

html5shiv

The html5shiv library enables support for HTML5 elements in older versions of IE browsers, in particular 6 to 8, and provides some basic support for IE9.

Also, this solution has another file named `html5shiv-printshiv.js`, which comes with a printable version included. It also allows HTML5 elements and their child elements to be styled, while being printed using IE6 to IE8.

You can use this by simply selecting the option as shown on Modernizr's download page and when the library is included in the project, it will apply the polyfill if the browser does not support that html5 element:

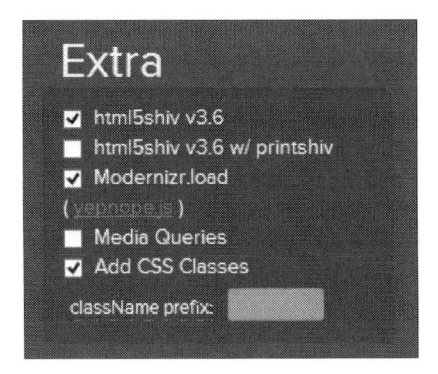

Polyfill implementations

There are hundreds of polyfills and shims already developed. And this list grows as soon as a new feature, element, or enhancement is created.

We will see some polyfill implementations right now, but it is important that you check the website `https://github.com/Modernizr/Modernizr/wiki/HTML5-Cross-Browser-Polyfills`, checking if there is a polyfill already developed before you start creating a new one.

MediaElements.js

MediaElements is a polyfill that creates a consistency of player designs for the `<video>` and `<audio>` elements being viewed in older browsers, using Flash technology that mimics the native HTML5 MediaElement API.

In the following example, we will apply this library to improve the browser's consistency when displaying videos. However, there is still a lot of work to get every browser to play your audio/video because they require hosting multiple versions of the file in different formats such as `.mp4`, `.webm`, and `.ogg`.

How to do it

After downloading the latest version from `http://www.mediaelementjs.com`, we may include the JavaScript library and the `stylesheet` file inside the `<head>` tag:

```html
<script src="http://code.jquery.com/jquery-1.9.1.min.js"></script>
<script src="../build/mediaelement-and-player.min.js"></script>
<link rel="stylesheet" href="../build/mediaelementplayer.min.css" />
```

The following code is used for offering more accessibility for different browsers:

```html
<video width="640" height="360" id="player2" poster="../media/echo-hereweare.jpg" controls="controls" preload="none">
   <!-- MP4 source must come first for iOS and webkit browsers -->
   <source type="video/mp4" src="../media/echo-hereweare.mp4" />

   <!-- WebM for Firefox and Opera -->
   <source type="video/webm" src="../media/echo-hereweare.webm" />
   <source type="video/ogg" src="../media/echo-hereweare.ogv" />

   <!-- Fallback flash player -->
   <object width="640" height="360" type="application/x-shockwave-flash" data="../build/flashmediaelement.swf">
     <param name="movie" value="../build/flashmediaelement.swf" />
     <param name="flashvars" value="controls=true&amp;file=../media/echo-hereweare.mp4" />
     <img src="../media/echo-hereweare.jpg" width="640" height="360" alt="" title="No video playback capabilities" />
   </object>
</video>
```

Then, you can initialize the player for any `<video>` or `<audio>` element in the document this way:

```html
<script>
$('video').mediaelementplayer({
   success: function(player, node) {
     $('#' + node.id + '-mode').html('mode: ' + player.pluginType);
   }
});
</script>
```

In the following screenshot, there is a sample of its default video player UI:

There is documentation with plenty of options in which we can configure the player when it is being executed. These options may be found at `http://mediaelementjs.com/#options`.

SVG

Scalable Vector Graphics (SVG) is an image format for vector graphics. There are a lot of advantages of its usage such as well compressed file sizes, scaling to any size without losing clarity, great appearance on retina displays, and allowing more interactivity by giving more control to designers.

However, its acceptance by browsers is not yet complete, requiring fallbacks. There is a technique made by *Alexey Ten* which is very interesting because it solves problems for browsers such as Internet Explorer 8 and Android 2.3.

Let's understand a better way to cover the SVG implementation.

How to do it

There are some different ways to put an SVG file on the site. We will approach them with the methods: background image, as the `svg` tag, and as the `img` tag.

SVG as a background image

Modernizr has an SVG test. So, you can declare a fallback with the class names that the Modernizr has injected into the HTML element:

```
.my-element {
  background-image: url(image.svg);
}
.no-svg .my-element {
  background-image: url(image.png);
}
```

SVG as the <svg> tag

This is the new technique where old browsers do not understand the highlighted term very well and display the .png file instead of the .svg file:

```
<svg width="96" height="96">
  <image xlink:href="svg.svg" src="svg.png" width="96" height="96" />
</svg>
```

SVG as a simple <img> tag

By using Modernizr, we will test if the browser supports the SVG before inserting the code. If not, the script will find the .png file which has the same name, and it will display the .png file instead of the .svg one.

```
<img src="image.svg" onerror="this.src=image.png">

<script>
if (!Modernizr.svg) {
  $('img[src$=svg]').each(function(index, item) {
    imagePath = $(item).attr('src');
    $(item).attr('src',imagePath.slice(0,-3)+'png');
  });
}
</script>
```

However, these consistent URL and filename patterns are required to keep the website working well, otherwise the script will not locate the correct resource.

Respond.js

Respond.js is a fast and lightweight polyfill for `min-width` / `max-width`, which enables media query to support as it is reinterpreting the stylesheet, after it has been loaded into a format that the Internet Explorer 6 to 8 browsers will understand.

All of our media queries do not require any extra change. We just need to ensure that our `@media` statements are written properly.

> Make sure to include `respond.min.js` after the CSS files if you have some.
>
> If our CSS is using `@import` or is coded inline, Respond.js cannot read it. Instead, use a typical `<link>` method. For example:
> ```
> <link rel="stylesheet" href="css/style.css"
> media="screen and (max-width:480px)" />
> ```

How to do it

At the bottom of DOM (before the `</body>` closing tag), we will need to include the Respond.js library, which can be downloaded at https://github.com/scottjehl/Respond. Make sure to include `respond.min.js` after the CSS files if you have any:

```
<script src="js/respond.min.js"></script>
```

And it is done.

Summary

In this chapter, we ensured the accessibility for viewers providing fallbacks. We have learned how to detect browser characteristics and supported features by using CSS Browser Selector and Modernizr. These libraries have helped us a lot by offering support to perform a progressive enhancement. Also, we learned interesting polyfills for HTML5, such as html5shiv, MediaElements, and techniques for `SVG` and `FileAPI`. `Respond`, a useful polyfill for CSS was included in this chapter too.

In the next chapter, we will see thousands of plugins for creating a good responsive website, complementing all of the chapters we have read so far.

11
Useful Responsive Plugins

With the constant evolution of technology and trends, there emerge new plugins every day, helping more and more in the development of responsive websites. It is important to keep yourself updated on them through blogs such as http://www.smashingmagazine.com/, http://bradfrostweb.com/blog/, and http://www.lukew.com/ff/.

In this chapter we will focus on showing different plugins by covering the following topics:

- Plugins for website structure such as Columns, Equalize, and Packery
- Plugins for menu navigation such as Sidr, EasyResponsiveTabstoAccordion, FlexNav, and other miscellaneous plugins

Plugins for website structure

In *Chapter 2*, *Designing Responsive Layouts/Grids*, we have seen plugins such as Fluid Baseline Grid System, 1140 Grid, and Foundation 4, which form a development kit that will help us to develop websites quickly. We need to keep in mind the objective to create a cohesive website and avoid wasting time recreating something that is already done.

There are some other additional plugins such as Columns, Equalize, and Packery which were not mentioned earlier in order to stay focused on building our website, but they are very useful.

Creating simple responsive structures using Columns

Let's start with the Columns plugin whose objective is to provide a quick creation of responsive layouts just as the Grid systems do. Its simplicity makes it lightweight and its learning curve is very fast. Columns has an MIT license, and works well on IE9 and modern browsers. If you want to use IE8, it will require polyfills for HTML5 and media queries.

This plugin is recommended for small websites where we just need a simple and quick responsive structure implementation. It does not mean it will not work for medium and large websites, but in this case other frameworks may provide more diversity of options and solutions that these websites may require.

In addition, there is an option to auto-adjust the minimum and maximum values for font sizes depending on the screen size.

For its implementation, we will need to access the website from `https://github.com/elclanrs/jquery.columns/` and download the files of this solution.

Then, let's insert the following code in the `<head>` tag of our DOM:

```
<link rel="stylesheet" href="css/jquery.columns.css">
```

Now, let's use this HTML code just as a sample to clarify the plugin usage, but feel free to try this plugin on your current HTML structure. Notice that classes such as `row-1` and `col` and IDs such as `content-1` and `content-2` will define how the structure will look depending on breakpoint:

```
<section id="slider" class="row-1">
  <div class='col'>
    <img src="http://fpoimg.com/1344x250" class="responsive" />
  </div>
</section>
<section id="content-1" class="row-2">
  <div class='col'>
    <h2>Maui waui</h2>
    <p>Lorem ipsum dolor sit amet...</p>
  </div>
  <div class='col'>
    <h2>Super duper</h2>
    <p>Lorem ipsum dolor sit amet...</p>
  </div>
</section>
<section id="content-2" class="row-4">
```

```
    <div class='col'>
      <h3>Something</h3>
      <p>Lorem ipsum dolor sit amet...</p>
    </div>
    <div class='col'>
      <h3>Nothing</h3>
      <p>Lorem ipsum dolor sit amet...</p>
    </div>
    <div class="col">
      <h3>Everything</h3>
      <p>Lorem ipsum dolor sit amet...</p>
    </div>
    <div class="col">
      <h3>All of it</h3>
      <p>Lorem ipsum dolor sit amet...</p>
    </div>
</section>
```

By defining the classes, such as `row-2` or `row-4`, we are defining how many columns are inside that section and IDs will give more control to display these columns differently later.

Basically, for this example we will use two breakpoints: 480 (standard for plugin) and 1024. At the bottom of DOM (before the `</body>` closing tag), we will need to include the jQuery code and the Columns script. Then, we will run the plugin by calling the `quickSetup` function and configure the column and breakpoint.

```
<script src="http://code.jquery.com/jquery-1.9.1.min.js"></script>
<script src="js/jquery.columns.js"></script>
<script>
$.columns.quickSetup({
  fontSize: [14, 16]
});
$.columns.setCols({
  'content-1': [ [1024, 1] ],
  'content-2': [ [1024, 2] ]
});
</script>
```

In this sample, the section `content-2` starts with four columns per row when the screen size is higher than 1024. Then, we set 2 columns per row when the screen size is less than 1024 pixels, and 1 column per row when it is less than 480 pixels.

Useful Responsive Plugins

Let's see the visual result of the plugin applied to a parent element viewed on desktop and tablet screens:

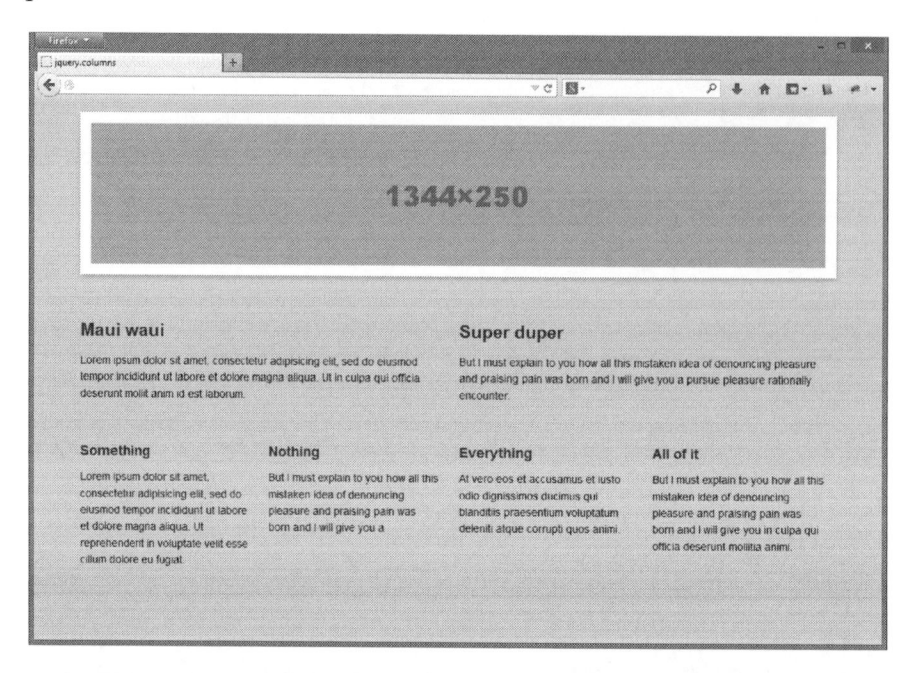

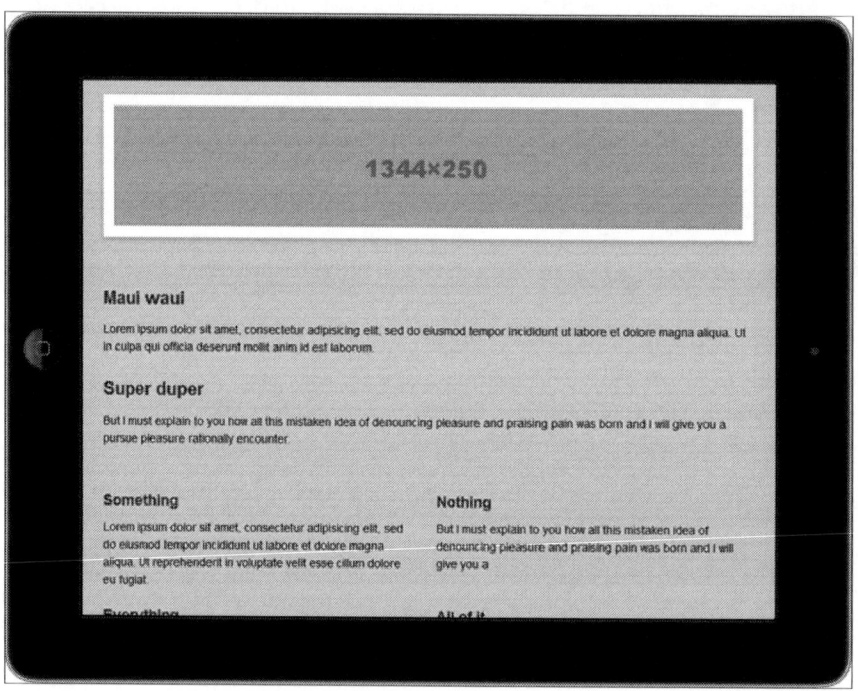

Also, the plugin allows you to add columns dynamically. But, to reflect this change, it requires to call `$.columns.refresh()` on code after adding it on DOM.

Using Equalize for element dimension adjustment

When customizing the page to look like cards, there is a common problem that occurs when loading the dynamic content whose dimensions may vary. We want to keep all the items with the same look.

If we float to the left of the list item elements, the content of each item will influence to breaking the row, and instead the second row that starts from left will start indented. So, the problem of undesirable layout card breaking will look as follows:

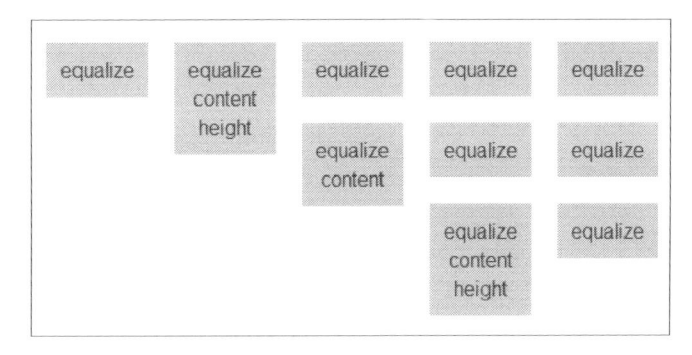

Or if we define the same dimensions of all items, we will lose the dynamic dimension. Something like that also happens to the width of the elements.

Equalize is created for equalizing the height or width of elements. It is a lightweight and very helpful jQuery plugin that only requires specifying the parent ID or class in order to be executed. Basically, it works by calculating the dimension of bigger elements and defining it to other ones, avoiding any floating issue.

Also, it accepts all the following jQuery dimension methods to resize elements: `height`, `outerHeight`, `innerHeight`, `width`, `outerWidth`, and `innerWidth`. The most used is `height`, which is set to default by plugin.

Let's try to reproduce the same example seen before to see this plugin in action. The objective is to implement the Equalize plugin, adjust all items to the same dimension of the bigger element, and keep the floating working responsiveness with no undesirable breaks.

After downloading it from https://github.com/tsvensen/equalize.js/, we will start by adding the following HTML code in our source code:

```
<ul id="equalize-height">
  <li>equalize</li>
  <li>equalize content height</li>
  <li>equalize</li>
  <li>equalize</li>
  <li>equalize</li>
  <li>equalize content</li>
  <li>equalize</li>
  <li>equalize</li>
  <li>equalize content height </li>
  <li>equalize</li>
</ul>
```

Then, at the bottom of DOM (before the `</body>` closing tag), we will need to include the jQuery and Equalize libraries. After that, we will execute the scripts for the `equalize-height` ID (parent of `<li>` elements).

```
<script src="http://code.jquery.com/jquery-1.9.1.min.js"></script>
<script src="js/equalize.min.js"></script>
<script>
$(function() {
  $('#equalize-height').equalize();
});
</script>
```

See the expected in the following figure:

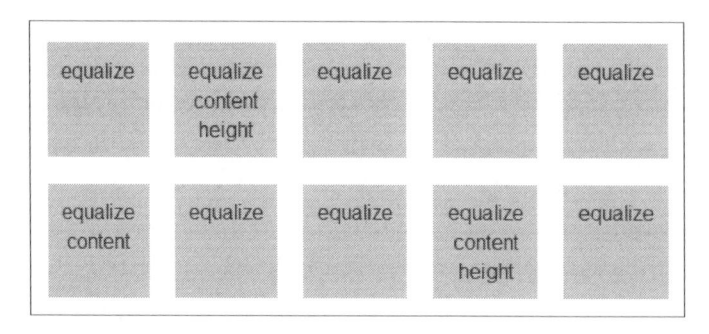

Implementing a card website layout with Packery

Packery is a jQuery plugin that uses an algorithm to fill empty gaps on website layouts based on cards, adjusting them gracefully. The trend of the layout based on cards came with Google+ and is gaining fans around the world.

> Packery plugin has a GPL v3 license for non-commercial, personal, or open source. If you want to use it on a public website, it will cost $25.

Its implementation is not too difficult, as we will see in the following example of its usage. But to do it, we need to download it first from https://github.com/metafizzy/packery.

Let's start by creating an empty HTML file. A packaged source file includes everything you need to use Packery. So, after downloading, let's include this suggested custom CSS on `<head>` tag to handle the card dimensions better:

```
<style>
img {max-width: 100%; height: auto;}
@media screen and (min-width: 1024px) and (max-width: 1280px) {
  /* DESKTOP - 4 columns */
  #container > div { width: 25%; }
  #container > div.w2 { width: 50%; }
  #container > div.w4 { width: 100%; }
}
@media screen and (min-width: 768px) and (max-width: 1023px) {
  /* TABLET - 3 columns */
  #container > div { width: 33%; }
  #container > div.w2 { width: 66%; }
  #container > div.w4 { width: 100%; }
}
@media screen and (max-width: 767px) {
  /* SMARTPHONE - 1 column */
  #container > div { width: 100%; }
}
</style>
```

After that, let's use this HTML code where each item represents a card:

```
<div id="container" class="js-packery">
  <div class="w4"><img src="http://placehold.it/1280x250"></div>
```

Useful Responsive Plugins

```
    <div class="w2"><img src="http://placehold.it/640x250"></div>
    <div><img src="http://fpoimg.com/320x250"></div>
    <div><img src="http://fpoimg.com/320x250img "></div>
    <div><img src="http://fpoimg.com/320x250 "></div>
    <div><img src="http://fpoimg.com/320x250 "></div>
    <div class="w2"><img src="http://fpoimg.com/640x250 "></div>
    <div><img src="http://fpoimg.com/320x250 "></div>
    <div><img src="http://fpoimg.com/320x250 "></div>
</div>
```

At the bottom of DOM (before the </body> closing tag), we will need to include jQuery and Packery libraries. Also, we will initialize the Packery script informing the container ID, the class used for child elements which will be relocated, and the desired space between columns (or gutter).

```
<script src="http://code.jquery.com/jquery-1.9.1.min.js"></script>
<script src="js/packery.pkgd.min.js"></script>
<script>
var $container = $('#container');
$container.packery({
   itemSelector: '#container > div',
   gutter: 0
});
</script>
```

And this is the visual result for tablets and desktops:

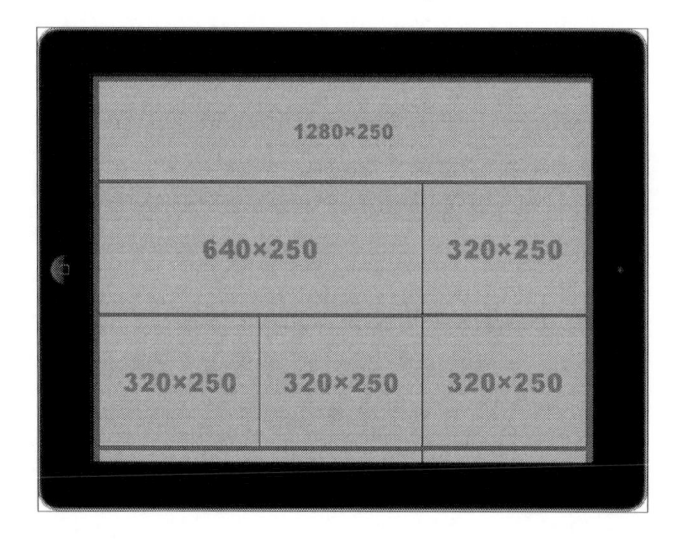

[198]

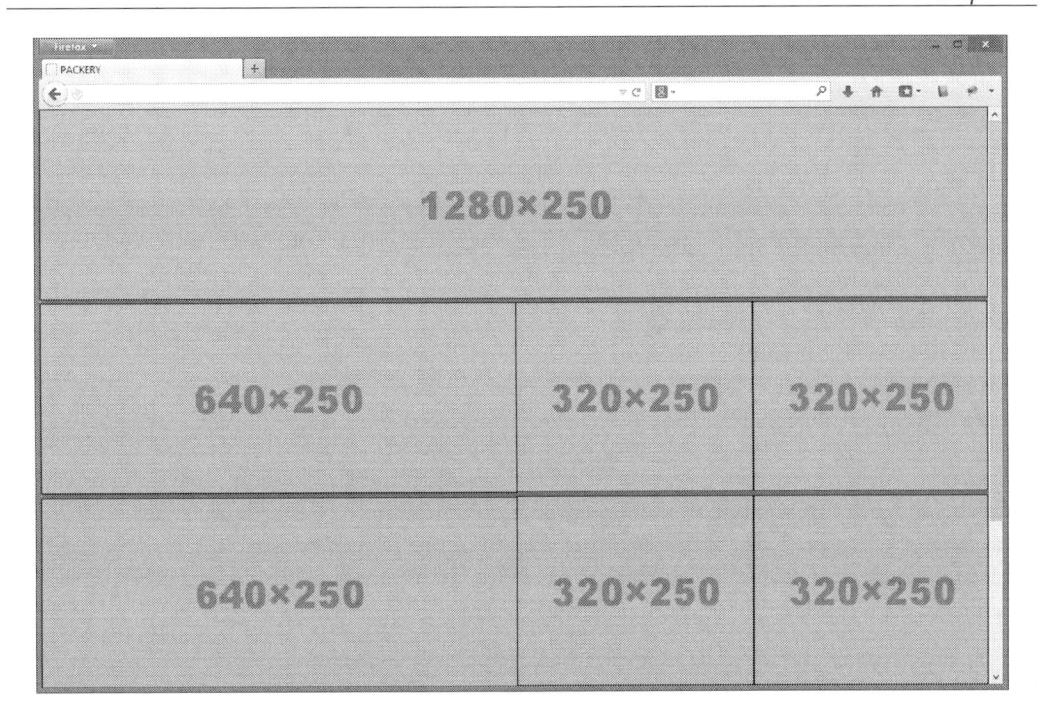

Plugins for menu navigation

In *Chapter 3*, *Building Responsive Navigation Menu*, we have seen eight different popular menu techniques, each one used for its own objective. There is no "jack of all trades" menu that works well in all situations, unfortunately.

In order to always stick together with the progressive user experience, we must research how to improve our website as a product, commonly found by using new JavaScript/jQuery plugins.

We will see three complementary plugins that bring small differences in approach if compared with plugins we have seen. They are Sidr, EasyResponsiveTabstoAccordion, and FlexNav.

Creating a side menu with Sidr

Sidr is a jQuery plugin used for creating side menus, which are very common on responsive websites. It also allows multiple Sidr menus (on both sides) and works with external content as well.

Let's try to implement the following example by creating a standard HTML file and adding the CSS file that is included in the plugin and may be downloaded from `https://github.com/artberri/sidr`. We will find two options to display the menu in a dark (`jquery.sidr.dark.css`) and a light way (`jquery.sidr.light.css`). We can use or extend them overriding some styles.

So, after including one of them on the `<head>` tag, we may set the initial style which will hide the menu header on screen sizes higher than 767 pixels.

```
<link rel="stylesheet" href="css/jquery.sidr.light.css">
<style>
  #mobile-header {
    display: none;
  }
  @media only screen and (max-width: 767px) {
    #mobile-header {
      display: block;
    }
  }
</style>
```

Now, let's use this HTML code just as a sample to clarify the plugin usage:

```
<div id="mobile-header">
  <a id="responsive-menu-button" href="#sidr-main">Menu</a>
</div>
<div id="navigation">
  <nav>
    <ul class="nav-bar">
      <li><a href="#">Menu item1</a></li>
      <li><a href="#">Menu item2</a></li>
      <li><a href="#">Menu item3</a></li>
      <li><a href="#">Menu item4</a></li>
      <li><a href="#">Menu item5</a></li>
      <li><a href="#">Menu item6</a></li>
    </ul>
  </nav>
</div>
```

At the bottom of DOM (before the `</body>` closing tag), we will need to include the jQuery and Sidr libraries. After that, we will bind the execution of Sidr with the menu button which is responsible for opening the side menu.

```
<script src="http://code.jquery.com/jquery-1.9.1.min.js"></script>
<script src="js/jquery.sidr.js"></script>
<script>
```

```
$('#responsive-menu-button').sidr({
  name:   'sidr-main',
  source: '#navigation'
});
</script>
```

The `#sidr-main` ID we have defined will be the ID of the sidebar menu `<div>`, and `#navigation` is the ID of the menu we selected to display inside of this sidebar.

In the following screenshot, we will see the result of this implementation. After clicking on the **Menu** link, the light-themed menu will appear on screens smaller than 767 px (this value was customized by us):

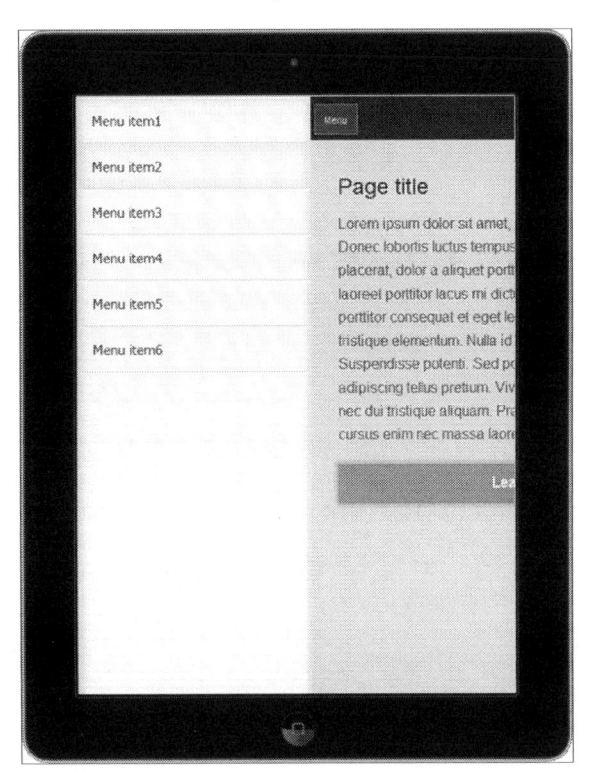

Knowing about EasyResponsiveTabstoAccordion

EasyResponsiveTabstoAccordion is a lightweight jQuery plugin which optimizes normal, horizontal, or vertical tabs to accordion especially when displayed on small devices such as tablets and smartphones.

Useful Responsive Plugins

The objective of this plugin is to adapt the element according to the screen size. Also, it prioritizes the content reading by starting to display the content of the first tab followed by others. The effect implemented on this plugin is entirely made by using jQuery which helps to provide cross-browser compatibility.

A better way to understand how it works is by practicing. After downloading it from `https://github.com/samsono/Easy-Responsive-Tabs-to-Accordion/`, let's create a standard HTML document and add the CSS file inside the `<head>` tag:

```
<link rel="stylesheet" href="css/responsive-tabs.css">
```

Now, we will use the following HTML code just as a sample of tab content:

```
<div id="mytab">
  <ul class="resp-tabs-list">
    <li>Tab-1</li>
    <li>Tab-2</li>
    <li>Tab-3</li>
  </ul>
  <div class="resp-tabs-container">
    <div>Lorem ipsum dolor sit amet...</div>
    <div>Integer laoreet placerat suscipit...</div>
    <div>Nam porta cursus lectus...</div>
  </div>
</div>
```

Then, at the bottom of DOM (before the `</body>` closing tag), we will need to include the `jquery` and `easyResponsiveTabs` libraries. After that, we will execute the scripts by informing the ID of our container element:

```
<script src="http://code.jquery.com/jquery-1.9.1.min.js"></script>
<script src="js/easyResponsiveTabs.js"></script>
<script>
$(document).ready(function () {
  $('#mytab').easyResponsiveTabs({
    type: 'default', //Types: default, vertical, accordion
    width: 'auto',
    fit: true,
    closed: 'accordion',
    activate: function(event) {
      // Callback function if tab is switched if need
    }
  });
});
</script>
```

This is the visual result of the plugin when viewed on smartphones and screen sizes more than 768 pixels:

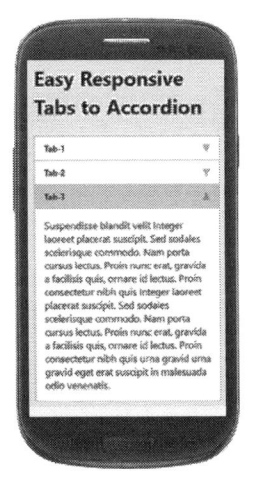

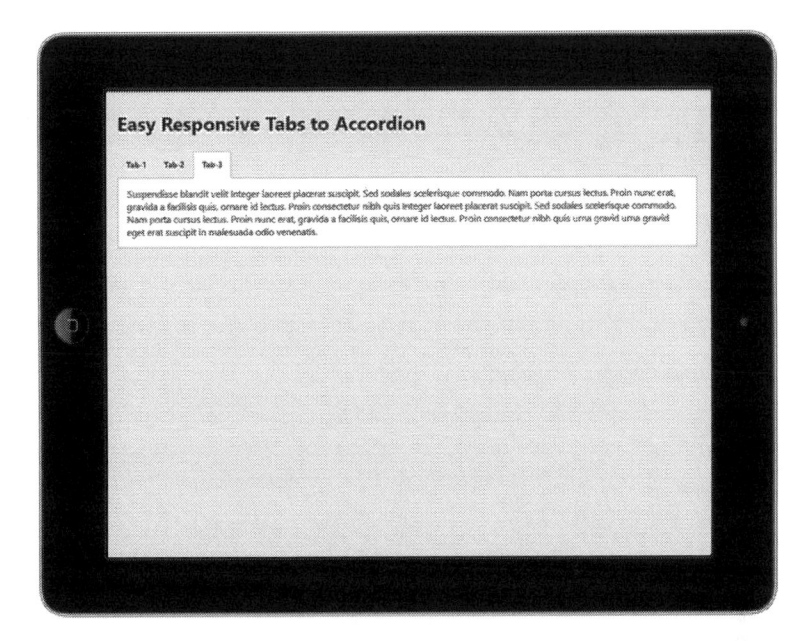

There are some optional parameters that would be informed when executing the script, such as:

- `type: 'default'`: It can be set as `default`, `vertical`, `accordion`
- `width: 'auto'`: It can be set as `auto` or any custom width
- `fit: true`: It helps fit the entire thing in a container
- `closed: false`: It closes the panels on start
- `activate: function(){}`: It is a callback function to include some custom code which fires when the tab is changed

Adding flexibility to your menu with FlexNav

FlexNav is a jQuery plugin that facilitates the creation of complex and responsive navigation menus without having to write many lines of code. It has the mobile-first approach which can reveal submenus for touchscreens just by tapping the target.

In addition to controlling these nested subitems in a device-agnostic way, this plugin has improved its accessibility for support navigation by keyboard tab and has provided a fallback for old browsers.

Useful Responsive Plugins

For its implementation you will find the downloadable files from `https://github.com/indyplanets/flexnav`. Starting with a standard HTML document, it is necessary to add this code in the `<head>` tag of code including the CSS file:

```
<link href="css/flexnav.css" rel="stylesheet" type="text/css" />
```

Now, we will include the following HTML code in a simple unordered list, adding in the class and data attributes:

```html
<ul class="flexnav" data-breakpoint="800">
  <li><a href="#">Item 1</a></li>
  <li><a href="#">Item 2</a>
    <ul>
      <li><a href="#">Sub 1 Item 1</a></li>
      <li><a href="#">Sub 1 Item 2</a></li>
    </ul>
  </li>
  <li><a href="#">Item 3</a>
    <ul>
      <li><a href="#">Sub 1 Item 1</a></li>
      <li><a href="#">Sub 1 Item 2</a></li>
      <li><a href="#">Sub 1 Item 3</a></li>
    </ul>
  </li>
</ul>
<div class="menu-button">Menu</div>
```

Then, at the bottom of DOM (before the `</body>` closing tag), we will include the jQuery and FlexNav libraries. After that, we will execute the scripts by informing the ID or class of the menu element which we want to transform into responsive.

```html
<script src="http://code.jquery.com/jquery-1.9.1.min.js"></script>
<script src="js/jquery.flexnav.min.js"></script>
<script>
$(".flexnav").flexNav();
</script>
```

This is a visual sample of what this plugin may offer if viewed on smartphones and tablets:

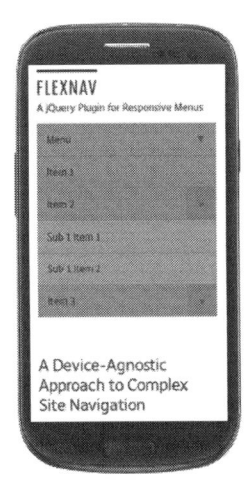

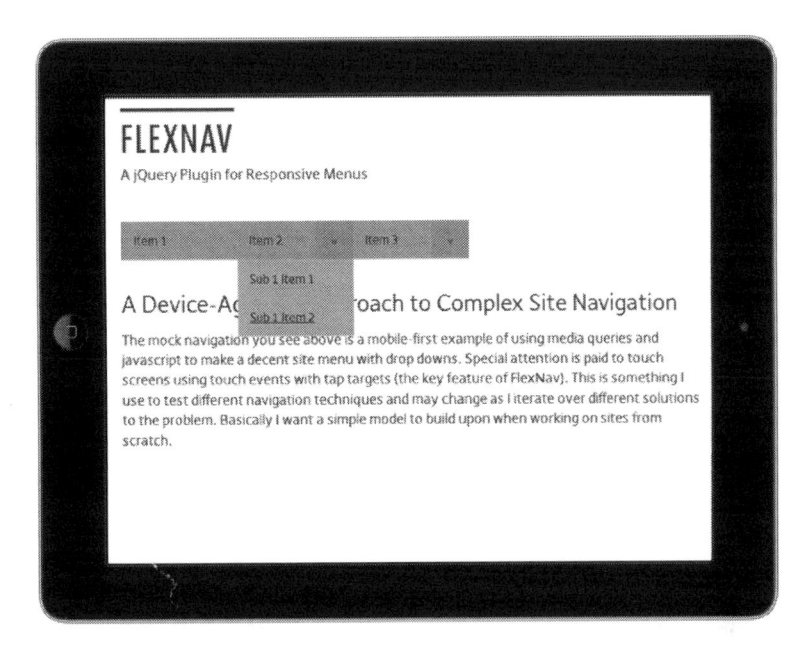

It is also possible to inform the plugin of a few options when we are executing the script, such as:

- `'animationSpeed':'250'`: This sets the speed of animations that accepts fast/slow too
- `'transitionOpacity': true`: This specifies default opacity animation
- `'buttonSelector': '.menu-button'`: This specifies the default menu button class
- `'hoverIntent': false`: This is used for hoverIntent plugin only
- `'hoverIntentTimeout': 150`: This is used for hoverIntent plugin only

For example:

```
<script>
$(".flexnav").flexNav({
   'buttonSelector': '.exclusive-button'
});
</script>
```

Miscellaneous

There is no specific category under which to regroup the following plugins we will see. They are SVGeezy, Prefix free, Magnific Popup, Riloadr, and Calendario.

SVGeezy

SVGeezy is a JavaScript plugin that handles SVG images for browsers such as IE8 and earlier and Android 2.3 and earlier. Its working is very simple because it only detects SVG images on our website and automatically searches for another image (in PNG format for example) as a fallback for it.

The fallback image must have the same filename. The change refers only to the file format. Also, it is not necessary to be a PNG file. This format may be specified when initializing the script.

If you need support for these old browsers, we will see how to do it. First, let's access and download the solution from https://github.com/benhowdle89/svgeezy.

Then, create a new standard HTML document and add the SVG image inside the `<img>` tag, as follows:

```
<img src="images/mylogo.svg" />
```

Later, at the bottom of DOM (before the `</body>` closing tag), we will include the jQuery and SVGeezy libraries. Then, we will execute the plugin by informing two parameters:

- The first one defines a classname which we can use if we do not have the SVG fallback image or simply do not want to provide a fallback for that specific image.
- The second one means that the extension of the image will be provided if the browser does not support display of SVG images. The PNG extension is the most common.

```
<script src="js/svgeezy.js"></script>
<script>
svgeezy.init('nocheck', 'png');
</script>
```

> We can also change `nocheck` to `false`, letting the plugin check all images.

Prefix free

Prefix free provides us the facility to use only unprefixed CSS properties; the plugin adds the current browser's prefix to any CSS code in a background service, only when it's necessary. In order to make prefixes code independently, we do not need to memorize what properties need prefixes anymore, and it may also avoid refactoring the code later only to remove or add new prefixes.

> This plugin is not necessarily responsive, but since its objective is to give more accessibility to the modern browsers, prevent the use of old prefixes and do not forget to use them when it is required.

It is not hard to start using it. First of all let's download it from https://github.com/LeaVerou/prefixfree.

For this example, let's re-use some HTML you already had and include prefixfree.js in the <head> tag of DOM (right after the CSS files):

```
<script src="js/prefixfree.js"></script>
```

> The plugin recommends including this in the header in order to minimize the blink effect that happens (also known as the FOUC effect).

This is the comparison between before and after, where we may notice how many lines of code we have saved.

This is how we commonly write a code:

```
#element {
  margin: 0;
  -webkit-box-shadow: 1px 2px 3px #999;
  box-shadow: 1px 2px 3px #999;
  border-radius: 10px;

  -webkit-transition: all 1s;
  -moz-transition: all 1s;
  -o-transition: all 1s;
  -ms-transition: all 1s;
  transition: all 1s;

  background: -webkit-linear-gradient(to top, orange 50%, #eee 70%);
  background: -moz-linear-gradient(to top, orange 50%, #eee 70%);
```

```
    background: -o-linear-gradient(to top, orange 50%, #eee 70%);
    background: -ms-linear-gradient(to top, orange 50%, #eee 70%);
    background: linear-gradient(to top, orange 50%, #eee 70%);
}
```

And this one shows, how we could write the same cross-browser code when using Prefix free:

```
#element {
    margin: 0;
    box-shadow: 1px 2px 3px #999;
    border-radius: 10px;
    transition: all 1s;
    background: linear-gradient(to top, orange 50%, #eee 70%);
}
```

We saved many lines of code. Incredible, isn't it? Try it on your document and check the benefits.

Magnific Popup

Magnific Popup is a jQuery plugin used for creating responsive popup windows which have multiple uses, such as:

- Single image/image gallery displayed in overlay window
- Popup with video or map
- Modal popup
- Dialog with CSS animation

It focuses on performance and providing best experience for users with any device. Regarding Internet Explorer browsers, Magnific Popups are compatible with Version 8 and earlier. It achieves it by providing a light and modular solution to be downloaded from `http://dimsemenov.com/plugins/magnific-popup/` and clicking on the **Build tool** link.

The use of CSS3 transition instead of JavaScript animations significantly improves the performance of animation. Also, this plugin has a kind of extendable microtemplating engine that re-uses existing elements responsible to speed up the popup loading when using the same pattern of popups (image gallery, for example).

Let's try to do this example by practicing it. We will start by creating a new standard HTML document. After downloading the solution from https://github.com/dimsemenov/Magnific-Popup, let's add the CSS file inside the <head> tag. This file is not required for its working, but inside of it there are some useful styles responsible for good effects:

```
<link rel="stylesheet" href="css/magnific-popup.css">
```

Now, we will add these two links on code displaying a simple image popup and, the other one, a video popup.

```
<p><a class="image-link" href="image-sample.jpg">Open popup</a></p>
<p><a class="popup-youtube" href="http://www.youtube.com/watch?v=0O2aH4XLbto">Open video</a></p>
```

Then, at the bottom of DOM (before the </body> closing tag), we will need to include the jquery and magnificPopup libraries. After that, we will execute the scripts twice and inform the classes (we specified one link previously) for each purpose:

```
<script src="http://code.jquery.com/jquery-1.9.1.min.js"></script>
<script src="js/jquery.magnific-popup.min.js"></script>
<script>
$(document).ready(function() {
  $('.image-link').magnificPopup({type:'image'});
  $('.popup-youtube').magnificPopup({
    type: 'iframe',
    mainClass: 'mfp-fade'
  });
});
</script>
```

The following is the visual of a simple image popup implementation viewed on smartphones and tablets:

There are many usage types which can be seen in detail in the plugin documentation at http://dimsemenov.com/plugins/magnific-popup/documentation.html.

Riloadr

Riloadr is a responsive plugin for image loaders. In this section we will see how it works with jQuery, although it is not required because it is framework-independent.

This plugin is an alternative solution to deliver contextual images in responsive layouts which use different image sizes at different resolutions in order to improve page load time and user experience.

Riloadr uses the `data-src` and `data-base` attributes in the image tag element instead of the common `src` attribute. So, this way we are able to handle the image element selecting the best image to be displayed before the browser renders the website.

There are some highlight features that differentiate it from other competitors, such as:

- Absolute control on process of image loading
- Unlimited breakpoints that may be set by using CSS properties, for example, `minWidth`, `maxWidth`, and `minDevicePixelRatio`

- Riloadr does not make multiple requests for the same image
- You can create different Riloadr objects (named groups) and configure each one to your needs
- Bandwidth testing to deliver high-resolution images only if the device has the connection fast enough to download it

After downloading it from https://github.com/tubalmartin/riloadr, the recommendation of the plugin is to let CSS and JavaScript files inside the `<head>` tag:

```
<script src="http://code.jquery.com/jquery-1.9.1.min.js"></script>
<script src="js/riloadr.jquery.min.js"></script>
```

Once the Riloadr is loaded, we may set up its image groups:

```
<script>
var group1 = new Riloadr({
  breakpoints: [
    {name: '320', maxWidth: 320},
    {name: '640', maxWidth: 320, minDevicePixelRatio: 2},
    {name: '640', minWidth: 321, maxWidth: 640},
    {name: '1024', minWidth: 641}
  ]
});
</script>
```

> The configuration of `minDevicePixelRatio` is related to the devices that support high DPI images and load up the image used for 640 px (with a dimension twice as large as normal).

Now, we will just add this `<img>` tag on our HTML code using `data-src` and `data-base`.

Notice that on `data-base`, we will use `{breakpoint-name}` as a dynamic value captured by Riloadr and identify on the breakpoint which has already been defined previously. This name may be used as a place to store images by dimensions without making a mess:

```
<div>
  <img class="responsive" data-base="images/{breakpoint-name}/" data-src="image-name.jpg">
  <noscript>
    <img src="images/320/image-name.jpg">
  </noscript>
</div>
```

When rendering the preceding code, the browser will detect the screen size and select the correct breakpoint that it fits. Then, it will be replaced by the content of the variable name we defined earlier, in this case, 320. The same thing happens if the browser identifies that the content of the variable name is 640, which fits better.

> If the browser does not support JavaScript or something wrong happens, the `<noscript>` tag will display the image we defined.

This following screenshot shows Riloadr in action, displaying images with different dimensions being loaded only when it is required by the browser (depending on breakpoints of 320 and 640 pixels):

Calendario

Calendario is a jQuery responsive plugin which was built to provide a suitable layout for improving a user's interaction with the calendar, keeping the calendar structure fluid for easy adaptation to different screens.

On large screens it displays a grid-based layout, while on smaller screens it converts it into a stack of the days of the month vertically, facilitating its visualization a lot.

> This solution will not work on all browsers yet because some of them do not support new CSS properties such as `calc()`. These browsers are Internet Explorer 8, Opera Mini, and Android Browser.

Calendario is available at https://github.com/codrops/Calendario.

Let's start by adding the CSS file that is included in the plugin:

```
<link rel="stylesheet" type="text/css" href="css/calendar.css" />
<link rel="stylesheet" type="text/css" href="css/custom_1.css" />
```

Now, we will include this structured HTML, adding classes and IDs for JavaScript handling later:

```
<div class="custom-calendar-wrap custom-calendar-full">
  <div class="custom-header clearfix">
    <h2>Calendario</h2>
    <div class="custom-month-year">
      <span id="custom-month" class="custom-month"></span>
      <span id="custom-year" class="custom-year"></span>
      <nav>
        <span id="custom-prev" class="custom-prev"></span>
        <span id="custom-next" class="custom-next"></span>
      </nav>
    </div>
  </div>
  <div id="calendar" class="fc-calendar-container"></div>
</div>
```

Then, at the bottom of DOM (before the </body> closing tag), we will need to include the jQuery and Calendario libraries. Then, we will initialize the script by setting the container ID and will create two useful functions for month navigation through the calendar:

```
<script src="http://code.jquery.com/jquery-1.9.1.min.js"></script>
<script src="js/jquery.calendario.js"></script>
<script>
$(function() {
  var cal = $('#calendar').calendario(),
    $month = $('#custom-month').html(cal.getMonthName()),
    $year = $('#custom-year').html(cal.getYear());

  $('#custom-next').on('click', function() {
    cal.gotoNextMonth( updateMonthYear );
  });
  $('#custom-prev').on('click', function() {
    cal.gotoPreviousMonth(updateMonthYear);
  } );
```

[213]

Useful Responsive Plugins

```
      function updateMonthYear() {
        $month.html(cal.getMonthName());
        $year.html(cal.getYear());
      }
    });
  </script>
```

The following is a screenshot of this calendar viewed on smartphones/tablets and desktops:

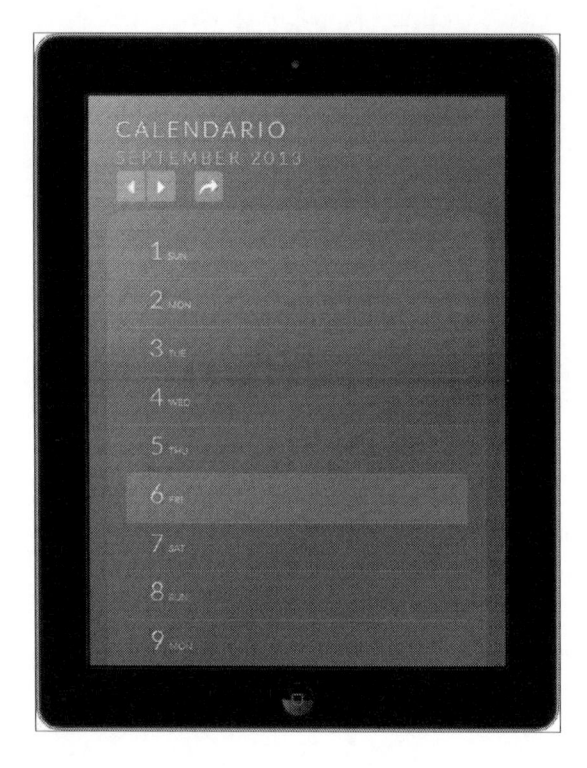

And how it may display on desktops:

Summary

In this chapter, we have learned about complementary plugins separated by three categories which are complementing the previous chapters. For structure plugins, we have learned how to use Columns for creating a simple responsive structure, Equalize for better distribution of floated element on page, and Packery for creating card layout websites. We have also learned different ways to display menus and tabs by using Sidr, EasyResponsiveTabstoAccordion, and FlexNav. In the *Miscellaneous* section, we have seen how to use SVGeezy, Prefix free, MagnificPopup plugin, Riloadr, and Calendario.

In the last chapter, we will see different techniques to detect how fast the website is loading. The performance topic is extensive, but since effective handling of this metric is very important, we will see some techniques to improve the performance when creating a responsive website.

12
Improving Website Performance

Loading time is a major contributing factor to page abandonment. Users will go elsewhere if pages take longer than 3-4 seconds to load.

The need for pages that load quickly is more acute for those on mobile devices because the users feel that the page loading takes longer than it does on desktops, and it happens with the majority of current websites (73 percent according to KISSmetrics, in their article *Loading Time*).

A good part of the loading time is spent on performing client-side processing and loading resources such as stylesheets, script files, and images.

In this chapter we will learn ways to improve the performance for responsive websites, by:

- Using a content delivery network
- Making fewer HTTP requests
- Reducing the size of the payload
- Optimizing client-side processing
- Using tools to check website performance

Using a content delivery network

A **Content Delivery Network (CDN)** is a collection of web servers distributed across multiple locations, making your pages load faster from the user's perspective.

The server selected for delivering content to a specific user is typically based on network proximity and this content delivery is achieved in the quickest response time. Also, this caches content into the browser so that it does not have to be retrieved again the next time, thereby saving on making requests to the server.

There is a cost-effective approach to use a CDN service provider, and some known service providers are Akamai Technologies, Mirror Image Internet, and Limelight Networks.

Making fewer HTTP requests

Decreasing the number of components included on a page reduces the number of HTTP requests required to load the website and it is not related to the number of KBs of each file only. There is also a problem that refers to the short time for which each HTTP connection is consumed by servers processing each request before delivering the file back to the browser.

We will see some techniques to achieve reduction in the number of requests:

- Using conditional loaders
- Combining multiple scripts into one script
- Combining multiple CSS files into one stylesheet
- Using CSS Sprites

Using conditional loaders

Conditional loaders such as RequireJS or yepnope.js, which we have talked about earlier in the book, will only load code that is required.

Consolidating and minifying resources (JavaScript and CSS)

The ideal result is that in production there will be a single CSS file and a single JavaScript file for the entire site.

The solution for this is to **consolidate** that bunch of JavaScript files into only one, reducing requests and speeding up page loading the first time, even though it may not be cached efficiently on mobile devices.

Minification is the best practice to eliminate inessential characters such as extra spaces, newline characters, indentation, and comments. Based on my personal tests, this improvement may reduce the file size by an average of 20 percent.

> This value is not accurate because it depends on the size of the file, the amount of white space, and so on.

This combo grants a good performance improvement, mainly because it is commonly executed before the site displays something.

There are several online tools to perform this task. My personal favorite is the YUI Compressor, which you can execute by accessing http://refresh-sf.com/yui/ and Google Minify from https://code.google.com/p/minify/.

The procedure to use YUI Compressor is really simple. You only need to select the files that will be consolidated, minify, and then click on the **Compress** button.

CSS Sprites

As we know, using CSS Sprites is a practice of image consolidation since it involves merging theme images into one. By combining (background) images, we can reduce the overall size of image files, and therefore reduce the number of HTTP requests made to the server.

> If you use Photoshop to create image sprites, once you have created these sprites, save the PSD source file for further changes. Later, if you want to include new icons in this image sprite, expand down and/or right-click on the blank area of this image.

The following is a sample of a Google image sprite:

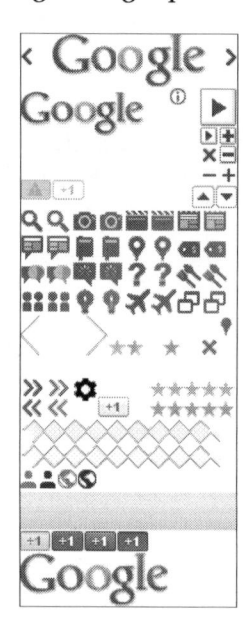

There are two online tools that I consider my favorites to create sprite images: Stitches (http://draeton.github.io/stitches/) and SpriteCow (http://www.spritecow.com/).

How to create sprites using SpriteCow

This tool generates the initial CSS code that you need to put in the CSS file later.

First of all, you need to create the image with all the buttons and icons (as we can see in the previous image). Then, at http://www.spritecow.com/, there is a button named **Open Image** that will upload the sprite.

Then click on the **Select Sprite** tool and make a square wrapping the icon you want to customize by clicking on it. Do not worry if your selection was not too near the icon because there is an automatic adjustment that improves this selection. Try yourself!

Reducing the size of payloads

After removing extra HTTP requests, it's time to reduce the size of remaining files as much as possible. Not only does this make your pages load faster but it also helps save bandwidth consumption.

Minimizing the payload size of both dynamic and static resources can reduce network latency significantly.

We will look at some practices to achieve this, such as Progressive JPEG, adaptive images, image optimization, and better use of HTML5 and CSS3.

Progressive JPEG

Progressive JPEG is not new. It was considered one of the best practices. However, with the improvement of Internet speed, this feature became unnoticeable for a while. But now, with limited bandwidths on mobile devices, this practice has surfaced again.

The difference between saving a normal JPEG image as a baseline and with the progressive option is represented in the following screenshot:

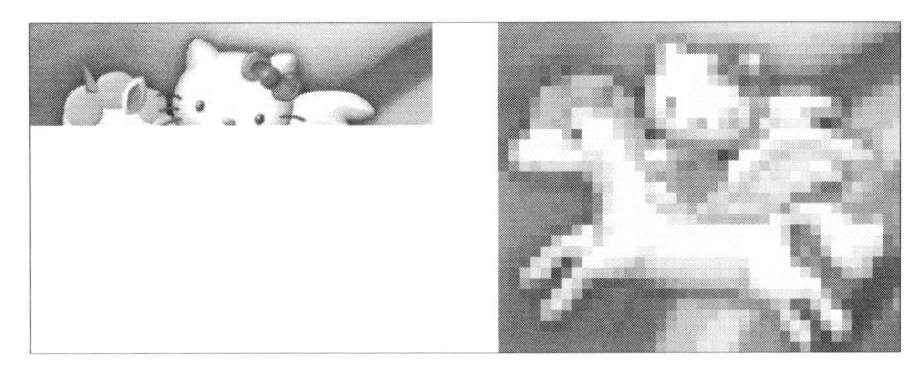

In terms of size, the progressive one has its size around 10 percent more for medium images when compared with the normal JPEG image. The loading time is almost the same or some milliseconds more.

But the preview effect of the progressive JPEG makes it seem a faster loading page on visitors' perception when compared to adaptive images.

On mobile devices, loading unnecessary high-resolution images is a massive waste of bandwidth, processing time, and cache space. To speed up page rendering and reduce bandwidth and memory consumption, replace images with smaller versions.

However, as we have learned in *Chapter 5, Preparing Images and Videos*, it is highly recommended to use solutions such as Foresight or Picturefill because they first check what the requesting device is and only then allow the browser to download any image.

Image optimization

Images usually contain certain amount of useless data that can also be safely removed while maintaining quality. There are two approaches to image optimization: lossless and lossy compression.

Lossless compression may remove extra information, such as embedded thumbnails, comments within the data, metadata about the photo, camera model, ISO speed, whether the flash was on or off, lens type, and focal length, and may save anywhere between 5 to 20 percent in file size.

The process of optimizing images is very simple because it just requires selecting which images should be changed.

There are plenty of tools available online to achieve this. Personally, I prefer using offline tools to remove this information because it gives more security on the legal rights of the image.

For PNG images, I recommend PngGauntlet (http://pnggauntlet.com); for Mac, Imageoptim (http://imageoptim.com).

Imageoptim also works for JPEG, but for Windows we may use RIOT (http://luci.criosweb.ro/riot/) to optimize JPEG images, which is almost as good as Imageoptim. However, if the image seems too big, such as a high-resolution picture, the best option is the JPEGmini tool (http://www.jpegmini.com/).

Simplifying pages with HTML5 and CSS3

The HTML5 specification includes new structural elements, such as `header`, `nav`, `article`, and `footer`. Using these semantic elements yields a simpler and more efficiently parsed page than using generic nested `div` and `span` tags.

Almost the same happens when using CSS3 features that may help create lightweight pages by providing dynamic artwork support for visual elements such as gradients, rounded borders, shadows, animations, and transitions. As we know, before CSS3, each of these mentioned effects required one graphical image that represented it and would require loading many images. Consider the following example:

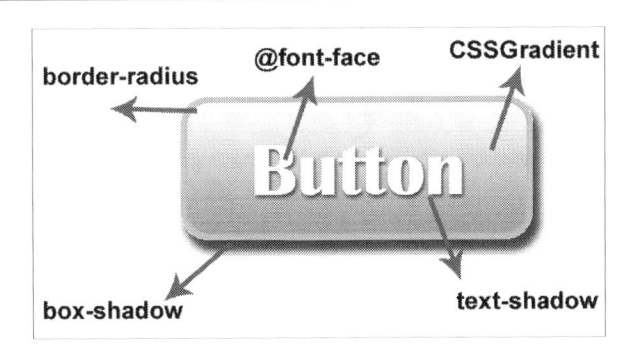

Testing website performance

We will see two browser tools, PageSpeed Insights and YSlow, focused on analyzing web pages and suggesting ways to improve their performance, based on a set of rules for high-performance web pages that are extremely professional and are in constant evolution.

Also, there are two online tools whose usage I recommend that run simple tests or perform advanced testing including multistep transactions, video capture, content blocking, and much more—WebPageTest and Mobitest.

> Testing website performance is key to maintaining a fast site; although it is outside the scope of this book, if you would like to explore this further, you may refer to *Instant PageSpeed Optimization* by *Sanjeev Jaiswal, Packt Publishing* or *Even Faster Web Sites* by *Steve Sounders, O'Reilly Media*, for more information.

PageSpeed Insights

PageSpeed Insights is an online tool built by Google to help developers optimize website performance. It evaluates the page's conformance to a number of different rules that cover general frontend best practices.

PageSpeed Insights gives tips and suggestions describing how we can best implement the rules and incorporate them into our development process.

You can try to use this tool yourself by accessing the website at http://developers.google.com/speed/pagespeed/insights/.

You can notice in the following screenshot that each notification shown has a summary content and it is expandable for more details and links for further information:

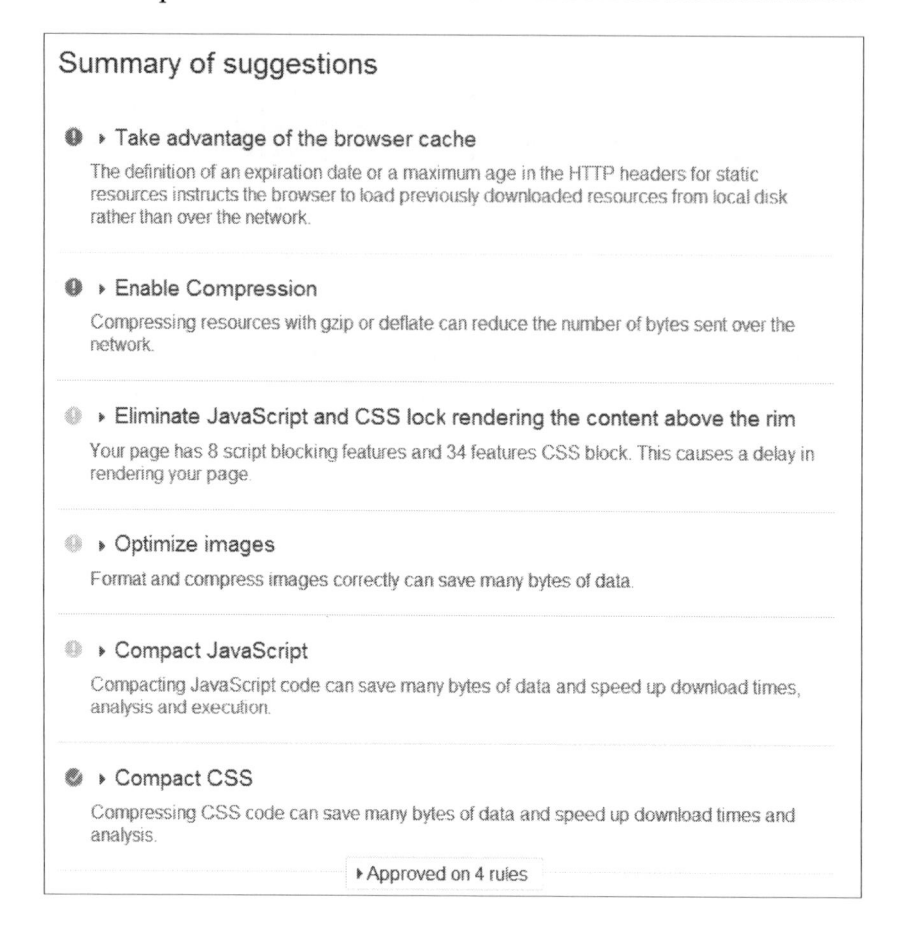

Summary of suggestions

- ▸ **Take advantage of the browser cache**
  The definition of an expiration date or a maximum age in the HTTP headers for static resources instructs the browser to load previously downloaded resources from local disk rather than over the network.

- ▸ **Enable Compression**
  Compressing resources with gzip or deflate can reduce the number of bytes sent over the network.

- ▸ **Eliminate JavaScript and CSS lock rendering the content above the rim**
  Your page has 8 script blocking features and 34 features CSS block. This causes a delay in rendering your page.

- ▸ **Optimize images**
  Format and compress images correctly can save many bytes of data.

- ▸ **Compact JavaScript**
  Compacting JavaScript code can save many bytes of data and speed up download times, analysis and execution.

- ▸ **Compact CSS**
  Compressing CSS code can save many bytes of data and speed up download times and analysis.

▸ Approved on 4 rules

YSlow

YSlow is a browser plugin developed by Yahoo! and is also focused on analyzing web pages and suggesting ways to improve their performance. Some of its features are as follows:

- Grades a web page based on a predefined ruleset or user-defined ruleset
- Suggests how to improve the page's performance and explains the reason in detail
- Summarizes the page's components, facilitating a faster search for critical issues

- Displays the overall statistics of the page
- Provides tools for performance analysis, including Smush.it™ (an online tool for image optimization) and JSLint (a code checker that finds common mistakes in scripts)

The plugin's website, which may be accessed from `http://developer.yahoo.com/yslow/`, displays a table with the default weight of each rule of the best practices so that we can prioritize critical issues before others (`http://yslow.org/faq/#faq_grading`).

Let's take a look at its interface and how each rule is described for us. Normally, only the small explanation about the rule (as shown in the following screenshot) is good enough for our comprehension before starting the fixes:

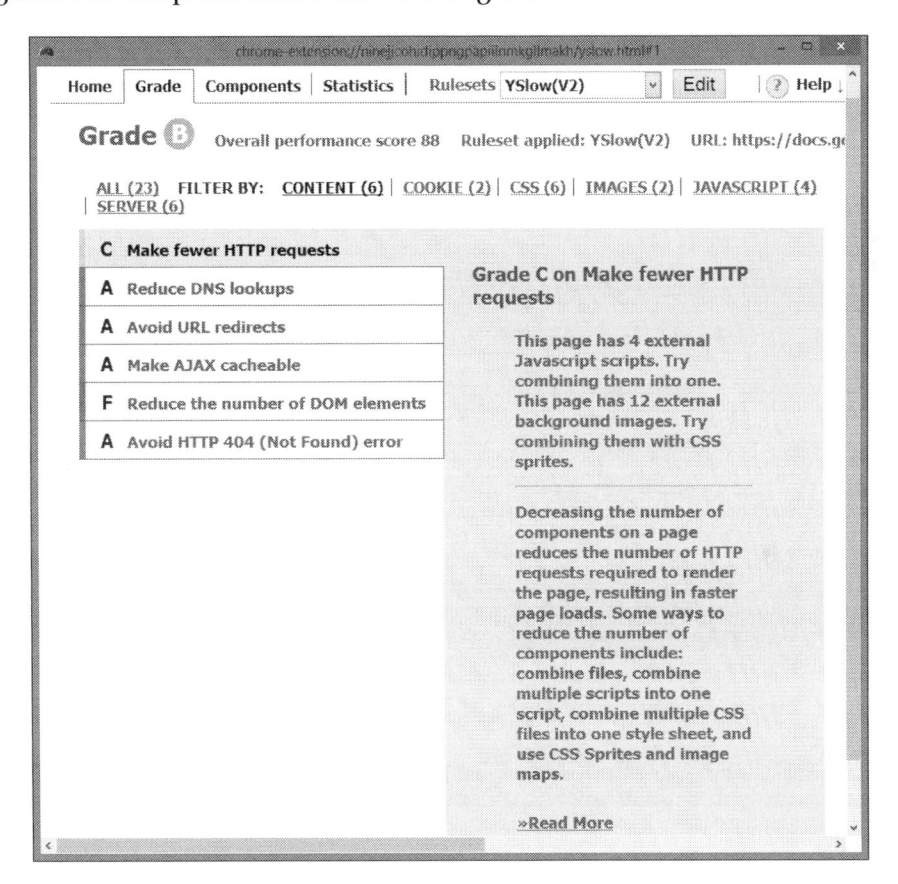

Improving Website Performance

WebPagetest

WebPagetest is a tool that was originally developed by AOL but is now supported by Google. We can use it by accessing `http://www.webpagetest.org/` and running a simple test or performing advanced testing, including multistep transactions, video capture, and content blocking.

The rich diagnostic information includes resource-loading Waterfall charts, page-speed-optimization checks, and gives suggestions for improvements that may be achieved once we enter a website URL. Then we will inform what site we want to test, the locale we want to test in, and the browser we want to use to do it. The following screenshot shows the WebPagetest's test result:

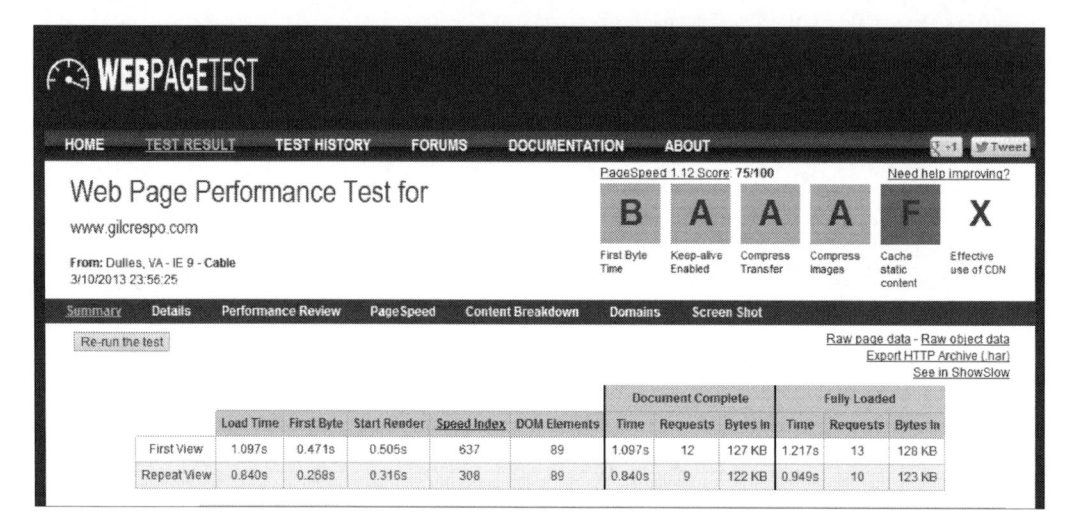

Mobitest

Mobitest is a great tool that simulates a real mobile device loading a website, capturing the page size, the total load time, and other performance-related stats. Although it is a great checking tool, it is no substitute for the real statistics that you would get from cell phone connections of limited bandwidth.

There is only one step to run the performance test after accessing `http://mobitest.akamai.com/`, which is to enter the website URL, choose one of the device/location options, and submit.

Sometimes it takes a long time to finalize the report, so the tool depends on the number of tests that are ahead of us in the queue.

The following is an example of a generated report:

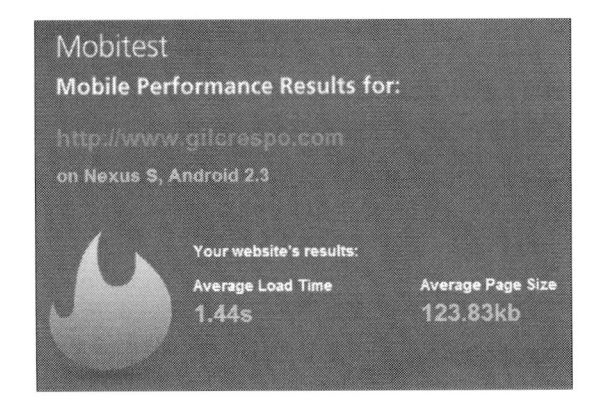

Mobitest
Mobile Performance Results for:
http://www.gilcrespo.com
on Nexus S, Android 2.3

Your website's results:
Average Load Time: 1.44s
Average Page Size: 123.83kb

Although this site is lightweight, it still has improvements that can be implemented. Let's see what the generated diagram of loading activity process, named Waterfall chart, indicates:

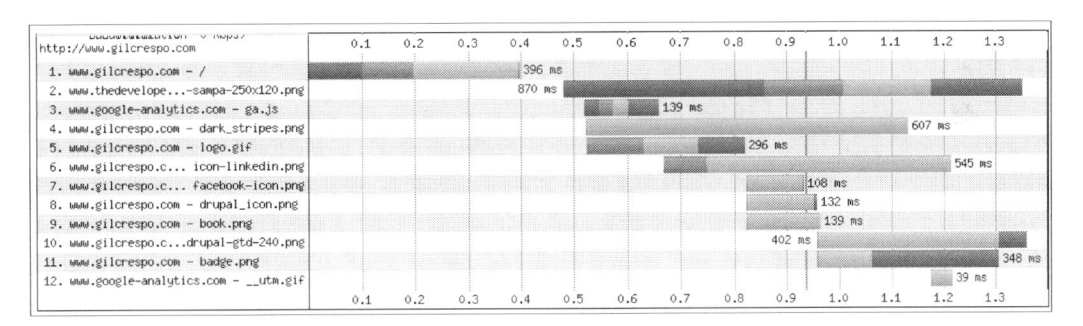

#	Resource	Time
	http://www.gilcrespo.com	
1.	www.gilcrespo.com - /	396 ms
2.	www.thedevelope...-sampa-250x120.png	870 ms
3.	www.google-analytics.com - ga.js	139 ms
4.	www.gilcrespo.com - dark_stripes.png	607 ms
5.	www.gilcrespo.com - logo.gif	296 ms
6.	www.gilcrespo.c... icon-linkedin.png	545 ms
7.	www.gilcrespo.c... facebook-icon.png	108 ms
8.	www.gilcrespo.com - drupal_icon.png	132 ms
9.	www.gilcrespo.com - book.png	139 ms
10.	www.gilcrespo.c...drupal-gtd-240.png	402 ms
11.	www.gilcrespo.com - badge.png	348 ms
12.	www.google-analytics.com - __utm.gif	39 ms

The Waterfall chart provided by Mobitest (image with horizontal bars) is demonstrating each resource being requested step by step, processed by server, and delivered back.

So, in the second line, the loading of a static image hosted in another website is taking a long time, which can be improved by adding the `expires` header and using CDN.

Summary

In this chapter, we learned some best practices, such as using a CDN to improve content delivery and cache static images, reducing HTTP requests by using conditional loading, file consolidation, CSS sprites, reducing the size of payloads by optimizing images, saving JPEG images as progressive, and simplifying page structure using HTML5 and CSS3. Additionally, we learned how to use tools such as PageSpeed, YSlow, WebpageTest, and Mobitest for performance testing.

Index

Symbols

3D flow style
  using, on Swiper 128
1140 Grid
  about 28, 29
  characteristics 29
  URL 28
<a> tag 57
</body> tag 48
.eightcol class 29
.elevencol class 29
.fivecol class 29
@font-face
  customizing 70
@font-face method 70
.fourcol class 29
<head> tag 51, 53
<nav> tag 46
.ninecol class 29
<noscript> tag 212
.onecol class 29
<picture> tag
  Foresight 92
  Picturefill 94, 95
.sevencol class 29
.sixcol class 29
.tencol class 29
.threecol class 29
.twelvecol class 29
.twocol class 29

A

adaptive features
  implementing 10
Adaptive Web Design 9
Adapt.js
  adopting 19
  adopting, pre-points 18
  characteristics 18
Anystretch
  about 96
  advantage 96
  data-stretch 97
  stretchMe 97
anystretch method 98
asNavFor option 117
autocomplete feature
  implementing 157, 158
  Magicsuggest, using with 156

B

Backstretch
  about 98
  responsive background slideshow, creating 99
Baseline Grid 27
Basic option 71
box-model 68
boxshadow property 183
box-sizing property 69
breakpoint settings 138
browser supporting features
  CanIUse.com 178
  checking 177
  MobileHTML5.org 178
  QuirksMode.org 179

C

Calendario plugin 212-216
CanIUse.com 178
CDN
  about 218
  using 218
centered column class 32
CMS (Content Management Systems) 114
Columns plugin
  used, for responsive structure creating 192-195
Content Delivery Network. *See* **CDN**
CSS
  used, for image resizing 86
CSS Browser Selector +
  about 181
  items 181
CSS Sprites
  about 219
  creating, SpriteCow used 220
  Google image sprite 220
Custom Screen Size button 172

D

data-base attributes 210
data-class attributes 139
data-hide attributes 139
data-ignore attributes 139
decision making
  influencing, factors 7
device simulating
  browser tools, using 169-172
  ScreenFly website tool, using 172
  Surveyor website tool, using 171
  Viewport Resizer website tool, using 170
div tag 32

E

EasyResponsiveTabstoAccordion 202, 203
Elastislide plugin
  about 108
  fixed wrapper with minimum of two visible images 111, 112
  minimum of four visible images 112, 113
  minimum of three visible images 109
  using 108, 109
  vertical with minimum of three visible images 110
element dimensioning
  improving, box-sizing property used 68, 69
em unit 66, 67
Equalize plugin
  used, for element dimension adjustment 195, 196
  using 195
expandable responsive tables
  transforming, from HTML tables 138-141
Expert mode 72

F

fallback 180, 181
feature detection tools
  about 181
  CSS Browser Selector + 181, 182
  Modernizr 182
featured homepage images
  different image versions, creating for 105
FitVids
  about 103
  using 104
FlexNav
  used, for adding menu flexibility 203, 205
FlexSlider2
  about 114
  basic slider 114, 115
  carousel settings 118
  carousel slider as navigation control 116, 117
Fluid Baseline Grid system
  about 25-28
  advantages 27
  Baseline Grid 27
  code 25
  Fluid Baseline Grid 28
  Fluid Columns 27
Fluid Columns 27
Fluid design 9
Focal Point CSS framework
  about 89-91
  defining 91

example 92
left-X/right-X 90
portrait 90
up-X/down-X 90
fonts
customizing 70
Font Squirrel tool
features 71
using 71-74
FooTable
extending 141-143
extensibility feature 141
FooTable jQuery plugin
used, for responsive table creating 152
footer anchor pattern
about 47
implementing 47-49
footer-only navigation
about 54
implementing 55
Foresight
about 92
right image, selecting 93
form inputs
attributes 156
types 155, 156
Foundation4
about 30-32
features 30
URL 30
using, for website structuring 36-41
full-table.css file 150
Function option 157

G

Guideguide plugin
about 33
URL 33

H

Hammer
about 134, 135
gestures 134
header section 43
high-density displays
dealing with 100, 101
Foresight, using 101
homepage title
customizing 82
horizontal overflow technique
header orientation flip 147-150
using 145, 147
html5shiv 184
HTML tables
converting, into expandable responsive tables 138-141
HTTP requests
conditional loaders, using 218
CSS Sprites 219
reducing, techniques 218
resources, consolidating 218, 219

I

IdealForms
about 163
implementing 163-166
URL 163
used, for contact form creating 166
image
resizing, CSS used 86
image breakpoints
using 86, 87
Imageoptim 222
image-set() function 92
image slider
creating, Swiper plugin used 135

J

JavaScript plugins
used, for touch event implementing 133
jPanelMenu jQuery plugin
URL 60
jquery library 151
jQuery plugins
used, for responsive background images 95, 96
JSON data source
No data source option 157
Static source option 157
URL option 157

K

Kernjs.com link 80
Kern.js tool 80

L

Launch button 173
lettering
  about 77
  Kern.js tool 80
  steps 78-80
  using 80, 81
Link to full-table technique
  about 150
  using 150, 151

M

Magicsuggest
  autocomplete feature 156
Magnific Popup plugin 208, 210
max-height property 50
MediaElements.js 185, 186
media queries
  specifying, features used 11
  using 10, 11
menu design, analyzing
  improving 43, 44
  item priority round 44
  page space round 44
  scanning round 44
  Topics and interests round 44
  visibility round 44
menu navigation plugins
  about 199
  EasyResponsiveTabstoAccordion 202
  FlexNav 204
  Sidr 199
meta tag of viewport
  setting 34
Mobile-first project
  designing 12, 13
  use case, analyzing 12
MobileHTML5.org 179
Mobitest
  about 226, 227
  generated report example 227

Modernizr
  about 182-184
  html5shiv 184
  YepNope.js 184
multi toggle pattern
  about 55
  implementing 55-58

N

No data source option 157

O

off-canvas menu pattern
  about 60
  jPanelMenu jQuery plugin 60-62
open-box class 135
open class 57
Opera mobile emulator 173
out of the box customization 138

P

Packery plugin
  used, for card website layout implementing 197, 198
PageSpeed Insights 223
pagination class 142
payloads size
  image optimization 222
  page simplification, HTML5 used 222
  progressive JPEG 221
  reducing 220
percentage
  about 20, 66
  advantage, over pixel 20, 21
  pixel, converting to 21-23
Photoshop plugin. *See* Guideguide plugin
Pickadate plugin
  about 159
  using 159-161
Picturefill
  about 95
  benefits 95
  URL 95
picture tag
  working 88

pixel
    about 20
    converting, to percentage 21-23
pixels per inch (PPI) 100
plugins
    Calendario 212
    Columns 192
    Equalize 195
    FlexNav 203
    Magnific Popup 208
    Packery 197
    Prefix free 207
    Riloadr 210
    Sidr 200, 201
    SVGeezy 206
PngGauntlet 222
polyfill implementations
    about 185
    MediaElements.js 185
    Respond.js 189
    SVG 187
polyfills 177, 180
Prefix free plugin 207, 208

Q

quickSetup function 193
QuirksMode.org 179
QuoJS
    about 133, 134
    gestures 134

R

relative units
    responsive text, converting to 65, 66
rem 67
Respond 11
Respond.js
    about 189
    adopting 20
    characteristics 19
    cons 19
    downloading 19
responsive background images, jQuery plugins used
    about 95, 96
    Anystretch 96-98
    Backstretch 98, 99
responsive form
    IdealForms, using 163-165
responsive grid system
    1140 Grid 28, 29
    about 24, 25
    advantage 24
    characteristics 25
    Fluid Baseline Grid system 25-27
    Foundation4 30, 31, 32
    using, need for 24
responsive images
    art direction, controlling 88, 89
    Focal Point CSS framework 89
responsive image sliders
    about 107, 108
    Elastislide plugin 108
    FlexSlider2 114
    ResponsiveSlides 119
    Slicebox 129
    Swiper 124
Responsive Measure
    about 81
    idealLineLength 81
    maximumFontSize 82
    minimumFontSize 82
responsive navigation patterns
    about 44
    footer anchor 47
    footer-only 54
    multi toggle 55
    off-canvas menu 60
    select menu 52
    toggle and slide 58
    toggle menu 50
    Top nav 45
Responsive Nav plugin
    about 50
    features 50
Responsive Nav window 52
ResponsiveSlides
    about 119
    examples 120-124
responsive structure
    creating, Columns plugin used 192-195

responsive tables
  about 137, 138
  creating, FooTable jQuery plugin used 152
responsive text
  about 65
  converting, to relative units 65, 66
responsive touch design
  about 132
  placement of controls 132
  touch target sizes 132
responsive video elements
  creating 102
responsive web design
  about 8
  issues, solving 17
  techniques 8
responsive websites
  design testing, tips 174
  testing 174, 175
Retina 100
Riloadr plugin
  about 210
  features 210, 211
root em 67

S

Scalable Vector Graphics. *See* **SVG**
screen
  adapting, with media queries 10, 11
ScreenFly website tool
  using 172
select menu pattern
  about 52
  implementing 53, 54
  TinyNav.js jQuery plugin 52
Select Sprite tool 220
Shims 181
Sidr
  used, for side menu creating 200
site
  adapting, JavaScript used 18
site, adapting with JavaScript
  about 18, 19
  Adapt.js, using 18
SlabText plugin 75, 76
Slicebox 129-131

Stackedtable plugin
  about 143
  desktop view 145
  small device view 145
  using 143-145
static source option 157
Surveyor website tool
  using 171
SVG
  about 187
  as background image 188
  as simple <img> tag 188
  as <svg> tag 188
SVGeezy plugin 206
swipe events 108
Swiper
  3D flow style, using on 128, 129
  about 124
  featured options 127
  used, for image slider creating 135, 136
  using 125, 126

T

The FitText plugin 74
TinyNav.js jQuery plugin 52
Toggle and slide pattern
  about 58
  implementing 58-60
toggle menu pattern
  about 50
  implementing 51, 52
  Responsive Nav plugin 50
  using 62
tooltip feature
  about 161
  advantages 161
  using 161, 162
Top nav pattern
  about 45, 46
  implementing 46
touch event implementation, JavaScript
  plugins used
  Hammer 134, 135
  QuoJS 133, 134
touch events
  implementing, with JavaScript plugins 133

U

URL option 157

V

vh (viewport height) 66
Viewport Resizer website tool
  advantages 170
  using 170
vw (viewport width) 66

W

WebPagetest
  about 226
  test result 226
website layout
  implementing, Packery plugin 197, 198
website performance
  Mobitest 226, 227
  PageSpeed Insights 223
  testing 223
  WebPagetest 226
  YSlow 224
website structure plugins
  Columns 191
  Equalize 191
  Packery 191
wireframe
  about 13
  layout design, creating 34, 35
  mobile-first development example 14
  URL 14
  using 13, 14

Y

YepNope.js 184
YSlow
  about 225
  features 224

[PACKT] open source
PUBLISHING
community experience distilled

Thank you for buying
Responsive Web Design with jQuery

About Packt Publishing

Packt, pronounced 'packed', published its first book "*Mastering phpMyAdmin for Effective MySQL Management*" in April 2004 and subsequently continued to specialize in publishing highly focused books on specific technologies and solutions.

Our books and publications share the experiences of your fellow IT professionals in adapting and customizing today's systems, applications, and frameworks. Our solution based books give you the knowledge and power to customize the software and technologies you're using to get the job done. Packt books are more specific and less general than the IT books you have seen in the past. Our unique business model allows us to bring you more focused information, giving you more of what you need to know, and less of what you don't.

Packt is a modern, yet unique publishing company, which focuses on producing quality, cutting-edge books for communities of developers, administrators, and newbies alike. For more information, please visit our website: www.packtpub.com.

About Packt Open Source

In 2010, Packt launched two new brands, Packt Open Source and Packt Enterprise, in order to continue its focus on specialization. This book is part of the Packt Open Source brand, home to books published on software built around Open Source licences, and offering information to anybody from advanced developers to budding web designers. The Open Source brand also runs Packt's Open Source Royalty Scheme, by which Packt gives a royalty to each Open Source project about whose software a book is sold.

Writing for Packt

We welcome all inquiries from people who are interested in authoring. Book proposals should be sent to author@packtpub.com. If your book idea is still at an early stage and you would like to discuss it first before writing a formal book proposal, contact us; one of our commissioning editors will get in touch with you.

We're not just looking for published authors; if you have strong technical skills but no writing experience, our experienced editors can help you develop a writing career, or simply get some additional reward for your expertise.

[PACKT] open source
community experience distilled
PUBLISHING

HTML5 and CSS3 Responsive Web Design Cookbook

ISBN: 978-1-84969-544-2   Paperback: 204 pages

Learn the secrets of developing responsive websites capable of interfacing with today's mobile Internet services

1. Learn the fundamental elements of writing responsive website code for all stages of the development lifecycle
2. Create the ultimate code writer's resource using logical workflow layers
3. Full of usable code for immediate use in your website projects
4. Written in an easy-to-understand language giving knowledge without preaching

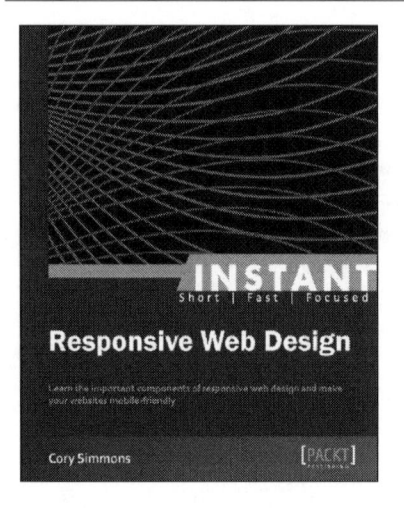

Instant Responsive Web Design

ISBN: 978-1-84969-925-9   Paperback: 70 pages

Learn the important components of responsive web design and make your websites mobile-friendly

1. Learn something new in an Instant! A short, fast, focused guide delivering immediate results
2. Learn how to make your websites beautiful on any device
3. Understand the differences between various responsive philosophies
4. Expand your skill set with the quickly growing mobile-first approach

Please check www.PacktPub.com for information on our titles

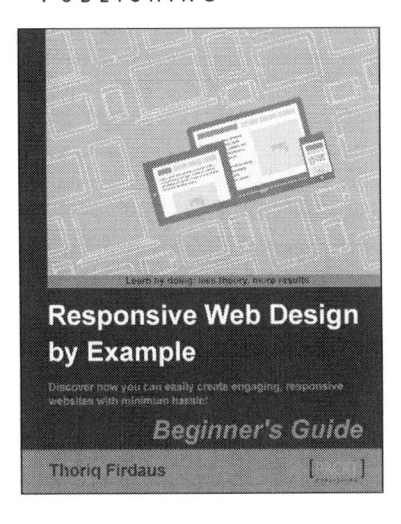

Responsive Web Design by Example

ISBN: 978-1-84969-542-8 Paperback: 338 pages

Discover how you can easily create engaging, responsive websites with minimum hassle!

1. Rapidly develop and prototype responsive websites by utilizing powerful open source frameworks
2. Focus less on the theory and more on results, with clear step-by-step instructions, previews, and examples to help you along the way
3. Learn how you can utilize three of the most powerful responsive frameworks available today: Bootstrap, Skeleton, and Zurb Foundation

HTML5 Enterprise Application Development

ISBN: 978-1-84968-568-9 Paperback: 332 pages

A step-by-step practical introduction to HTML5 through the building of a real-world application, including common development practices

1. Learn the most useful HTML5 features by developing a real-world application
2. Detailed solutions to most common problems presented in an enterprise application development
3. Discover the most up-to-date development tips, tendencies, and trending libraries and tools

Please check www.PacktPub.com for information on our titles

Printed in Great Britain
by Amazon.co.uk, Ltd.,
Marston Gate.